# THE PRINCIPLES OF COMPARATIVE PHILOLOGY

# THE PRINCIPLES OF COMPARATIVE PHILOLOGY

A H SAYCE

GYAN

*Published by*

Gyan Publishing House
5, Ansari Road
Daryaganj, New Delhi-110002
Phone: 011-47034999, 9811692060
E-mail: books@gyanbooks.com

*Distribution Network*
gyanbooks.com
India, USA, Canada, UK, Australia



ISBN: 978-93-7447-051-0 (PB)

First Published, 1885

2nd Impression 2025

*Printed at:* Gyan Press, Delhi.



**THE PRINCIPLES OF COMPARATIVE PHILOLOGY**
Author: A H SAYCE

# COMPARATIVE PHILOLOGY

THE

# PRINCIPLES OF COMPARATIVE PHILOLOGY.

BY

A. H. SAYCE,

FELLOW AND TUTOR OF QUEEN'S COLLEGE, OXFORD;
MEMBER OF THE ROYAL ASIATIC SOCIETY, OF THE SOCIETY OF BIBLICAL ARCHÆOLOGY, AND OF THE GERMAN ORIENTAL SOCIETY;
*Author of "An Assyrian Grammar," "An Assyrian Elementary Grammar and Reading Book," &c. &c.*

Third Edition, Revised and Enlarged.

LONDON:
TRÜBNER & CO., LUDGATE HILL.
1885.

TO

*PROFESSOR MAX MÜLLER,*

WHOSE WORKS FIRST KINDLED MY INTEREST IN THE

STUDY OF LANGUAGE,

AND

WHO HAS SINCE BEEN TO ME A TEACHER,

GUIDE, AND FRIEND.

# PREFACE TO THE THIRD EDITION.

SINCE the publication of the second edition of my work in 1875, a revolution has taken place in the Comparative Philology of the Indo-European languages. Sanskrit has been dethroned from the high place it once occupied as the special representative of the Aryan Parent-Speech, and it has been recognised that primitive sounds and forms have, on the whole, been more faithfully preserved in the languages of Europe than in those of India. The old theory which derived flection from an earlier period of agglutination has been rudely shaken, and Professor Delbrück, its latest advocate, in his "Introduction to the Study of Language," after admitting that the "agglutinative theory" has "not been verified in individual cases," rests his defence of it solely on the resemblance of the first two personal pronouns to the first two personal terminations of the verb. Professor Fick, so long the leading authority on the doctrine generally received in regard to roots, now rejects it completely ("Gött. gelehrte Anzeigen," Ap. 6, 1881), and speaks of "the obsolete point of view" of Paṇini, with its "empty chatter of roots and suffixes" ("Gött. gelehrte Anz.," Nov. 9, 1881). He believes the Aryan verb to have originally consisted only of infinitives and infixes. Following the example of Benfey, he has further shown that the present stems of verbs like λείπω, ἔχω (σέχω), are older and more primitive than the contracted stems of the aorist, ἔλιπον, ἔσχον, which are the result of a retrogression of the accent. The axiom laid down by the so-called "Younger Grammarians' School," that a phonetic law admits of no exception, has brought about a recognition of the truth of the views I have maintained in the last chapter of this book: it is analogy and assimilation, not phonetic decay, which have been the main causes of change in language.

But it is in the domain of primitive Aryan phonology that the most important revolution has been effected. The labours of Brugman, Osthoff, Johannes Schmidt, Collitz, Fick, and more especially De Saussure, have proved that I had good reason for saying that "the original alphabet which is supposed to have been possessed by our remote ancestors . . . is, like the root-language, a logical, not an historical starting-point." Instead of the few and simple sounds to which the words of the Indo-European dialects have been reduced by etymological analysis, we now know that the Parent-speech possessed an alphabet which was very rich in both consonants and vowels. By the side of *k*, *g*, and *gh* existed the velar gutturals *k'*, *g'*, and *gh'*, which were pronounced, as I believe, *kw*, *gw*, and *ghw*.

Schmidt would add to these *κ′*, *γ′*, and *γh′*, represented in Sanskrit by *s′*, *j*, and *h*, in Zend by *ç* and *z*, and in Old Bulgarian by *s* and *z*. The Greek *θ* (Sanskrit *h*) is the descendant of two different sounds which appear in Old Bulgarian as *z* and *ž*, while Osthoff has made it probable that the Parent-speech contained two sibilants, one sonant and the other surd.

It was above all in vowels that the primitive Aryan alphabet was most rich. The monotonous *a* of Sanskrit is an amalgamation of at least three sounds, which Brugman, the real author of this discovery, would represent by $a_1$, $a_2$, and $a_3$. Collitz, rightly as it seems to me, prefers to substitute for these three symbols the European letters *ĕ*, *ă*, and *ŏ*. But the *ŏ* itself, as De Saussure has observed, was not a single sound. There was an *ŏ* which is found in the Greek *πόσις* and the Latin *potis*, and a second *ŏ* which interchanges with *ĕ*. The correlation of these two vowels has been explained by Fick; where we find *ĕ́* and *ŏ* alternating with one another, as in *λέγο-μεν* and *λέγε-τε*, the first (*ŏ*) represents an originally unaccented syllable, while the second (*ĕ*) takes the place when the syllable receives the accent. Just as there were two *ŏ*'s, there must also have been two *ĕ*'s.

The discovery of these primitive vowels has produced a revolution in etymology. Not only has it shown that Sanskrit is not that standard of European phonology it had been imagined to be; it has also proved that the phonetic laws which govern the equivalence of vocalic sounds are as strict as those which govern the equivalence of consonantal ones, and that consequently roots containing *ă*, *ĕ*, and *ŏ* must never be confounded together. Henceforward it becomes impossible to derive *magnus* and *μέγας* from the same root.

Another phonetic discovery of equal importance is due to the researches of Brugman and De Saussure. This is the existence of sonant liquids, labials and nasals in the Parent-speech. The primitive Aryans possessed a sonant *r*, *l*, *m*, and *n*, which became *αρ*, *αλ*, *ρα*, *λα*, (*αν*,) *α* in Greek, *or*, *ul*, *em*, *en* in Latin; *aúr*, *aúl*, *um*, *un* in Gothic. Here again the progress of language has been marked by successive simplifications; the old distinctions between sounds have been lost, and the many has been reduced to the one.

It was inevitable that amid so many discoveries my own opinions should have undergone modification upon several points during the nine years that have passed since the appearance of the last edition of my book. Although the theories and principles I have maintained seem to me to have been verified and confirmed by recent discoveries, there are many points of detail in which I should to-day express myself somewhat differently. Two of these I would specially signalise, since they concern questions so important as those of verbal flection and the origin of gender.

As I have said above, the latest defender of the old agglutinative theory of Bopp finds himself compelled to rest his support of it on the supposed resemblance between the first two personal pronouns and the corresponding personal terminations of the verb. According to Professor Delbrück, this resemblance proves that the terminations of the verb are old pronouns which have become mere signs of flection. Until lately, I was inclined to be of the same opinion, and I would willingly have continued to explain the resemblance, as I have done in the present volume, on the ground that the noun being older than the verb, the verbal suffixes were modelled after those of the noun, and that the personal pronouns attached to the verb conformed in time to the general inflected type of the language.

But the theory which sees in the person-endings of the verb the relics of the personal pronouns, is open to grave objections which to-day seem to me to be insuperable. The verbal stem cannot be distinguished from the nominal stem: *ἄγο-μεν* and *ἀγό-ς* are one and the same. Every attempt to explain the terminations of the third person of the verb has failed; equally fruitless has been the endeavour to discover the pronominal suffixes of the dual and plural in the dual and plural of the verb. The second person singular of the verb loses all external likeness to the second personal pronoun as soon as we remember that the original form of the last was *tw*(*ŏm*) and not *σύ* as in Greek; while, on the other hand, the same person was also characterised by the termination -*θα*, which not only does not correspond with any personal pronoun, but serves to denote the first person of the plural in the forms -μεσ-θα and -με-θα. The researches of Scherer and Brugman, moreover, have proved that the Greek and Latin forms of the first person singular in -ō have nothing in common with the forms in *-m* and *-mi*, but are due to a fusion of the final vowel of the stem with the vowel *a*. It is scarcely needful to observe that we know of no pronoun *a* with the meaning of the first person.

On the other hand, the person-endings are all nominal suffixes, many of which belong to abstract substantives and infinitives, and the infinitive, it must be remembered, is frequently employed in the place of the finite verb. The third person of the singular φέρε-τι, when compared with a noun like γένεσις, can hardly be anything else than an abstract noun, used either in the locative, or as a bare stem like the infinitives in -μεν and -Fεν (φερε-Fεν = φέρειν). The third person of the past tense in Turkish is similarly an abstract noun. The third person of the plural φέρο-ντι may be connected with the present participle, φέρο-ντι standing to φέρε-τι as the Sanskrit *bhárantam* to *bharatás*. I fancy the analogy of the second person plural, where the terminations *-tĕs* and *-tĕ* were used side by side, brought about the change of φέροντες into φέροντε, this form in its turn being afterwards assimilated to the singular φέρε-τι. In Turkish, as in the Semitic languages, the third person of the verb is expressed by the present participle. As for the first person, I see no way of deriving the so-called secondary termination *-m* from the primary *-mi;* neither phonology nor analogy would allow it. If, however, we admit that the secondary termination is the older, there would be no difficulty in supposing that it has been assimilated in the present tense to the vocalic termination of the third person (in *-i*). Now the secondary termination is simply the suffix of the accusative or objective case of the noun, and like it can appear under the form of the sonant *ṃ*. The same explanation will hold good of the second person of the singular; here also the secondary *-s*, which serves not only as the suffix of the nominative singular and plural and accusative plural of the noun, but also as the suffix of abstract stems, will be the primitive termination. Consequently, the ideas "I bear," "thou bearest," would have been originally expressed by *ĕghŏm bhĕrŏm, twŏm bhĕrĕs*, which answer exactly to the Latin *ego verbum, tu scelus.* It was only by degrees that the signification of the phrase, which at first depended on the context and the position of the words, was transferred to the terminations of the words themselves, and thus became the origin of the verbal flection. A true verb is still wanting in many of the languages at present spoken in the world, and in the Polynesian idioms it is still position and the cases of the noun that take the place of the verb and supply its functions. If we now consider the plural, we shall find *-μεν*, *-με* (Sanskrit *-ma*), and *-μες* used to denote the first person, although *-μεν* is a well-known suffix of the infinitive, like *-Fεν*, which seems related to the

*-va* and *-vas* of the first person dual in Sanskrit. In the middle voice, the suffix *-θα* is attached to *-με* and *-μες* just as *-σι* is attached to the nominal suffix -(ε)ς in a word like *πόδεσ-σι*, and since according to Apollonios Dyskolos, the Æolic form of *-μεθα* was *-μεθεν*, while *-θε* is the suffix of the second person of the plural, it is clear that we have to do with the same nominal suffix as that which appears in *οὐρανόθεν* and *ὕπαιθα*. In the imperative we even have the nominal *-θι*. I therefore find myself compelled to agree unreservedly with Fick's conclusion that not only forms like *bháve*, the first person singular of the Sanskrit middle, are really old infinitives, but that the other forms of the verb are infinitives as well. However, I cannot assent to his further conclusion—at least in the terms in which it is stated—that the forms have been differentiated by means of infixes. I doubt whether infixes, or, as they are sometimes called, pleonastic letters, have ever been introduced into the body of an uncompounded word except by the aid of analogy.

On the other hand, Fick, following herein a suggestion of Benfey, has clearly shown, as it seems to me, that what is termed the present stem is older than the stem of the aorist. In *πείθω*, for instance, the "root" appears under a more primitive form than in *ἔ-πιθο-ν*, where the vowel of the stem has been shortened in consequence of the accent having been originally on the last syllable. The so-called "strong aorist" ought, therefore, rather to be termed the "weak aorist," since it presents the verbal root under a weakened form. As Benfey was the first to point out, it is really the imperfect of a weak present stem, and hence it was that the Greeks were unable to determine whether ἔλυον were an aorist or an imperfect. As a matter of fact, there were three present stems in the Parent-speech, a strong stem as in πείθω, a weak stem and a reduplicated stem, and it is possible that the strong stem as well as the weak one admitted of reduplication. These stems cannot be referred to any anterior "root," partly because the weak stem is merely the result of the rapid pronunciation of a word which already had its full form, partly because in the case of words like σπέσθαι or σχεῖν, the "roots" would have to be the purely consonantal groups σπ, σχ, which is absurd. Moreover, it is impossible to separate nouns like ἀγό-ς from verbs like ἄγο-μεν. Here the common "root" would be αγο, which, when used with certain suffixes in a certain context, would be regarded as a nominal stem, while with other suffixes and in another context it would be a verbal stem.

The second point to which I wish to refer briefly is the question of gender, a subject on which my views have been slightly modified since the first publication of this work. I still see no reason to doubt that Bleek was right when he regarded the classes into which the Kafir noun is divided as being substantially the same as the genders of the Aryan and Semitic languages. But I should now explain the development of generic distinctions in these two families of speech in the following way. There was a time, I believe, in the history of the Aryan family when no specific suffixes had as yet been set apart to denote the distinctions of gender. As in the agglutinative languages, there existed the idea of sexual gender only, and not of grammatical gender. Nouns were generically distinguished one from the other only in so far as they denoted males and females, like the pronouns which referred to them. Since uncivilised man is prone to personify the objects of nature he sees around him, most nouns came to be classed as either masculine or feminine; but this classification depended solely on their signification and on the pronouns which were used with them. We may find traces of this period in the history of language in common words denoting relationship, like "father" and "mother," which continued to be declined in exactly the same manner in the Indo-European languages without any distinctive mark of gender. Similar traces may be discovered in words which form exceptions to the general rule, that stems in *-ŏ* are masculine and stems in *-ă* are feminine. Thus the Greek *ὁδός* and the Latin *humus* bear witness to an epoch when the terminations *-ος* and *-us* were not yet associated with the idea of the masculine. Gradually, however, small classes of nouns began to be formed, which accidentally had the same suffixes, and referred to the same sex. Nouns, for instance, the stems of which terminated in the vowels *i* and *ya* (*yĕ*, *yŏ*), were used more especially of persons of the feminine sex, or of objects assimilated to these persons. Hence certain groups of nouns grew up, which by the help of analogy tended to assimilate other nouns referring to the same sex or furnished with the same suffixes. Stems in *i* and *ya* all tended to be classed among feminine nouns, those in *-ŏ* among masculine nouns. The result was that sexual gender became grammatical gender, the pronouns which were associated with masculine and feminine nouns becoming themselves masculine and feminine, and causing other nouns with which they were associated to become also masculine or feminine. The Semitic languages stopped here. The primitive personification of natural objects on the one hand, and the influence of analogy on the other, extended further in this family of speech than in the Aryan languages, and ended by relegating all nouns to one or other of these two classes. In the Aryan languages, however, a certain number of words still remained without gender. On the one hand, the object could be employed as subject with a passive verb, in which case the accusative became a nominative; on the other hand, as soon as the primitive sentence had been analysed, and the relations of grammar had in some measure been extracted from it, a certain number of nouns was left which, when used as subjects, were without suffixes indicative of gender and case. When these nouns clearly represented ideas like those of "father" or "mother," they were naturally treated as masculines and feminines; but when this was not the case, they were collected into a distinct class, which comprised such nouns as *μέθυ* in Greek or *virus* in Latin. To the same class were also referred nouns which, although used as the subjects of a passive verb, were really objective cases, and consequently could not be regarded as denoting persons of either the masculine or the feminine gender. Three great classes of "gender" were thus formed, among which nouns were distributed; it only remained for phonetic decay and assimilation to work further changes by transferring nouns from one class to another. Thus in German the loss of the final *n* of *Sonnen*, "the sun," caused the word to be associated with feminines in *-e*, while *Mond*, "the moon," was for similar reasons transferred from the class of feminines to that of masculines. But up to the last the classes into which words were divided continued to resemble the classes of nouns in Zulu, and were distinguished one from the other by the pronouns with which they were construed.

I must not conclude this Preface without saying a word or two about the First Appendix, which I have left just as it was written ten years ago. The main conclusion it seeks to establish remains unaffected by recent discoveries; but the views embodied in it in regard to the original home of the Aryans, and the relations of the Aryan languages to one another, can no longer be supported. I must avow my entire conversion to the theory, first propounded by Latham, and of late years ably defended on anthropological and linguistic grounds by Poesche and Penka, that the Aryan race had its first seat, not in Asia, but in the Baltic provinces and Scandinavia. Here the Aryan languages grew up, and from hence they spread along with the spread of the tall, blue-eyed, light-haired dolichocephalic people who spoke them, and who succeeded in impressing their supremacy and speech upon races either alien or allied to them only through intermarriage. The Eastern Aryans of India and Iran were the latest and most distant branch of the race, who had followed the course of mighty rivers until they eventually found themselves among the streams of the Punjâb. In Europe the Keltic and Italic dialects claim the closest affinity one to the other, and presuppose a time when the ancestors of the Aryan Kelt and the Aryan Italian still lived side by side. Greek, on the other hand, looks towards the East, and will probably find its nearest kindred in Armenian, which is itself but an offshoot of the Phrygian and Thrakian stock. The idyllic life of our Aryan forefathers, painted for us by Pictet and his followers, has become a pleasant dream of the past; Otto Schrader ("Sprachvergleichung und Urgeschichte") has shown that the annals of language, when rightly questioned, tell a very different tale, and that the primitive Aryan was really a coarse and squalid savage, defending himself against the inclemencies of the climate with the skins of wild beasts, and unacquainted with the use of metals.

A. H. SAYCE.

QUEEN'S COLLEGE OXFORD,
*November*, 1884.

# PREFACE TO THE SECOND EDITION.

THE present edition will be found little more than a revision of the first. Two or three inaccuracies of statement have been corrected, as well as a few misprints, which I much regret. What additional matter there is has been thrown into footnotes and appendices. Appendix I. is added not only for the sake of the illustration it affords of the way in which the forgotten history of the past may be restored by the help of language, but also in support of the views I have propounded in regard to the Lyḳian inscriptions. The main part of the new matter is contained in Chapters III., IV., and V., especially Chapter IV.; beyond this there is little that is fresh except the note on the story of the Kyklôps in Chapter VIII.

I need hardly say that the opinions contended for in the first edition have undergone no change or modification. I find, however, that what I have said on the subject of roots has given rise to misconceptions, and that my meaning has been obscured by the ambiguity of the terms "roots" and "root-period." I fancied that I had sufficiently guarded myself against being misunderstood; but since this does not seem to have been the case, it is as well to state explicitly the precise doctrine on the matter which I hold. Roots, then, in the lexical or grammatical sense of the term, are those ultimate phonetic elements discovered by an analysis of groups of allied words, and they stand in the same relation to words or derivatives as letters and syllables do to them. Just as words are reduced into a limited number of letters or syllables, not in spoken language, but by the reflective labours of the grammarian, so roots also are the product of the lexicographer's study—the elements into which he chemically decomposes all speech. Now if the philologist assume that the roots so arrived at ever constituted a real *language*, he would make the same mistake as a chemist who held that his simple elements existed separately and independently—not before the existence of the compounds into which they entered, but—in those compounds themselves; that oxygen and hydrogen, for instance, are distinguished by nature in the water itself after it has been made. The chemist, however, must artificially analyse the material with which he has to deal; and so too must the Glottologist; and for scientific purposes he is perfectly justified in speaking of a "root-period," meaning thereby a period in the history of speech of which the roots he has extracted from the dictionary may give us a faint idea. So far as the root-period is made synonymous with the results of his labours, it is purely imaginary, existing only in the reflective brain of a modern scholar; but since this root-period is the best representative that we can get of an early synthetic stage in the development of language, it may also be used to signify the latter. In this case the root will be a sentence-word, summing up in one whole what a later stage of language would break up into separate words or forms, the name of an individual object implying and including subject or object and "verb" as well. Hence there would be as many sentence-words as momentary impressions made upon the senses by a particular object; and if language rests upon onomatopœia or the like, sentence-words applying to the same object might be expected to resemble one another, and in this resemblance allow the philologist to discover those types of sound which he calls roots. Each class of languages will have its own roots, and there is no more reason for assuming that the roots of all languages are the same than there is that the languages themselves are the same. Of course, in so far as roots are constituted merely by resemblance of allied sentence-words, that is, in so far as they are the results of lexical analysis, they will be similar all the world over; but if we use "roots" in the sense of the sentence-words which lie at the bottom of all developed speech, our only knowledge of the characteristics of them will be derived from the phenomena of each known language, and the roots will differ one from the other in exactly the same way as the known languages do. The characteristics of a Chinese or Aryan root (when considered as part of a spoken language) are the characteristics of a Chinese or Aryan word; and the Aryan root of the grammarian is as unlike a Chinese word as is the grammarian's Chinese root itself.

It will be seen that what I believe to be the true doctrine of roots depends upon the axiom that language starts with the sentence, not with the isolated word. When my book was published last year, I imagined that the axiom was formally enunciated for the first time, and had no idea that any clear statement of it was to be found elsewhere. Since then, however, I have come across the highly instructive passage in Waitz's "Anthropologie" which is quoted in a footnote to Chapter IV. of the present edition, as well as a remarkable but long-forgotten work published in 1831 by an anonymous author, and entitled "An Outline of Sematology; or, An Essay towards Establishing a New Theory of Grammar, Logic, and Rhetoric." The philological ideas of the writer are naturally extremely crude; but the theory upon which the whole work is based, though arrived at, it would seem, from an *à priori* point of view, is substantially the same as my own, and is worked out with great clearness and vigour. He lays down that language has originated out of natural cries, each cry comprehending what we should now call a sentence, the several parts of which came in time to be limited and determined by one another, and so passed into words. In this way, it is argued, perceptions became knowledge; and the writer adds with great truth (p. 39)—"It is not *what* a word signifies that determines it to be this or that part of speech, but *how it assists other words in making up the sentence.*" (The italics are his own.) Further on he observes (p. 55) that: "The (separate) words of a sentence are significant only as the instrumental means for getting at the meaning of the whole sentence or the whole discourse. Till that sentence or oration is completed, the WORD is unsaid which represents the speaker's thoughts." And he afterwards points out that the separate syllables of a word (like *un*, *mis*, *con*, *ness*, or *fy*) may be as significant as separate words.

As soon as we admit that language begins with the sentence, and that the synthetic is prior to the analytic—an admission which the *facts* of philology seem to me to force upon us—we are driven to the conclusion that, from one point of view at any rate, the agglutinative languages, which analyse the primitive sentence and distinguish its parts one from the other, are in advance of the inflectional; so that, were the development-theory true, the inflectional would have developed into the agglutinative, and not the converse. We might then go on to infer that the civilisation of the agglutinative races is higher than that of the inflectional races,—a position, indeed, which could be defended on the ground that the oldest civilisations of which we know were those of Turanian Accad, of China, and of Egypt, and that the beginning of culture implies a higher mental effort than the perpetuation of it. At all events, civilisation and the development of language are so intimately connected as to be practically inseparable. Language is the reflection of society, creating and created by it, as well as the outward expression of thought; there can be no progress, therefore, in language without a corresponding progress in the society which moulds it and the thought which underlies it. The great masters of philological science saw of what vital consequence to the development-theory was the relation between the several stages of language and the civilisations which were supposed to answer to them; and it is on this account that I have devoted so much space to the endeavour to show that this relation cannot be maintained. If the parent Aryan or the inflectional Hottentot had previously been isolating and agglutinative, the society which they represented would have already passed through two stages of civilisation analogous to the civilisations of China and Accad.

Professor Max Müller, in his highly important and suggestive lecture on "Chronology as applied to the Development of Language," has laid down (1.) that only where a sound and rational analysis of flection has been made can it be asserted that flection has arisen out of agglutination; and (2.) that all the three classes of language, isolating, agglutinating, and inflectional, trespass occasionally on one another's ground, and partake in some measure of the characteristics which distinguish each. Thus Chinese exhibits inflectional as well as agglutinative phenomena, and a sentence like *je le vous donne*, though divided artificially in writing, can scarcely be said to differ from a form of the Basque verb. Here, as elsewhere in nature, one species or family passes insensibly into another, and the boundary-line between them cannot be sharply defined. But this does not affect the general character of the language, although those who look to the individual word—the product of the latter age of reflection, analysis, or literature—instead of to the sentence may be puzzled how to distinguish between the three great classes of speech. The existence of these three great classes, however, is a fact; but it is equally a fact that in each of these phenomena occur which characterise the other two. The advocates of the development-theory would do well to consider this, and explain how it is that, in spite of the occurrence of inflectional phenomena, the agglutinative family has always remained agglutinative, the isolating family isolating. Chinese possesses forms which may be classed as agglutinative, and yet throughout the whole course of its long historical existence it has continued as true to its primitive type as the isolating dialects of barbarous Taic tribes. The Finnic verb may be called inflectional, but for all that the Finnic group is not less agglutinative than the Accadian of 4000 years ago. Aryan has always been inflectional, so far back as our verifiable facts allow us to go, and to postulate for it a preceding era of agglutination is an hypothesis which has all history against it. The cases of the Semitic noun were formed, not by juxtaposition, not by agglutination, but by the adaptation of vowel-differences; in the Aryan family itself certain instances of flection can be proved to have originated in mere euphonic distinctions of sound; and, as Westphal remarks ("Vergleichende Grammatik der indogermanischen Sprachen," p. xvii.), we ought not to ask, "Can agglutination become flection?" but, "Why has it not become so?" If the gradual growth of the preposition to the verb in composition or the history of the augment show that our family of speech was originally agglutinative, what explanation can be given of the fact that the Finnic idioms are still agglutinative though the verbal forms are inflectional? A language remains true to its type and makes the new products of speech conform to it by the power of analogy, but analogy is powerless where there is no type to which to conform. The development-theory is an hypothesis, unproved and unprovable; as a merely working hypothesis it has no doubt done good service; but it is time we should awake to the discovery that, though it explains some facts, there are other facts which it not only does not explain, but which are wholly incompatible with it. Perhaps the truth which it has shadowed forth, with exclusive regard to the outward material of speech, would be better expressed by keeping the eyes fixed on the inward and mental, and holding that, whereas in the first stage of language thought was, as it were, absorbed in its expression, the two factors being equally balanced in the second stage, in the third stage expression has to give way to thought, and we are conscious of the meaning rather than the phonetic sound of our utterances.

There is one point more to be noticed. The convenient distinction between derivative and flectional suffixes is as much the work of a reflective grammarian as is the so-called root. To convert the logical into the historical, and declare that the difference which analysis has drawn between the two kinds of suffixes was once an historical fact, is quite unwarranted. It hangs together with the attempt to transmute all the case-endings from the very first into pronominal, or at any rate independent, words. So far as I can see, many of the flections were formative suffixes before they were turned to their later use. The objective, the oldest case of the noun, still shows traces of its origin even in Aryan, and the case-endings of the Semitic languages bear their purely euphonic descent upon their face. The distinction between the formative and flectional part of a word was worked out gradually by the developing thought, which found phonetic machinery in plenty already existing for its expression. One of the earliest contrivances of language for elaborating the relations of grammar out of the sentence was the combination of a class-word with some other that served to define it. Such determinatives are still employed largely in the Taic languages of Further India, and out of the 44,500 words in the Chinese Imperial Dictionary of Kang-hi, 1097 begin with (or are formed upon) *sin*, "the heart." Even in Accadian, words may be lengthened by a final vowel like *babbara* by the side of *babbar* without any necessary change of signification.

A. H. SAYCE.

*March* 1875.

# PREFACE TO THE FIRST EDITION.

THE substance of the first eight of the following chapters was originally delivered in the form of lectures at Oxford in the early part of 1873. The last chapter is a subsequent addition, which should strictly be regarded as an appendix of the first. The detailed treatment of a single philological principle in it is so disproportionate to the general plan of the book, that its introduction can only be defended on the double ground of the great and far-reaching influence of analogy and the scant attention it has hitherto received. In tracing its action, I have had to review all the various parts of the science of language; and practical illustrations of this kind may be more efficacious than pages of abstract argument in showing clearly what I believe to be comprehended within the limits of Glottology, and in summing up the results I have tried to make good in the preceding chapters.

For the sphere and subject-matter of Comparative Philology are very liable to be unduly narrowed. The danger lies not so much with the followers of

Steinthal, who consider language too exclusively from the psychological and *à priori* point of view, as with those who, treading in the footsteps of Schleicher, would assimilate its study to the fashionable physical sciences, and demand a place for it by the side of chemistry or physiology. The belief that philology is etymology has passed away, only to be succeeded by the belief that it is phonology. But this belief, whether consciously or unconsciously held, cannot be too strenuously resisted. Etymology and phonology are parts of Comparative Philology, but they do not constitute Comparative Philology. This is a science of far more comprehensive reach; a science, too, which takes its start not from matter, but from mind. Glottology is an historic, as opposed to a physical, science; and its object is to trace the development of the human intelligence as expressed in the outward and enduring monuments of speech. Language is at once the creator and the mirror of society; and it is in and through society that the human mind has attained its present level of civilisation. Our science, therefore, by comparing the linguistic relics of social change and thought, by classifying sounds and words and sentences, by tracing out the history of forms and syntax, and determining the laws which govern speech, will work back to the progressive intelligence that produced them, and will tell us with the certainty of scientific knowledge, better than all the flints of Abbeville or the skulls of Bruniquel, how "man, the speaker," first raised himself above the level of the brute, how society progressed from an hive-like communism to the republics of Greece and the kingdoms of modern Europe, and how the fairy world of mythology, the instincts of an unrevealed religion, the philosophic systems of East and West, have grown out of the manifold imaginings of the mind as it struggled to express itself in language. To understand the present and to provide for the future we must know the past; and the key to this is given us by scientific philology. The very problems which face the logicians of our day, as they once faced Aristotle and Bacon, will never be solved until it is recognised that, instead of building up a so-called science on a narrow basis of empiric observation like the great Stagirite, or determining like Hegel the laws of being from the standpoint of modern European speech, we must begin at the opposite end, and learn from Glottology how the framework and character of our thought originated, and wherein it differs from that of other races in the past and present.

Phonology and letter-change, comparative grammar and comparative mythology, the history of words and their meanings, the origin of flection and the nature of roots—such are the subjects with which scientific philology has to deal; and the construction of an universal language is the practical object towards which it aims. Under the head of Comparative Grammar is included comparative syntax, a most important branch of study, but one which is only beginning to be worked. A thoroughgoing investigation of it may throw light on the difficult question as to the possibility of a mixed grammar; and Mr. Edkins already believes that he can detect the influence of Semitic idiom upon the doctrine of the relative and the definite article in Greek. The origin of language itself must be left to other sciences to reveal, but there is no reason to despair of our eventually determining this problem of problems. Glottology, however, has to postulate the existence of conscious and articulate speech; all that it can do is to point the way to the true solution of the riddle, to show what is the conclusion towards which its body of facts and evidence is tending. But this does not prevent the solution of the riddle being of the utmost importance to it; on the contrary, like the law of gravitation in astronomy, a knowledge of the genesis of speech will bind together the empirical generalisations of language, and give the reason for their special character. We cannot properly be said to know a subject, or to trace the course of its development, until we are able to resolve it into its original elements, and to discover how and out of what it arose.

The following pages, it will be seen, are rather critical than constructive. New theories have, indeed, been put forward in regard to mythology, and such points as gender and number; but the chief feature of the first seven chapters of the book is a criticism of certain generally received hypotheses which underlie a good deal of current philological reasoning, but which do not stand, as it seems to me, the test of facts. These hypotheses may be reduced to three axiomatic assumptions, against which the present rough-hewn work, however devoid of the graces of style, and bristling with uncouth words, is intended to be a protest. The belief that the Aryan languages are the standard of all others, and that the generalisations gathered from their exceptional phenomena are laws of universal validity; the substitution of the mechanical and the outward for the intellectual and the inward; the confusion between the convenient classifications of science and actual divisions into natural "families"—these are the three assumptions which, though maintained unconsciously, and rejected by most students when presented in their crude form, are yet the real causes of certain fashionable theories, which have even been elevated into "the most unquestionable results of modern philology." First and foremost among these is the doctrine of a graduated evolution of speech through an isolating and agglutinative into an inflectional stage—a doctrine which rests upon the second assumption, and explains the forms of grammar by the accidents of phonetic decay. When will it be recognised that the growth of most of our present flections out of independent words indicates not a primitive agglutination, but a preexisting inflectional instinct or analogy, which they could but follow, and that the near approach of certain members of the agglutinative group—the Finnic idioms, for example—to some of the phenomena of inflection only proves the fixed character of their mental point of view, which remained true to its agglutinative type, although the outward crust of language, the phonetic expression of the inward thought, had done its utmost to bring about a change?

Had it been remembered in what language really consists, we should have heard less of letters and more of sounds, less of outward form and more of inward meaning, less of phonetic decay and more of analogy; the philologist would have betaken himself to the study of living speech rather than of dead literature, and have learned that, instead of starting with the written crystallised word, he should have begun with the only actual whole of which language knows—the sentence. Had the sentence been made the basis of research, little would have been said of an agglutinative background to Aryan speech, or of a time when men talked with one another in roots. But, in fact, the larger part of the strange hypotheses which the discovery of roots has called forth are mostly dependent on the first assumption. I feel confident that the world would never have heard of "pronominal roots" had the Turanian tongues been the primary subject of inquiry; nor would the supposed necessity of finding biliteral radicals have made such wild havoc in the Semitic family. Even the term "family" itself calls up erroneous ideas.

The days are past, indeed, when philological and ethnological unity were imagined to be identical, but we still picture to ourselves a "family of languages," like a family in social life, except that it springs not from two ancestors, but from one. Such pictures, however, are but the convenient symbols of working science, and, if pressed too literally, lead to conclusions the reverse of the truth. Simplicity and unification are the latest result of time, and instead of forcing all the known dialects of the world under a few neatly labelled classes or "families," we should rather wonder that more waifs and strays have not come down to us out of the infinite essays of early speech.

The arguments with which I have endeavoured to combat these and similar views are founded upon three or four postulates. Language is social, not individual, interpreting the society of the past, and interpreted by the society of the present; it starts with the sentence, not with the word; it is the expression of thought; so that all explanations of its phenomena which rest contented with its outward form alone must be inadequate or erroneous; and its study, if carried on by the light of the comparative method, ought to embrace all the manifold operations and products of thought which are embodied in spoken utterance. These are the principles which underlie the following pages, and will furnish the key to what I have written. Throughout I have presupposed an acquaintance with Professor Max Müller's

"Lectures on the Science of Language," to whose world-wide popularity Comparative Philology owes its present position and its present charm. My indebtedness to their wealth of illustration will be apparent to every reader, and the familiar character of the work has relieved me of the necessity of encumbering my book with frequent references to it.

A. H. SAYCE.

QUEEN'S COLLEGE, OXFORD,
*May* 1874.

# CONTENTS.

# ANALYSIS OF THE CHAPTERS.

I. DATA OF GLOTTOLOGY ACCESSIBLE TO EVERY ONE—language the characteristic of man—objects of a science—Glottology still young and forced to put forth provisional hypotheses—these must be tested from time to time—nature of scientific hypotheses—scientific knowledge is *comparative*—the science of language, therefore, is the application of the comparative method to phonology and sematology—not to be confused with "scholarship"—not an exact science—uniformity of nature assumed—words (or derivatives) and languages compared and classified, grammar and structure forming the basis of classification—the laws of the science determined thereby—the laws (1) primary and (2) empirical—action of both affected by the two principles of Laziness (Phonetic Decay) and Emphasis—nature and effects of phonetic decay—and of emphasis (which embraces Dialectic Regeneration)—Glottology defined as an inductive historical science—historical more complex than physical sciences; but yet possible—language social, not individual; therefore an object of scientific treatment—the facts of the science are words or judgments; we can trace its laws only where these exist—definition of Comparative Philology, and relation of Psychology and Phonology to it—its relation to other sciences, especially the social ones—its laws (especially the empirical) verified by History (whence the value of modern European languages) and Psychology—starting-point of Comparative Philology, and relation of Physiology to it—does not treat of gestures or the origin of language—Rules to be observed by the student—significant change—name of the science and its relation to special philology.

II. Nature and use of hypotheses—Aryan philology made the standard and key of all philology—reasons of this idolum—sometimes not even all Aryan philology embraced—instances of false theories which rest on the assumption that the laws of Aryan philology are of universal validity—(1) that the roots of all languages are monosyllabic—(2) that all roots were originally verbal —(3) that grammar and vocabulary are similar among all members of the same family—the origin of the verbal expression in Aryan can be understood only by a comparison of other groups of languages.

III. Causes of a desire for unity—all things summed up in "the world"—meaning of the term—wish to trace all languages to a single source or two or three centres—all the facts against this—Aryan and Semitic not from a common source—what the facts are: structure, grammar, and vocabulary must be alike, with a regular interchange of letters—only a general likeness in all language: allied "families" the exception—no argument from the fluctuating state of savage speech—Lykian and Etruscan cannot be legitimately classified—

or the Caucasian dialects—Georgian, though inflectional, not Aryan—modern languages, like modern races, the selected residuum of infinitely various extinct species—slang and "new tongues" a reversion to primitive productiveness—savage communities isolated and small, and constantly change their languages—a language breaks out into dialects when it ceases to be literary—separate societies imply separate languages—civilisation unifies—conclusion.

IV. THEORY OF THREE STAGES OF DEVELOPMENT IN THE HISTORY OF SPEECH—definition of a *word*—language based on the *sentence*, not on the isolated word—hence flection really belongs to an earlier stage of development than agglutination—languages differ in the conception of the sentence—agglutinative languages, though presenting the phenomena of inflection, remain agglutinative; flectional languages, though admitting agglutination, remain inflectional—the idea that the existence of flectional phenomena must lead to flection due to our speaking inflected languages—different races have different potentialities—the development-theory disproved by history—Chinese and Accadian civilisation show that mental development does not imply "development" of language through the three stages; but since language is based on the sentence, and reflects society, it *must* imply this development were the theory true—the polysynthetic and incorporating languages overlooked by the theory—the theory suggested by a (grammatical) analysis of Aryan flection—verbal flection has grown out of agglutination—case-flection not successfully analysed—Professor Curtius's arguments answered—the cases have not grown out of "pronominal roots"—not so formed in agglutinative languages—*meaningless suffixes adapted to express a new case-relation when first struck out*—the Semitic cases distinguished by vocalic differences only—verb later than the noun—meaning of words first determined by their position in the sentence; then attached to their hitherto meaningless suffixes—hence the same suffix denotes different cases in different Aryan languages or in the same language—these meaningless suffixes shown to have existed in Aryan and Semitic—the case-endings like the suffixes—independent words when used symbolically made to conform to the inflectional character of the language—the inflectional instinct less strong now—no proof that some of the case-suffixes were independent words—if they were, it would imply retrogression—"pronominal roots" imaginary—historical proofs that new inflections arise by adapting old suffixes to mark a new relation—the synthetic and complex prior to the analytic and simple; what is *logically* first not *historically* so—Aryan languages always inflectional *so far as we know*—arguments against a primitive isolating stage stronger than against a primitive agglutinative one—men could not talk in roots—Chinese words not roots—roots contain no sentences; therefore could constitute no language—roots discovered by grammatical analysis no real *language*—language is an organism only metaphorically—the different stages of development in language represented by different races.

V. LANGUAGE TEST OF *social contact*, NOT OF *race*—examples—a whole language not necessarily borrowed—possibility of a mixed grammar—*idioms* borrowed—also the relation of subject and attribute—the Pehlevi inscriptions—the North Indian and North African dialects—*words denoting the relations of the noun may be borrowed when a language becomes analytic*—pronunciation influenced by neighbouring languages—borrowed words reveal the relations of nations and civilisations to one another—*but do not prove a negative*—objects known by the same name in different languages must have been known to the speakers; *but the converse does not hold good*—a borrowed word may be subjected to the laws of *lautverschiebung*—borrowed words not to be confused with words accidentally similar in sound—we must know on which side the debt lies—examples.

VI. LANGUAGE, THE REFLECTION OF SOCIETY, ORIGINALLY COMMUNISTIC—words have been differentiated out of sentences—compounds of late growth—the original types of language discoverable by comparison—nature of these roots—*roots differ in different languages*—if spoken, could not have had an abstract meaning—objects named from their (sensible) qualities—the name of the individual could be expressed only as part of a sentence—the Epithet-stage of language—implies fixity—ceremonial languages—period of the creation of the personal pronouns—period of analysis—sentences changed according to the momentary impression upon the senses; hence sentence-words innumerable—*lexical roots the residuum of numberless sentence-words*—roots dissyllabic—attempts to explain the origin of language—the question not insoluble or useless, but beyond the sphere of Glottology—decomposition of Aryan "roots"—views of Pott and Curtius—analysis not to be carried too far—some natural cries polysyllabic—clicks—phonetic decay (or regular letter-change)—indistinctness of primitive sounds—the oldest roots purely sensuous—theory of Pronominal Roots examined—roots peculiar to different dialects of the Aryan family—what lexical roots really are.

VII. MEANING OF "METAPHYSICS OF LANGUAGE"—first Greek grammar by Dionysius Thrax—belief in the conventional origin of grammar—how the conceptions of grammar are to be analysed—outward form symbolic—illustrations: Gender originates in different pronoun suffixes; the Dual prior to the Plural; the Objective case the most primitive form of the noun; the origin of the Genitive, and of the Persons of the verb—conclusion.

VIII. THOUGHT AND LANGUAGE CANNOT BE SEPARATED—words may influence thought—original meaning of words forgotten and new meaning assigned—names when first given sum up existing knowledge—as society and knowledge progress they become misleading and produce Mythology—Mythology, therefore, must be explained by the history of words, the fossils of the past strata of society and knowledge—"faded metaphors"—but only external side of mythology explained by words; not Religious Instinct, which underlies and preserves it—our knowledge of the development of this religious instinct derived from language—difference between a Religion and Mythology—mythology precedes a religion, and generally colours it—the dogmas of religion explicable by the history of language—hence both Comparative Mythology and the Science of Religions branches of Glottology—the records of the oldest religions locked up in dead languages—*religion the expression of society and the history of society given by language—only those myths to be compared which are supported by etymological evidence*—the Iliad—similar myths arise independently among uncivilised races—*history cannot be extracted from myths where historical evidence is wanting*—the "Nibelungen Lied"—Euhemerism—what is native and borrowed must be distinguished in mythology—story of the Kyklôps—Allegory and Fable contrasted with Myth—origin of Totemism—Eponymous ancestors—the religious instinct first shows itself in *the worship of dead ancestors*—hence origin of Serpent-worship—*animal wants instigated worship*—Fetichism, second stage of development—germs of a mythology—worship of Nature coeval with Epithet-stage and a developed Mythology—why few myths about the moon—objects of nature anthropomorphised—this perpetuated in language (*i.e.*, mythology)—objections to Comparative Mythology: (1) too high, and (2) too feeble an imagination presupposed in early man—solar origin of some myths *proved* by the Rig-Veda and non-Aryan mythologies—other objections—Dogmatology: how religions must be compared.

IX. Importance of the principle of analogy, and relation to it of phonetic decay—what is meant by *false analogy*—analogy acts upon both the Form and the Content of speech—the action of analogy due to Laziness and Imitation—roots which differ in meaning not necessarily unallied—changes effected by analogy in Accent, in Quantity, and in Phonology—explanation of

Grimm's law—false analogies in the Homeric poems—analogy creative in the *material* of language (euphonic differences made significant)—vowel-change as originating flection in Aryan—effect of analogy on Grammatical Forms; on Structure; and on Syntax—position of the verb—influence of analogy on the meaning of words—popular etymologies: analogy and mythology—mistaken etymologies in Homer—affectation of archaism in the Odyssey—modern English spelling—origin and nature of Poetry and Rhyme—conclusion.

# THE PRINCIPLES

OF

# COMPARATIVE PHILOLOGY.

## CHAPTER I.

### THE SPHERE OF COMPARATIVE PHILOLOGY AND ITS RELATION TO THE OTHER SCIENCES.

AMONG the many new departments of study which have been called into existence by the extension of the scientific method, there is none that possesses greater interest than Comparative Philology. It is, on the one hand, so closely bound up with the history of mankind in general, while, on the other, it enters so largely into the life of the private individual, that there are none whose attention it ought not to excite. We have no need, as in ethnology or botany, to collect from outside the preliminary facts upon which the science is built: the facts of Comparative Philology are literally in the mouths of every one; they are the words which we speak, the thoughts which we clothe in articulate language, the indispensable links of union which bind together a civilised society. While we are thus favourably placed in regard to the materials of our study, the study itself appeals at once to our reason, our imagination, and our curiosity. Language peculiarly belongs to man; it is the most characteristic mark of distinction between him and the brute; and the careful examination of it seems therefore especially appropriate to him. The object of all science, it may be presumed, is twofold: to obtain such a knowledge of nature and its laws as shall enable us to combine and control them practically for our future use and benefit. Years have not deprived the old Delphic oracle of its truth, and a knowledge of ourselves is still the most important that we can acquire. The improvement of the species, the amelioration of society, the well-being and happiness of the individual, are the most pressing questions of our age. But to answer these satisfactorily, we must know the laws which govern the race and the individual, and the way in which we have arrived at our present condition. Every new discovery confirms the theory of progressive development: man was not once what he now is; and the long series of centuries that lie behind us have seen him slowly changing with changing circumstances, and gradually moulded by the experiences and habits of former generations. It is not the outward form of man that concerns us now; that, indeed, may have altered, and the long ape-like jaw of the primitive savage have contracted into the mouth of a Cleopatra or a Mary Queen of Scots. But the change of external shape has little interest for the politician and philanthropist; it is rather an index of deeper spiritual changes than the cause of them; and with these more secret and subtle changes the student of society has alone to do. It is the development of the moral and intellectual life of mankind, a knowledge of which is so necessary if we would understand the present state of society, and rightly set about its improvement. But over the first beginnings of this moral and intellectual life—the very foundations of it, without which all the superstructure is but half intelligible—there is drawn, as it were, the veil of Isis, and the veil can only be lifted by the interpreter of the symbol. Such an interpreter is language, the mediator between the spiritual and the physical, which records the varying phases of human thought in enduring symbol and sensuous metaphor, like the rocks which bear witness to the climate and zoology of remote geological eras. If we are to look anywhere for the solution of some of the highest problems connected with the history of our species, it must be, above all, to the science of language. Already much has been done by it; not the least good being the clearance of many old prepossessions and beliefs that blocked up the path of inquiry, and distorted all the evidence that might be presented to the mind.

But it must be remembered that the science is still in its infancy, and more has been expected from it than its present stage of advancement would legitimately allow us to demand. Many causes have combined to give an impetus in the present day to the investigation of the historical sciences—those, namely, which deal with man and his works, and to the study of social phenomena. Ready conclusions and rapid generalisations are wanted; answers to the many questions which are starting up on all sides cannot be waited for; and the Comparative Philologist is accordingly called upon to furnish the key or suggest the solution of numerous difficulties. His situation is a tempting one. Knowing, as he does, how much certain ground has already been won, and acquainted with a further range of data from which he is only too well disposed to draw hasty inferences, he is ready to take his seat on the tripod, and deliver dogmatic statements which are received by the general public as so many ascertained facts. If put forward as provisional hypotheses only, intended to represent the sum total of the evidence upon some particular subject which the inquirer had at his disposal, such statements would have great value; but the mischief done is immense when they are made and received as of equal authority with the ground-principles of the science, and become so many propositions which may not be contradicted. It is, indeed, the lot of all new sciences; but none the less necessary on that account to be foreseen and guarded against.

A man's foes, it has been said, are those of his own household. Comparative Philology has suffered as much from its friends as from its opponents; and now that it has at last won its way to general recognition and respect, there is a danger that its popularity may lead to the cessation of sound and honest work, and to an acquiescence in theories which, however plausible, are not yet placed upon a footing of scientific certainty. The great names to whom the scientific study of language owes its origin are passing away from among us, and there is reason to fear that their places may be taken by patient plodders, content to work out small details, and to walk in the paths already traced for them, rather than to criticise and re-examine the magnificent generalisations of their masters, and to further the progress of the study by fresh hypotheses of their own. Newton was followed by a century of stagnation, and Aristotle's successors were the grammarians of Alexandria. Geniuses are rare, and it is much easier for the ordinary man to fill in by patient elaboration what has already been sketched for him in outline, than to venture upon a new line of discovery, in which the sole clue must be the combinative powers of his own imagination and comprehensive learning. And yet, now as much as ever Comparative Philology has need at once of bold and wide-reaching conceptions, of cautious verification, and of a mastery of facts. It is true the science is no longer struggling for mere life, and the time is gone by for proving the possibility of its existence. But it is still young, scarcely, indeed, out of its nursery; a small portion only of its province has hitherto been investigated, and much that is at present accepted without hesitation will have to be subjected to a searching inquiry, and possibly be found baseless after all.

Scientific hypotheses do not pretend to do more than explain all those phenomena which are known at the time of their formation: they supply the mind with a clue for further researches; they serve to connect the isolated facts, and to simplify the bewildering maze in which we find ourselves; and however erroneous they may eventually turn out to be, they will yet be of use, like will-o'-the-wisps, in warning future students from what has been proved to be wrong. But they can do no more than this; with the accession of further facts and the enlargement of the boundaries of the science, they have to be continually modified, and often to be given up altogether. A science consists of hypotheses more or less nearly related; and its aim is to make these hypotheses correspond more and more closely with the observed facts. It is evident, therefore, that while a science cannot progress without the formation and testing of hypotheses, a young science, like that of Philology, will put forward many which maturer knowledge will show to be untenable.

Now, it is necessary to bear in mind what is meant by science and scientific knowledge. Scientific differs from the ordinary knowledge of practical life in being *comparative.* In order to know an object or be conscious of a sensation, we have to compare and contrast it with some other object or sensation. The more accurately this act of comparison is performed, the more nearly shall we approach to scientific certainty. For this purpose a standard of comparison is required, some third term with which we may compare our two other terms. In other words, to use Mr Herbert Spencer's language, the distinction between scientific and unscientific knowledge is, that the one is *quantitative*, the other *qualitative*. The primitive savage knew the qualitative difference between hot and cold water; his senses told him that much: a scientific knowledge of the matter began with the thermometer, which enables us to measure the amount of heat in each case.

It is easy enough, then, to see wherein a scientific treatment of language differs from that haphazard charlatanry at which Voltaire directed one of his epigrams. Language is the expression of thought and feeling through mechanical means; and just as it has been found possible to construct a science of thought and feeling, so with greater reason should we expect to discover law and order when that thought and feeling has been subjected to the restraints of physiological conditions, and expressed in articulate speech. Every sound emitted by the human voice is the result of the physical formation of the vocal organs, and of the manner in which these are brought into contact with the breath; while, on the other hand, the laws which govern the development of the human mind will necessitate the expression of thought and its relations in a particular way. Language is limited as much on the psychological as upon the physiological side: a knowledge of this twofold limitation will constitute its science. And inasmuch as the two sides can be as little separated from one another in actual speech as oxygen and hydrogen in water, or colour from the objects about us, the general laws of the science must relate to the combination, although, for analytical purposes, it may be advisable to investigate the two separately. But we must never forget that such a separate investigation is preliminary only. Neither linguistic metaphysics nor phonology by themselves represent philology, but a combination of both. We may have laws of phonology like that of Grimm, or laws of linguistic metaphysics, such as that every predicate must have a subject. But these are only empirical, subordinate, and partial, forming the scaffolding of the higher and more comprehensive generalisations of the master-science itself. This, however, is a truth often forgotten, and more will be said about it further on.

Now, in being scientific, Philology must be comparative; and it is simply the application of the comparative method to the phenomena of language that has brought the new science into being. The attempt to study a language without reference to any other is futile. A certain number of empirical rules may indeed be found peculiar to the language in question, but the reasons of the existence of these, and the more important and general laws to which the language conforms, can only be discovered by a methodical comparison with other dialects, while many of the fancied facts of "scholarship" will turn out to be the most portentous errors. Hence originated such beliefs as the derivation of Latin from the Æolic dialect, the misconception of the locative case, the idea of the priority of the passive to the middle voice in Greek, the identity of *καλέω* and "call," *ὅλος* and "whole," or the grotesquely wrong meanings assigned to such Homeric words as *διερὸς* and *μέροπος*,[1] not to speak of Buttmann's endea-

[1] The old grammarians connected the Homeric *διερὸς* with *διαίνω*, and so identified it with the post-Homeric *διερὸς*, "wet." Accordingly, *διερὸς βροτός* (Od. 6, 201) was explained to mean "a mortal filled with the juices of life," and *διερῷ ποδί* (Od. 9, 43), "with juicy," *i.e.*, "quick foot!" *Μέροψ* was derived from *μείρομαι* (or rather, *μερίζω*) and *ὄψ* in the sense of "dividing the voice," *i.e.* "articulate," in disregard of the fact that *μέρος* and *μερίζω* do not occur in Homer, the allied *μόρος*, *μοῖρα*, and *εἵμαρται* only implying "apportionment," not "division" (Curtius, Grundzüge d. Griech. Etymol., p. 104). *Διερὸς* really comes from the same root as *δίω*, *δῖνος*, Sansk. *dî*, "to hasten," whence by an easy transition of meaning we get also, *δεινός*, *δέος*, *δείδω*, and *dirus;* while *μέροπες* must be "the snatchers," connected with *μάρπτω*, like *στεροπή* and *στέροψ* with *ἀ-στράπτω* (Fick iu Kuhn's "Zeitschrift für vergleichende Sprachforschung," xx. 3, 1871). Confinement to the resources of a single language not only brought about such absurd etymologies as abound in Plato's "Kratylus," but sometimes resulted iu the invention of a purely imaginary word. Thus the Scholiasts, after exhausting all possible references to *τρίτος*, to the Libyan lake Tritônis, or to the Bœotian torrent Tritôn in *τριτογένεια*, the Homeric epithet of Athena, coined in their despair a word, *τριτώ*, which was put down as an Æolic term for "the head" (Schol. Aristoph. Nub. 989, Tzetz. Lycophr. 519). The origin of *Tritogeneia*, however, does not seem far to seek. I would connect it

vour to get ἄφνος out of ἄφθονος.[1] Until a common quantitative standard was applied, until it was recognised that language, like everything else in this world, obeys undeviating laws of its own, excessively complicated though these may be, such mistakes were inevitable. As in other things, so in language. We cannot really understand a single dialect unless we study it in the light of others. For literary and artistic purposes this may not be necessary, but then we must not confound such a study with philological knowledge, and believe that we know a language because we can successfully imitate the idiosyncrasies of a few of its literary men.[2]

with the Vedic deity *Trita*, who is said to have harnessed the sun-horse (see Rig-V. i. 163, 2, 3). Now Trita has long ago been shown by Burnouf to be the Thraêtaona, son of Athwya, of the Avesta, who finally became transformed into the Feridún of Firdusi, the slayer of Zohák, or *Aji daháka*, "the biting snake" of night and darkness. "Trita-born" would be a fitting title for Athena, the dawn-goddess.

[1] Ἄφνος or ἄφενος is akin to the Sansk. *ap-nas*, "possession," Lat. *ops*, *op-es*, *op-ulentus*, *in-ops*, and *copia* (=*co-op-i-a*).

[2] Dr Wagner, in the President's Annual Address to the London Philological Society for 1873 (p. 33), says (speaking of German scholars), "We have passed the stage of a sentimental admiration of the ancient authors, such as we find it in the editions of Heyne and his school. Our eyes are fully open to the shortcomings and failings of Latin literature when considered æsthetically, nor do we any longer attribute to this literature the 'humanising' influence so *naïvely* believed in by former centuries. There is among us very little of that which may be termed *elegant* scholarship—which is all very nice, but perfectly useless; in fact, we do not work

In calling Comparative Philology a science, we must not, of course, think of it as an exact science like astronomy. Here the phenomena are comparatively but little complicated, and have been studied for a considerable number of years. The generalisations obtained from them by a comparison of instances have been so far simplified as to be resolved into the one primary law of gravitation, which serves as the starting-point of deductively determining the relations of new astronomical phenomena. Other sciences have not yet reached this exactness; chemistry seems likely soon to find its primary law, but meteorology, sociology, and many more in which the phenomena are extremely complex, are very far indeed from such perfection. Here we can only collect, compare, and classify, thankful if we can bring the isolated phenomena under some general heads which may bear more or less relation to one another. The process is strictly inductive; we assume the uniformity of nature, and generalise from the facts in

like ladies, but like men mindful of a serious purpose, which is, in the first line, to trace the intellectual life of the great Roman nation in its literature; and secondly, to show and follow the connecting links between this literature and the other nations of Europe and Asia. To attain this end, it is necessary to pursue the most minute investigations, but not to generalise without sufficient data and foundations. But the days in which it was held the height of Latin scholarship to write a splendid Ciceronian style, and to turn neat Latin verses, are past, and will never return."

accordance with what we see at present going on around us, testing these generalisations by fresh instances and combination of instances. Thus in Philology the facts with which we have to deal are thoughts expressed in speech. So far as these will carry us, we can proceed with our generalisations. We assume that the same mental processes were involved in the first attempts at language that are involved now, and that, given a certain arrangement of the vocal organs, the same sound will always have been produced. In other words, we assume the uniformity of nature in regard to language. With this assumption we proceed to our comparisons, classifying the like together and separating the unlike. It is the object of the science to discover the limits of this classification, and to create an ideal type, as in natural history, around which we may group the several phenomena which resemble one another. Thus we put the so-called Indo-European languages into a class apart by referring them to a hypothetical Aryan parent-speech; and we throw together a number of derivatives, or a series of ideas, by assuming a common root or a common primary notion. In this way we come to know the typical marks by which similar instances may be recognised. The analogy of the other sciences would lead us to infer that these typical marks are by no means those which first meet the superficial view; and, in fact, one of the first results of Comparative Philology was to lay down that mere similarity of sound could constitute no basis for a sound comparison. Language is not phonology only; if we would seek the true marks of difference and resemblance, we must penetrate below the surface, and find some surer guide to our first attempts at grouping than the shifting modifications of sound. Speech is uttered thought; grammar and structure therefore must lead the way to the examination of the lexicon. When we have formed our groups by comparing the grammatical characteristics of the languages under review, we may complete the process by comparing the vocabularies, knowing the limits within which the resemblance of letters is due to identity of origin, and not to accident. The groups thus formed will then have to be compared with one another, and the general laws of the science determined thereby. It is evident that such a comparison must be as wide as possible; the greater the number of facts brought together, the more diversified in time, and space, and circumstances the languages compared, the safer and more general will our conclusions be. To confine our attention to a single family of speech, much more to two or three members of the family, will lead us into many errors and false generalisations.

No idiom, however obscure and barbarous, can be despised by the comparative student. The most precious facts of the science will often lie in dialects whose very names are almost unknown, and whose speakers stand upon the lowest level of humanity. It is in these, however, and not in the polished periods of a classical literature, that we can trace the fundamental laws and working of primitive speech, and detect those simple contrivances which have elsewhere been obliterated. Science desires truth, not beauty, although in the end the true is always the beautiful.

The laws or generalisations which we are called upon to observe are of two kinds—empirical and ultimate or primary. So long as we confine our attention to one part only of the subject, we meet with a number of rules which are always complied with, though we cannot account for their existence. Thus we find that a Gothic *g* almost invariably answers to a Greek $\chi$, a Latin *h* or *f*, a Sanskrit *gh*, and a Slavonic *g* or *z*; but why this should be we cannot at present tell.[1] We only know that such is the case; it is an empirical law, the immediate result of observation, which

[1] These phonetic changes have, it is true, been brought about by the influence of climate, food, laziness or the reverse, analogy, and fashion; but we are still ignorant of the relative power of these causes, and the precise manner in which they affect the phonology of a language.

will have to be explained by some higher and more comprehensive law. These subordinate laws have to be made out before the primary can be deduced from them by comparison; but the primary laws alone belong to Comparative Philology properly so called, the subordinate ones relating to the preliminary subdivisions of the science, such as Phonology. But the action of both kinds of law alike is affected by two great principles or causes of change in language. These cannot be called laws themselves, since they do not act in an invariable manner; but they make a science of language possible, by preventing it from being stationary, and by bringing about that constant movement and development in speech which allows the action of the several laws to take place. These two principles may be named Laziness and Emphasis. The first of these has been made familiar to every one by Professor Max Müller under the name of Phonetic Decay. Words become clipped and shortened in the course of time, until it may happen that nothing is left of the original, some secondary termination alone remaining. Thus the Latin *pilus* has passed the various stages of the Spanish *peluca*, the Italian *perruca*, the French *perruque*, and the English *perwiche*, *periwig*, into the modern *wig*. Rapid speaking, an imperfect ear or pronunciation, and the common desire to save time and trouble, will inevitably wear away the words of everyday life. Where little care is taken of language, where there is no literature, and no standard or court dialect, the vocabulary will be like the drift boulders that line our valleys, or the sand and gravel of ancient beaches. The lower we descend in the scale of culture, the more rapid and extensive will be the process of decay. The Berlin workman has contracted *ich* into *i*, like our own countrymen; and the waggoner's *wo!* and *way!* are the last relics of *withhold* and *withstay*. In spite of artificial attempts to preserve the full forms of the words, and the adoption of Greek metres by a literary coterie, the curt colloquialisms of the plays of Plautus and Terence, or the *cauneas* with which the contemporaries of Cicero[1] scandalised the purist, became the models after which the Romance languages shaped themselves.[2] It may not be a distant period at which the *don't*, the *I'll* and the *isn't* of conversation take their

[1] Cic. de Div., ii. 40, 84: "Quum M. Crassus exercitum Brundisii imponeret quidam in portu, caricas Cauno advectas vendens, *Cauneas* clamitabat. Dicamus, si placet, monitum ab eo Crassum, *caveret ne iret*."

[2] Thus, in Heaut. v. 5, 16, scansion requires us to pronounce, "Gnáte m'yó pol tí do póllam lépidam quám tu faíl amés;" and in Adelphi, iii. 2, 20, "Ad'lescént' ips' érip'r' œílos: pósthac præcip'tem darém," where we are reminded of the French *œil*. (See Donaldson, "Varronianus," pp. 524-527.)

authorised place in books; and if *ain't* is never able to lose its taint of vulgarity, it will be due to the printing-press and the schoolmaster. Children are the best representatives that we have of the infantile and barbarous state of society, and the language of childhood is one of maimed and half-pronounced words. Such nursery names as Tom, Harry, Bob, Peggy, have become so many household terms. But phonetic decay is especially accelerated by the contact of two languages. The attempt to speak a foreign idiom leads to the rejection of all difficult sounds. Thus the final guttural in our *enough, through, though,* has been softened and lost; and languages such as the Hawaian, which do not suffer two consonants to follow one another, turn words like "steel" into *kila* (for *tila*). Indeed, contraction and decay may be carried so far as to become an idiosyncrasy of a particular language. This is pre-eminently the case in French, which persistently modifies the pronunciation of every foreign word which it has to adopt, in accordance with its principle of rejecting the final letters. Thus London must be Londres, and Biarritz Biarri', in spite of local usage. The terminal consonants have been lost in the majority of words, and the rest of the vocabulary has had to follow the general fashion.[1] Analogy has immense power

[1] The Chinese similarly reduce foreign words to one syllable

in language, and whatever once becomes a distinguishing feature of a dialect forms a type after which every exception is gradually forced to model itself.[1] As poetry is better remembered than prose, so the rhythm of analogy fixes itself upon the memory, and the ear and will, once accustomed to a particular association of sound and idea, instinctively demand the sound when the idea has to be expressed. Irregularities constantly tend to disappear, more especially if no artificial means are employed to perpetuate them. The Æolic dialect assimilated the accentuation of every word to the general rule which threw the accent back upon the antepenultima; our own tongue is replacing the strong preterites of our verbs by the secondary perfect in *-ed*, originally *dide* (did), the reduplicated past tense of *do*; and an English child whom I knew, born and brought up in France, and speaking French only, conjugated all the verbs regularly, saying, for instance, *avrai* for *aurai*, and *allerai* for *irai*. In fact, we

when they have to repeat them. The Pigeon-English of Canton offers numerous examples of this; and the Chinese at San Francisco, I am told, invariably say, "Morn' Mis' Stan'," instead of "Morning, Mr Stanford."

[1] M. Ancessi ("L'*S* causatif et le thème *N* dans les langues de Sem et de Cham," p. 72) asks why French for some time past classes all its new verbs, however derived, and of whatever meaning, under the first conjugation. No one "would dare to pronounce *électrisoir*, *chloroformir*, *photographire*." See Chapter IX.

may lay it down as an universal rule that the oldest grammatical forms are those which are rarest in a language; so that when we find in Sanskrit only a very small number of verbal roots, such as *as-mi, ad-mi,* which affix the personal endings without any intervening element, we may regard them as going back to the most ancient period of the speech. The influence of analogy had been continually narrowing the province of the formation, until only those verbs which constituted the most necessary stock-in-trade of everyday life were able to resist the encroachments of other later but more popular forms. If, however, we really want to see the principle of Phonetic Decay in its full activity and importance, we must turn our eyes to unwritten dialects rather than to that particular dialect which has accidentally been stereotyped into the standard language of literature. Here the various processes which change and devolop language go on unchecked; and unless we can compare dialect with dialect, it is often obviously impossible to settle the original form, and therefore the true etymology, of some word in the special idiom we are examining. The wear and tear of time alters so completely the face of words, that where we are not able to apply the scientific method of comparison by the help of cognate dialects, our attempt at derivation is likely to be nothing more than an unscientific guess. It is this want of allied dialects that makes Latin etymology a matter of such difficulty and uncertainty; and we have to be thankful for the fragments of Oscan, Umbrian, and Sabellian which we can recover from a few inscriptions or the scanty notices of grammarians. When we remember that it is only our extensive knowledge of the languages which are, as it were, the daughters of Latin that enables us to trace such a word as the French *même*, for instance, through the Portuguese *mesmo*, the Old French *meïsme*, the Provençal *medesme*, and the Old Provençal *smetessme*, to the Latin *semetipsissimum*, we may well despair of making out the true ancestry of words when such an assistance is not available. Even the Turanian or Ugro-Altaic languages,[1] which do not so readily admit of

[1] The term *Turanian* must be confined to those Ugro-Altaic languages which, as it seems to me, have been proved by Schott and others to be related to one another (extending from Finland on the one side to Manchuria on the other). Under the Ugrian dialects are classed Finnish, Lapp, Mordvinian, Tcheremissian, Votiak, Zyrianian, Vogulian, &c.; while the Altaic comprise the three great sub-classes of Turkish-Tatar, Mongolian, and Tungusian. The Samoiedian idioms stand midway between the Ugric and the Altaic. With this family Basque has also been grouped. Prince Lucien Bonaparte, Charencey, and others have tried to show that this interesting language more or less closely agrees with Ugric in grammar, structure, numerals, and pronouns. M. Antoine d'Abbadie, in d'Abbadie and Chaho's "Études Grammaticales sur la Langue euskarienne" (pp. 17, 18), has pointed out as far back as 1836 the resemblances that exist between Basque

phonetic decay as the inflectional families of speech, are kept living by the same active principle, and without dialectic comparison we should be altogether unable to penetrate their secrets. It is thus that we can analyse the verbal forms in Magyár, Mordvinian, and Vogul, which incorporate the objective pronouns or trace the original forms of the Turanian numerals; and if Basque is to be added to the group, the importance of an acquaintance with a variety of dialects becomes still more manifest. The Basque verb presents the phenomenon of incorporation to an astonishing degree; not only the objective cases of the pronouns, but the datives and the index of the plural as well, are inserted into the body of the word, and the whole has been fused together by the influence of phonetic decay into a hardly distinguishable unity. A comparison of the several Basque dialects—Labourdin, Souletin, High and Low Navarrese, Guipuscoan, and Biscayan—is equally indispensable for the vocabulary. Basque has existed for centuries as an unwritten language, separated from the rest of its kindred, and struggling for existence in a small tract of country. If

on the one hand, and Magyár and Lapp on the other. The resemblances, however, are general, not special; and how wanting Basque really is in the characteristics of a true Ural-Altaic language may be seen from Vinson's edition of Ribary's Basque Grammar.

we are to discover the affinities of its lexicon, it must be by knowing what were the primitive forms of its words. The larger part of the dictionary is, indeed, derived from Spanish or French; but when we find that the natives of S. Jean de Luz[1] ordinarily drop *r* and *d* between vowels, without even the substitution of the aspirate, thus making *harits* (oak) *haits*,[2] *aditu* (heard) *aïtu*, *baduzu* (have you) *bauzu*, *emadazu* (give me) *emāzu*, we may well be cautious even when we are dealing with a member of the agglutinative family of speech.

Of course, phonetic decay attacks principally those portions of a word or sentence upon which

[1] That is, the Labourdin dialect.

[2] The aspirate is frequently lost, and we have *aits* for *haits*, and *iri* (town) for *hiri*. *H* often stands for *g* (as in *bihar*, "to-morrow;" *ihes*, "flight"), and *k* (according to Prince Lucien Bonaparte and M. Vinson), especially at the beginning of a word (*e.g.*, *hill*, "to die;" *hume*, "child," in *ar-kume*, "lamb," *ema-kume*, "woman"), often also for *n* between two vowels (thus *liho*= "linum," *ohore*= "honorem," *diru* (for *diharu*)= "denarium"). It is possible that *harits* may be a loan-word, since a dialectic variation gives us *aretcha;* and so the word might be traced back to the Latin *quercus*. (See Vinson, *Revue de Linguistique*, v. 1872.) Van Eys, however ("Dictionnaire Basque-Français," pp. viii.-xi.), disputes the priority of the guttural to the aspirate; and though the change of *h* into *g* or *k* is contrary to the usual phonetic law in language that the harder sound passes into the easier, and not the easier into the harder, the arguments of so profound a Basque scholar require a careful examination.

no emphasis falls.[1] The accented syllable remains untouched, and when this is a secondary derivative, and not part of the root, sometimes causes the entire loss of the root itself, as in *age* from *ætaticum*, where the first letter only claims connection with *ævum*, *αἰών* (Etruscan *aiv-il*), our *ever*, Sansk. *âyus* "like."[2] In a case of this kind we have another principle besides laziness brought into play. It is the striving after clearness and distinctness, the second cause of change in language, which I have called the principle of Emphasis. It works in the contrary direction to Phonetic Decay, and, as it were, counterbalances the latter. The use of language is to make ourselves intelligible to others; and the more intelligible we wish to be, the more careful we are in our pronunciation, and the greater stress we lay upon those words or syllables to which we would particularly direct the attention. If we find that a foreigner does not understand us, we instinctively raise the voice and speak with slowness and precision. There can be little doubt that the principle of Emphasis loses in force with the

[1] The general rule may thus be laid down, that the accented syllable is never lost; and, consequently, derivations like that of *dîner* (*disner*), *dine*, from *desinere*, have to be rejected.

[2] Max Müller, "Lectures on the Science of Language," i. 304.

progress of culture and intelligence. Education makes us readier in catching the meaning of those with whom we are conversing, and our mastery over ideas gives us the clue to many of which only a fragment, only a suggestion, has reached the ear.[1] The modern Englishman of the upper classes, particularly if he belong to the south of the island, is notorious for closing his lips and lazy indistinctness of speech. It is quite otherwise with savage races. They lack that quickness in seizing the signification of what is set before them which is characteristic of the civilised man, even though they do not display that hopeless bewilderment which Mr Galton's African Dammaras showed when required to count beyond three.[2] The meaning of their words has to be eked out by gesture and gesticulation, and the muscular effort called forth by these necessarily extends to the elocution also. If we would speak

[1] This principle of Emphasis lies at the root of that repetition of the negative which is so striking in Greek. Vulgar English emphasises and strengthens a negation in the same natural way, and it is only the growth of culture that has made two negatives express an affirmative instead of a stronger negative. This intellectual laziness and economy, the syntactical analogue of phonetic decay, has proceeded to its most extreme point in cases like the French *pas*, *point*, *jamais*, where the negative is dropped altogether, and has to be supplied by the mind.

[2] See Sir J. Lubbock's "Origin of Civilisation and Primitive Condition of Man," pp. 333-336, and Galton's "Tropical South Africa," p. 132.

clearly, we must take the trouble to exert our muscles in the endeavour.[1]

Now the principle of Emphasis acts upon language in many ways. First of all, it lies at the bottom of what Professor Max Müller entitles Dialetic Regeneration, which he seems to set up as the counterbalancing principle to Phonetic Decay. The words, however, and still more rarely the grammatical forms, which from time to time find their way from the so-called dialects into the literary language, are too few and unimportant for the process to be raised into a principle, much less a principle co-extensive with that of Laziness. We want one which is the same in kind; one, namely, which is due to the general constitution of our nature. Moreover, Dialectic Regeneration principally applies to literary languages only, not to the mass of human speech. And even in these its action is extremely limited, and, unless we can find the motive of it, at once accidental and capricious. The motive, however, is the desire to give additional strength and clearness; to make the language employed more forcible, and therefore

[1] M. Antoine d'Abbadie has informed me of a curious custom among the Gallas. A Galla orator marks the punctuation of his speech by lashing a leathern whip which he holds in his hand. Thus a slight stroke denotes a comma, a harder cut a semicolon, a still harder one a full stop, while a note of admiration is represented by a furious cut through the air.

more distinct and plain. A new word, taken up from the fresh fountain of living speech, carries with it new ideas, and impresses itself upon the mind more vividly than the familiar expressions which have become nothing except dead, insipid symbols. We read of the "four points of the compass," with a full understanding of what is meant, but without picturing it to ourselves in any way; but when Carlyle talks of "the four airts," at once our attention is aroused, and our imagination engaged. Our mechanical association of sound and sense can alone be broken through by novelty, and the excitement of realising the complete force of a term which has come up from the patois where the life of language is still vigorous, and words have not become mere counters and conventional signs. Another mode of arresting our attention and giving distinctness to the thought which has to be expressed is by setting two synonymes side by side. This is especially frequent in a language like English, the vocabulary of which owes as much to Latin as to Saxon; and much of the charm of the authorised version of the Bible is due to the fact that the translators have usually tried to bring out the meaning of a Greek word by using two English equivalents, one from a Romanic, the other from a Teutonic source. In this way we are obliged to dwell upon the conception intended, and to contrast and define the two synonymes. Somewhat similar is the origin of that analytical tendency which distinguishes our modern European languages. The difficulty of mutual comprehension on the part of the Roman provincials and their Teutonic conquerors necessitated the distinct expression of each grammatical shade of meaning by a separate word. The old broken-down inflections would no longer suffice. The idea had to be clearly marked out, not merely suggested, for a people whose ear and mind were unaccustomed to the language with which they came in contact. *Amabo* did not sufficiently convey the conception of futurity to the Frank: the termination allowed him neither time nor opportunity to consider what it intended to signify; and in order to have the tense-distinction clearly presented to his view, it was necessary to go back to the definite representation of futurity—*ama-fuo*—out of which *amabo* had grown, and analyse the concept into *aimer-ai*, "I have to love." Even this was not enough; the personal pronoun had to be prefixed, and no longer implied only in the form; and when *j'aimerai* itself had become familiar and conventional, a new mode of expression, in which the attention might be fixed upon the fact that future time was denoted, had to be invented in *je vais aimer*. The influence of Emphasis will again show itself not only in the preservation of sounds that would otherwise be subject to phonetic decay, but also in the introduction of expletive ones. The insertion of the dental and labial in such Greek words as ἀν-δ-ρὸς and μεσημ-β-ρία may indeed be ascribed to the first principle rather than to the second, since their addition facilitates pronunciation; but this cannot be said for the final *d* in our own *sound*, *lend* (A.-S. *lænan*), *riband* (Fr. *ruban*), and the like. The same letter has also crept into *thunder* (A.-S. *thunor*), *tender*, and *jaundice* (Fr. *jaunisse*). The effort to be distinct has again produced *thumb* out of *thum-a*, *behest* out of *behæs*, *amongst* out of *amonges*, *tyrant* from the Old Fr. *tiran*, *parchment* from *parchemin*, *ancient* from *ancien*. So, too, *citizen* has come from *citoyen*, though this may have been due to an orthographic mistake. Hardly so, however, the inserted letter in *impregnable*, from the French *imprenable;* and the cases of an intrusion of an *n* or *r* into the middle of a word are numerous. Thus *nightingale* represents in the A.-S. *nihtegale*, *messenger*, *passenger*, and *popinjay* are the Old Fr. *messagier*, *passagier*, and *papigai;* *groom* and *horse* are the A.-S. *guman* and *hôs*, *cartridge* is the Fr. *cartouche*, *corporal* is *caporal*, *culprit* comes from *culpa*. Similarly *n* has been added in *bittern*, A.-S. *butore*, and *marten*, A.-S. *mearth*, and the Fr. *perdrix* (our *partridge*) goes back to the Latin *perdix*.[1] The same principle is at work, but in conjunction with phonetic decay, whenever the loss of a sound is compensated by the lengthening of the adjoining syllable, as in *mellis* for *melvis* (stem *madhu?*), *μᾶλλον* for *μᾶλyον*, or *feci* for *fefeci*. But the principle appears by itself in lengthened forms, such as *μανθάνω*, *λαμβάνω*, where the secondary inserted syllable—*αν*—arises from the wish to attach greater clearness and emphasis to the action of the verb. Much the same account must be given of the expletive *w* and *y*, which, like our vulgar *kyind* for *kind*, or the Italian *luogha* from *locus*, have played so great a part in Greek grammar, and in bringing about phonetic changes.

The extension of *πόλις* (Sansk. *puri*) into *πτόλις* and of *πόλεμος* into *πτόλεμος* is a further illustration of the same tendency. But perhaps the chief exhibition of the power of Emphasis is to be found in its regulation of accent and intonation. We naturally accentuate the syllable or word to which we would give prominence and definiteness; and the less cultivated the language, the more important is the employment of accent. As has been well remarked,[2] accent and tone vary inversely as syntax;

[1] See Morris, "Historical Outlines of English Accidence," pp. 63-73.

[2] Rev. J. Earle on the "Revision of the English Bible."

and we may gauge the development of syntax in a language by its use or disuse of accent. Chinese depends almost wholly upon tone, and its syntax may be compressed into a few lines; English, on the contrary, which is so rich in syntax and idiom, is correspondingly poor in intonation. We may say that tone or accent is to the primitive man what syntax is to his civilised successors.[1] In other words, what civilisation expresses by intellectual processes, barbarism expresses by the physical management of voice and muscles. Accent goes along with gesticulation; and action is still needed by the orator who has to appeal to the passions and not to the reason of his hearers. The important part played by accent in the early history of speech is still but inadequately recognised. The *guṇa* and *vṛiddhi* of the Sanskrit grammarians are as much the result of it as those diacritical marks which were invented by Aristophanes of Byzantium. A considerable proportion of the phenomena which we observe in Aryan grammar is the effect of accentuation; and many of the changes undergone by the flections are due to the attempt to lay the accent on the modifying

[1] Tones in Chinese, however, seem to be rather the result of an attempt to counterbalance the action of Phonetic Decay in cutting off final letters. Mr Edkins stated before the Oriental Congress at London, in 1874, that it takes about 1200 years to produce a new tone.

element of the word. Why, for instance, we may ask, do we have οἶδα, οἶσθα, οἶδε, in the singular, but ἴστον, ἴσμεν, ἴστε, ἴσασι, in the dual and plural? And why is this distinction in the length and quality of the vowel in the two numbers preserved in all the cognate languages, so that Sanskrit gives us *vèda, vêttha, vêda,—vidwá, vidathus, vidatus; vidmá, vidá, vidús*; and Gothic, *vait, vaist, vait, vituts; vitum, vituth, vitun*? Accent alone can answer the question. When the vowel of the singular was *gunated,* that is, raised in clearness and emphasis, the terminations of the singular had grown into such common and familiar use as to convey the ideas which they denoted without the aid of any distinguishing sign or stress. It was otherwise, however, with the terminations of the dual and plural. These still had a somewhat strange sound, and required a greater effort of intelligence to connect them with the conceptions they denoted; consequently they were brought out into distinct relief by placing the accent upon them.[1] Something not unlike this has been the

[1] In the same manner we must explain the Greek rule which throws the accent upon the first member of a compound whenever possible. The Aryan languages, which prefix the genitive relation, necessarily lay greater stress upon the second word, the last spoken in point of time; and the first word of a compound is consequently in danger of being slurred over. This is prevented by its receiving the accent. Perhaps the apparently arbitrary difference in the

procedure of those languages which, like the Tibetan dialects, form the present tense out of the aorist by doubling the last consonant and adding a firm vowel; as in *ngá gyeddo*, "I do," from *ngá gyed*, "I did." Here the indefinite time of the aorist is made definite by a prolongation of the syllable, and the distinctness of the idea of present time marked out by an emphatic dwelling upon the uttered word.

But these are not all the results that may be traced to the principle of Emphasis. The origin of poetry itself may be referred to the wish to set

accentuation of *πέντε* and *ἑπτὰ*, which is also found in the Sanskrit *pánchan* and *saptán*, is due to the attempt to distinguish between two vocables of similar meaning, which were set apart to denote numerals at successive epochs. The final *n* or *m* of *panchan* was original whatever be its derivation, unlike that of *saptan*, which is perhaps derived from the root *sap* (*sak*, *sequor*, ἕπω), "following." It is possible that the primary meaning of *panchan* was still remembered when *saptan* was taken to signify "seven;" and the two numbers were accordingly marked off from one another by a change in the position of the accent, much as we distinguish, by a similar contrivance, between the substantial and verbal uses of words like *tórment* and *tormént*, *cómpact* and *compáct*, or between two words of the same form but different signification, such as *íncense*, and *incénse*, *mínute* and *minúte*. The Latin *quinque*, when compared with the Greek *πέντε* and the Sanskrit *panchan*, is clearly the result of assimilation, the original form being *penque*, or, if the termination of *panchan* is not due to assimilation to that of *saptan*, *penquem*. Since the Gaelic form of the numeral is *coic*, the assimilation of the initial syllable of *quinque* must have taken place before the separation of the Italians and Kelts.

forth in clear and distinct language the ideas which possess the mind. The more primitive language is, the more rhythmical we discover it to be; in fact, early speech may be called a lyric. It is not surprising, therefore, that verse should be the first form in which literature clothes itself. The deep strange thoughts which, with the force of a new revelation, are struggling to find expression in the soul of man, must be invested with all the strength and distinctness of which language is capable; and as language itself is poetry, symbolising the impalpable things of the spirit under the veil of metaphor, so the earliest form of conscious language must be poetical. Now poetry at the outset possesses melody, and not harmony; the notes must follow one another, each distinct, clear, and independent; and the monotonous rhythm which meets us in the verse of uncultivated tribes is generally characterised by alliteration. But alliteration is not only useful as an assistance to the memory; it serves to force a particular sound upon the attention, and to afford so many resting-places, as it were, in which the mind may take in clearly all that lies between. Throughout the course of its development, literature remains true to its primary instinct. So long as books are recited or read, not to convey knowledge solely, but to communicate thought and feeling, distinctness of pronunciation will be of the highest moment. It is only in an age of science, when we read not for the sake of the style, but of the matter, that the principle of Phonetic Decay takes the place of the principle of Emphasis. While thought and its expression are but the two sides of the same prism, while the language is regarded as an end in itself, and not a mere instrument for the imparting of scientific truths or statistical facts or commercial instructions, every syllable will be watched with jealous care, and its due weight and meaning assigned to each. It is in this way that we can explain the precision and crystallisation of the literary language of Rome, so different in this respect from the ordinarily spoken Latin dialects amongst which Phonetic Decay reigned supreme. The pronunciation of Virgil and Horace was regulated by the spelling; and the tendency of Latin poetry was more and more to avoid elisions. It was this stereotyped, unreal condition of literary Latin, as has been acutely remarked,[1] which has caused the same phenomenon to reappear in modern literary Italian. Modern Italian is the dialect of Tuscany, and Tuscany, screened as it is by mountains, was the part of the Peninsula least affected by the inroad of the Teutonic nations. The Tuscan population long preserved the relics of

[1] Donaldson, "Varronianus," pp. 530-2.

the old Roman literature and civilisation, and "the studied accuracy with which the Romans of the Augustan age pronounced their Græcised poetry" still lingers in that standard Italian language, of which it has been so truly said that it cannot be pronounced both well and quickly. We must go to the other dialects of Italy to find Phonetic Decay in unrestricted action.

Both Phonetic Decay and Emphasis, however, have their root in the same utilitarian object: both are intended to aid the memory. As laziness would save trouble not only to the breath but also to the recollection, so the effort to be distinct has the same end in view. As we should burden the memory by a needless string of sounds which are not wanted as soon as the understanding has seized the idea, so we should burden it equally were we not to furnish it with the means of easily determining what idea it is that is intended. To give too much or too little to the comprehension, in order that it may take in and remember the meaning of what is suggested by symbolic speech, is alike contrary to the economic provisions of nature. Hence arise the two great principles which underlie the working of all those laws of language which it is the business of our study to ascertain by careful observation and accurate verification.[1]

[1] In correspondence with what I have termed Phonetic Decay,

Comparative Philology, then, must be defined as an inductive science, pursuing the same method of inquiry as geology or biology, and engaged in the discovery of laws or regulative generalisations which may possibly be some day applied deductively. But there is one point in which, in common with the other sciences which concern the human mind, Comparative Philology differs from geology. It is an historical, as distinguished from a physical, science. In the one case, the sum of the forces at work remains always the same—the same processes and the same results operate still upon the surface of the earth that operated millions of years ago; in the other case, the sum of the forces increases in an accelerated ratio. Every new generation is influenced by the preceding one; and that influence is a fresh element of motive power introduced into our calculations. Human volition is the result of so many

Emphasis, and Analogy, Mr Henry Sweet, in his valnable work on "The History of English Sounds," 1874, lays down (p. 7) that all changes of sonnd may be classed as—1. *organic*, 2. *imitative*, and 3. *inorganic*. "Organic changes are those which are the direct result of certain tendencies of the organs of speech: all the changes commonly regarded as weakenings fall under this head. Imitative changes are the result of an unsuccessful attempt at imitation. Inorganic changes, lastly, are caused by purely external causes." A little further on he remarks, that some changes "do not reqnire the hypothesis of muscular economy, but even run quite counter to it; as when an open consonant is converted into a stop, a by no means uncommon phenomenon in the Teutonic languages."

obscure and complicated causes, as to appear at first sight mere caprice and chance; and an historical science like Philology is eminently subject to the will of man. Then again we have to admit the influence of the individual, who may invent and give currency to new words or change the social condition of a country, though, strictly speaking, this is only another way of regarding the element of volition. In short instead of the simpler, unvarying processes of nature, which, for the most part, can be tested by experiment, we have to deal with the infinitely complicated developments of human thought and action, in which observation alone can be our guide. Language, as we find it, is as much the creation of man as painting or any other of the arts; and thus all possibility of forming a science out of what would be dependent upon the arbitrary caprice of the individual would seem to be out of the question. Such, however, is not the case. It may be true that the individual exercises some influence upon speech; that individual writers, for instance, such as Neckar and Reichenbach, have brought in new words like *sepals* and *od force*, but this influence after all is infinitesimally small. Language belongs to the multitude; it is the medium of communication between man and man; and consequently must be the combined product of causes and influences which affect all alike. Now, these causes can only be general; and if on the one side they are psychological, they are on the other side still more physical. The constitution of the human mind is fundamentally the same at all times and in all places; every one, be he savage or civilised, must become conscious of objects in much the same way, and must express his first needs in a similar manner. Once grant the power of forming articulate speech, and there can never be much difference in the attempts to realise it. All men have at bottom the same primary instincts and passions, otherwise they would not be men; and the primitive experiences of all races must have been almost identical. The life and necessities of the barbarian of to-day differ but little from those of the barbarian of yesterday. Even greater than the psychological similarity is the physical similarity. We are all cast in the same mould. We are all given the same physical machinery for producing sounds; and that machinery has everywhere the same restrictions. We cannot speak without opening our lips. How far this machinery may be modified by food, climate, and education, is a question which will have to be considered hereafter: in this place it is sufficient to notice that it can only be modified, never radically changed. Such modifications, moreover, cannot be individual;

they must affect a whole people, for language is social and national, not individual.

Language exists for the sake of society: the self-sufficient man would have no need of such an instrument of intercourse with his kind. We speak in order that we may be understood; and consequently we are obliged to say what is intelligible to those around us. The child learns the idiom of his parents, and cannot unlearn it if he would. It becomes part of himself and his nature before he has arrived at an age to think about it: and so long as he remains a member of a particular society, he is bound to talk the language of that society. The invention of a new language would be an useless waste of labour; he could not expect any one else to learn it, and so the whole *raison d'être* of language would be lost. The individual as such, has no language: language is the product and instrument of society, whose fortunes it represents, whose law it obeys, and whose progress it shares. As particular societies tend to lose their insulation, and to be more and more assimilated to each other with the advance of civilisation, so also it is with the dialects which severally belong to them.

Thus it is that the element of individual uncertainty is eliminated from the study. Although in one sense the creation of man, language is yet the outgrowth of general causes, and governed by general laws, partly mental and partly physical. By extending the area of our comparision, we are enabled to make these laws more and more general, and thus more and more to exclude the caprices and idiosyncrasies of particular nations. It is true that these idiosyncrasies will have to be explained; but it can only be done by the light of the general laws: we can only recognise and understand the exception by knowing the rule. Hence our inductions ought to be as wide as possible, and our collection of facts of the most extensive character.

Now, these facts are words, or rather judgments expressed in words; and since these are the outward embodiments of thought, the reflections of the passing phases of the mind subjected to the restrictive conditions of our physical nature, it is clear that, just as thought is progressive, and can only be studied historically, so words also must be subjected to an historic treatment. In so far as thought is stationary, it is unconscious, and must be treated physically like the rest of brute nature: with consciousness, history begins. It is the same with language: consciousness first shows itself in the period of roots, and with this period accordingly Comparative Philology commences. Behind lie the unconscious, instinctive beginnings that led to articulate speech, but our linguistic data do not carry us so far; the investigation of this primeval age of humanity belongs to physical science, not to Glottology.

Here, then, is one of the boundaries of the science to which I have alluded. Our data are limited to the words that can be collected from the mouths of living speakers, or have been committed to the safe keeping of writing. It is only where a group of cognate languages has changed but little that we can go back much beyond the invention of writing. Practically, therefore, we are bounded, so far as time is concerned, by the earliest written records which we possess, whether in Egypt, Babylonia, or China, or by a literature like that of the Rig-Veda, which has been stereotyped by traditional recitation. It is absolutely necessary that our facts should be accurate, that is, that we should know the exact forms and meanings at any given period of the words with which we are dealing; and this can only be done by the help of contemporaneous evidence, or by the inductions built upon this. It has been thought possible to construct a dictionary of the primitive Aryan language; but this is only because the cotemporary evidence we possess of the different branch-languages of the Aryan family of speech is sufficiently large to enable us, by the use of the comparative method, to determine what must have been the parent sound which alone could have given rise to the several varieties of the same word. And, after all, much in this dictionary must remain uncertain; we cannot always be sure of the original form of a vocable, and words possessed by the parent language may often have been lost altogether, or have left but slight traces behind them. Of course, in this work of reconstructing parent languages, or of probing language in general to its roots, we obtain additional light and assistance from other sciences, such as psychology, prehistoric archæology, or physiology.

From all this it will be evident to every one what is the object and scope of Comparative Philology.[1] It is an historic science, which traces

[1] Professor Whitney, at the beginning of his lectures on "Language and the Study of Language," p. 6, thus admirably describes the work of "the linguistic student:"—"To assemble, arrange, and explain the whole body of linguistic phenomena, and as thoroughly to comprehend them, in each separate part and under all aspects, is his endeavour. His province, while touching, on the one hand, upon that of the philologist, or student of human thought and knowledge as deposited in literary records, and on the other hand, n that of the mere linguist, or learner of languages for their practical use, and while exchanging friendly aid with both of these, is yet distinct from either. He deals with language as the instrument of thought,—its means of expression, not its record; he deals with simple words and phrases, not with sentences and texts. He aims to trace out the inner life of language, to discover its origin, to follow its successive steps of growth, and to deduce the laws that govern its mutations, the recognition of which shall account

the gradual evolution of human thought and action as photographed in the enduring monuments of language—the outward expression of that thought and action—and which has its roots far down in the dawning consciousness of primitive man. So far as man is man, so far, that is to say, as he has emerged from a mere brute life and has awakened to consciousness, he has a history, and that history may yet be recovered, either wholly or in part, from a scientific study of language. The facts with which this study deals are words or stereotyped thoughts; these it has to compare and classify, and thus determine the general laws to which they are subject. The general laws, made up of a variety of subordinate ones, belong partly to psychology, partly to phonology; the first lays down the conditions under which the awakening and developing mind views objects and their relations; the second, the conditions under which sounds are produced by the human voice, and the mind is enabled to express itself. Phonology is of the highest importance for getting at the laws of speech, since it ascertains the relation of sounds one to another, and thus

to him for both the unity and the variety of its present manifested phases; and, along with this, to apprehend the nature of language as a human endowment, its relation to thought, its influence upon the development of intellect and the growth of knowledge, and the history of mind and of knowledge as reflected in it."

explains the changes and kinship of words; but it must not be made synonymous with Comparative Philology, as is so often implicitly done. It is one of the chief and most valuable instruments of the science, but it is not commensurate with the science. The outward and physical is the most accessible to observation, and, therefore, to comparison; but words may often be phonetically identical which yet have nothing to do with each other, like the sounds set apart by most languages to denote "father" and "mother," or the roots *dhê*, to "suck," and *dhe*, "to place," in our own family of speech. This mistaken conception of the place of phonology is the modern representative of the notion that etymology is the beginning and end of philology, and that when a word had been tracked back through cognate dialects to the most original form attainable, nothing further was needed. This was the error of the lexicographer, just as the phonological misconception is the error of the grammarian. Words are of no value in themselves except to a dictionary-maker; they are only valuable in so far as they reflect and embody thought; and the object of a true philological etymology is to illustrate or discover the laws which have governed the evolution of thought, or rather the way in which that evolution has been determined by material and social circumstances. It is hardly likely that we shall ever attain to a perfect knowledge of these, and lay bare the whole mystery of the origin of roots and the history of grammatical relations. Should we do so, Comparative Philology would become an exact deductive science, and we should be able to predict the future destiny of language and languages. Meanwhile, we have to be content with an examination of the past or the present, so far as this is open to us, testing our conclusions by the facts of history and psychology, and by the laws which control the utterance of sounds.

To explain more clearly what is meant, we may quote, by way of example, the general law that all languages have a period of roots in which the several distinctions between the parts of speech lay undeveloped in a kind of embryonic common sound. The empirical laws of phonology enable us to trace the words of a civilised community back to this common source; and the law itself is verified by what psychology teaches us of the gradual growth of the mind, and by the facts of ethnology, with its illustrations of modern savage intelligence, and of prehistoric archæology, with its rough-hewn flints and other evidences of childish ignorance.

Thus, on all sides, Comparative Philology is

brought into contact with its sister sciences. If language is the reflection of common thought, it is at once the product and the mirror of society. It will, therefore, bear the impress of every movement of society, and its phenomena consequently will in large part be explicable only by means of the social sciences. Why, for instance, is Lithuanian, one of the least advanced members of the Aryan family, more conservative in its retention of many primitive grammatical forms than even Sanskrit; while, as a general rule, tribes in a low state of civilisation, like the Ostiaks or the Bushmen, are continually changing the character of their idioms, so that in the course of a single generation two neighbouring villages become mutually unintelligible? Why, again, did the Northmen give up their language in France, and retain it in Ireland? Comparative Philology alone cannot furnish the answer. Similarly we must go to physiology, if we would investigate the influence of food and climate upon the organs of speech, important as this question is to the philologist, who finds that every Polynesian syllable must end in a vowel, or that the Chinese have to turn every foreign *r* into *l* before they can pronounce it, or that Portuguese is more closely related to French than the intervening Spanish, or that the Teutonic coast population from Denmark to Flanders drops the final *d* of a syllable, while English, on the contrary, tends to introduce an expletive one, as in *sound* and *compound*. One of the most important problems which now await solution is to explain the causes of that regular *shifting* of sounds which words undergo in different cognate languages. Why, for example, must a Latin *d* answer to an English *t* and a High German *z*?[1] or what brought about the loss of a guttural before a labial in some dialects, and the retention of it in others? Some common cause must have been at work to produce *apa-s* in Sanskrit, *eau* in French, and *aua* in the Romansch of the Engadine, by the side of the Gothic *ahva*, Latin *aqua*, Italian *acqua*, and Spanish *agua*.[2] It is scarcely an answer to say

[1] Mr Sweet's admirable monograph on this subject (in the Appendix to his edition of "Gregory's Pastoral Care," pp. 496-504), ought to be studied. He remarks that "the oldest changes of *t* into *d*, and *d* into *t*, must have occurred simultaneously. . . . The phenomenon is, in fact, a case of simple confusion or interchange, as familiarly exemplified in the vulgar *hair* for *air* and *'are* for *hare*, when heard, as is not unfrequently the case, from the same mouth."

[2] The retention of the guttural cannot be ascribed to the influence of a colder, more northern climate, since the natives of Durham and Yorkshire say *wick* for *quick*, *wicken* for *quicken*, and a proverb current among the inhabitants of the Engadine assigns them nine months of winter and three of cold; nor to the mountainous nature of the country, since the Greeks, with their ἵππος and ἕπω dwelt in an incomparably more rugged region than the Latins, the people of "the plain," with their *equus* and *sequor*. There is here no question of an original inability to distinguish between *k* and *t*, such as is quoted by Professor Max Müller (Lectures, ii. pp.

that this cause was laziness, the general principle of phonetic change, because we want to know why this cause should have acted in some cases and not in others.

It may be said that the reason will be furnished by history. This is perfectly true. If we had a complete history of the movements of society, we should have a key to the changes of language which are its expression and reflection. But such a history would be nothing more than an exposition of the laws which govern society; and as we do not and cannot possess it we must endeavour to find out these laws by some other method. When once the laws have been discovered, that fragmentary and superficial series of biographies which we term history can be applied for the purpose of verification. It is thus that the generalisations of an historic science are tested. As in the physical sciences we verify our conclusions

167, 168, 182) as existing among the Sandwich Islanders, and which reappears among the lower classes in Canada, who say *mékier* for *métier*, *moikié* for *moitié*. This confusion of sounds merely shows the near relationship of the dental and guttural, like our own common pronunciation of *at least* as *a'cleast*, or the conversion of *charcutier* in the Parisian dialect into *chartuticr*. What we want to know is why some tribes should have chosen the guttural and others the dental or labial? Why should the Wallachs, the successors of the Roman soldiers who settled in Dacia, say *apa* for *aqua?* We can hardly grant, as Professor Max Müller suggests, that they all came from those Oscan districts of Italy in which the *qu* had lost its guttural and changed the accompanying labial into a *p*.

by an appeal to experiment, so in philology, our inductions can be verified by a reference to the known facts of history. The clear traces of a Teutonic influence in French point to a German occupation of the country, and this we know from history was actually the case. Arabic words in Spanish afford evidence of a contact with the Moors; and the relation of the Romance languages to Latin necessitates philological conclusions which are borne out by the statements of annalists. Such general principles even as the ascription of phonetic decay to laziness may be confirmed by historical instances like the Norman conquest of England, where the loss of inflections was accelerated by the attempt of a foreign population to speak the language of the country with the least possible trouble to themselves. From cases like these, which can be tested by a direct appeal to history, we may proceed by analogy to others in which such a test cannot be applied. But it is evident that the further we recede from cotemporaneous history, and the more unable we are to verify our inductions by its means, the more hazardous and provisional will our conclusions be. Hence some of the primary laws of the science can best be obtained from a study of modern European languages, though we must be upon our guard against applying the results gained from these to languages which are not occidental, or which do not stand upon the same level of civilisation and religious progress.

History is especially valuable in corroborating the empirical laws which we discover, those, namely, of which the reason cannot be given, but which fall under some higher and more general law. Psychology has more to do with the general laws, in so far as these relate not so much to the external accidents as to the inner meaning and structure of language. In fact, just as a philosophy of history, in which the attention is turned to the motives and connection of outward events, depends upon psychology, so also does philology, which displays the laws that govern our mental development, not in action, but in speech. Physiology, on the other hand, deals with the external, and is therefore mostly applicable to phonology alone. Here we have to ask it to help us in determining what sounds may pass into one another, and under what conditions they may do so. To look too exclusively at this side of the science, however, is to repeat the mistake of the last century, and to see nothing but mechanical materialism everywhere. We require the aid, not only of those sciences which are concerned with the external framework and circumstances of man, but yet more urgently of those which trace the growth of his spiritual life, like jurisprudence or history, however much these may lead us back to a dim starting-point, where the distinction between matter and spirit, between nature and consciousness, seems almost imperceptible.

But dim as it may be, we must remember that it *is* a starting-point. Comparative Philology cannot get beyond the range of its facts, beyond the commencement of conscious articulate speech. Language for it is not the language of gesture, but the language of articulated utterance. The investigation of language, in the wider sense, as including looks, play of features, modulation of voice, and gesticulation, to say nothing of the finger-language of the deaf and dumb, must fall under a more comprehensive science. The examination of this inarticulate speech belongs to physiology; and Mr Darwin, in his work on the "Expression of the Emotions in Men and Animals," has already broken ground in this direction. But it is one of those sides of physiology which most directly bear upon our science, and from which we may hereafter expect the most important aid. In fact, if ever we are to solve the problem of the origin, not of language in the philological sense of the word, but of articulate speech itself, the subject-matter of philology, it can only be by special physiological researches upon this head.

Häckel has endeavoured to trace the earliest utterances of man to the cries of the ape; and, as Professor Benfey points out, the physical accessories of speech, as we may call them, "make the purely human origin of articulate speech more easily intelligible; for we must certainly credit them with the power of assigning to any sound or combination of sounds the meaning which the first man who joined together these articulations and their accessories was impelled or intended to express by them." Looks and modulation of voice seem to agree in all nations, gestures only in part, thus forming the bridge by which we may pass over into spoken language, the dividing element in human history. The first three are common to man and the lower animals; articulate language alone, whatever may be its ultimate source, draws the impassable line between us and the beasts, and makes man man. This is the justification of a science of Comparative Philology taking its rank among the historical sciences, and not being merged in a general science in which the brute and the human are coupled together.

In applying its laws, the practical rules to be deduced from them lie upon the surface. If the facts with which we start are judgments expressed in words, it is obvious that the grammar and structure of a language will afford the only sound basis of comparison. It is not mere sounds that we have to compare, but the processes of thought involved in them. Thought is relative, and these relations may be viewed in different ways. Only those languages which agree in their mode of viewing these relations can be grouped together. When once agreement in grammar and structure has determined the connection of two tongues, we may proceed to compare their lexicons. The first words to be brought under scientific treatment are the pronouns and numerals, which constitute a link between grammar and vocabulary. They are the earliest attempts to reduce the abstract to the concrete, to embody thought; and the need of their frequent use will better preserve them than is the case with other words. At the same time, the very frequency of their use subjects them all the more to the influence of phonetic decay, and so renders a knowledge of their history the more necessary. Now, the history of a word can only be made out by a comparison of dialects, and an acquaintance with the older monuments of the language; so that until we have traced back a word to the most ancient form attainable, we have no right to employ it for the purposes of comparison. We may compare roots, but not derivatives. Words derived from the same radical will often assume different forms in different languages, or even in the same one; while words derived from different radicals will, on the other hand, often assume the same form in different languages, or even in the same one. Before we compare, we must know the history of a vocable. It is equally important that the words should be found in some written language. In no other way can we obtain documentary evidence of their older forms, and compare the latter with the forms of the same words in modern dialects. We shall never know the roots of the Polynesian idioms, since we can only bring dialects together which are still spoken, and the most primitive forms to which such a comparison will conduct us are relatively modern. Similarly, our area of comparison must be wide and varied, and not confined to a group of dialects which all flow from one and the same mother speech, like the manuscripts of Sophokles from a single tenth-century original. Unless we are aided by the sub-Semitic dialects of Africa and the old Egyptian, our comparative researches into the Semitic family will remain as unsatisfactory as would be the case with the Romance languages were all the cognate idioms, past and present, utterly extinct and lost. Written languages, moreover, guarantee a systematic pronunciation. We are not obliged to take our materials from one observer who represents the French *un* by *a*, and from another who represents it by *one*. But above all, we must not compare roots together, unless the meaning as well as the sound agree,[1] or apply to

[1] Significant change, though of almost equal importance with phonetic change, has been hitherto but scantily attended to. The changes of meaning undergone by words through the influence of the general principle of analogy have been due to two causes, which are of the same nature as Phonetic Decay and Emphasis. The first of these causes is mental laziness, or the inability to understand the full and proper signification of a term; the second, the addition of new force and meaning to the content of a word. One of the few writers who have devoted much care to the subject, the determination of which Curtius calls "much harder" than that of phonetic mutation ("Grundzüge der Griechischen Etymologie," 2d edit. p. 87), is Professor Whitney, in his lectures on "Language and the Study of Language." He there sums up the processes whereby words change their meaning under the two heads of—(1) Specialisation of general terms; and (2) Generalisation of special terms (p. 106). A more thorough-going and highly suggestive discussion of the subject will be found in Pott's Introduction to the fifth and last volume of his great "Wurzel-Wörterbuch der indogermanischen Sprachen." After drawing attention to the fact that the same conception is expressed in different languages, sometimes in the same way, sometimes dissimilarly, he groups the causes of significant change in seven classes. (I.) Words may become defined by either the narrowing or the widening of their meaning. (Thus ἄλογον, "the irrational brute," is confined to the "horse" in modern Greek, like *deer* (the German *thier*, "fera") in English, and *emere*, which originally meant "to take," came to be restricted to the sense of "buying.") (2.) Metaphor is a very common cause of change of signification. (Thus the use of the prepositions has been transferred from space to time.) (3.) The meaning of a word will vary according to its application to persons or things (as in the adjective "beautiful," for example), to what is good or bad (whence the change in meaning in *silly* and *fortuna*), or to what is great or small. (4.) Words, again, will change their signification according

one group of languages the phonetic rules and possible interchanges of letters which belong to another. The last error is a fatal one, but is not unfrequent under the disguised form of attributing a phonetic law peculiar to a special language to allied dialects or the common parent of them all. Thus, because Sanskrit may drop an initial short *a*, Pott assumes, in his theory of roots, that the primitive Aryan could do the same; and the Latin habit of changing *s* into *r* has been quoted by

to their use as active and passive, nominative and accusative. (It is of some consequence, for instance, whether we use *venerandus* in reference to the object of veneration or his admirer.) (5.) It makes a considerable difference whether an idea is expressed by a compound or by a simple word. (Thus the Latin *nepos* is the French *petit-fils*. Collectives imply no small power of abstraction; and the fact that the derivatives of Aryan are replaced by compounds in Taic shows not only the mental superiority of the former, but also the fundamental contrast between their respective modes of thought.) (6.) The same word may be differently applied, and this relativity of meaning has important consequences. Hence come the idioms which form the characteristic feature of a dialect or language, and make a literal or exact translation impossible. (Compare the variety of senses in which the word "heart" is used.) (7.) (α) Though change of pronunciation may cause no change of meaning, the converse is often the case. (β) Words or parts of words get lost, necessitating the introduction of new ones with a more or less varying signification. (So *equus* in the Romance languages has been replaced by *caballus*.) (γ) The vocabulary, and therewith the stock of ideas, may be increased by new formatives or loan-words, which bring about slight changes of meaning in old words. To these seven causes of change may be added an eighth, that of ignorance or false analogy, of which more will be said in the ninth chapter. Cases like that of *impertinent*, which has almost lost its original sense, will best fall under Pott's third class.

K. O. Müller and others to support an extraction of πελασγοί in Greek out of πελαργοί (from πέλω and ἀργός = ἀγρός [1]).

In conclusion, a few words must be said about the name of the science with which we are concerned. "Comparative Philology" is at once long and misleading; it perpetuates the idea that its subject-matter belongs to a higher and more comprehensive philology. Apart from Comparative Philology, however, there can be no scientific study of articulate language; and if philology means something other than this, it would be absurd to rank the scientific under the unscientific. But this is what is popularly done—philology signifying sometimes a dilettante acquaintance with the canons of taste and polite literature, and, in fact, with everything that is not the science of language; sometimes classical scholarship, in which the correction of a MS., or the close imitation of an Augustan writer, is the highest result aimed at. Now these are all very good things in their way; but it cannot too often be repeated that they have nothing in common with Comparative Philology. Classical scholarship may, indeed, contribute much

[1] Pischel, in Kuhn's Zeitschrift (vol. xx. p. 369, 1872), has somewhat boldly tried to explain πελασγοί from the roots which we find in Sanskrit *param*, Greek πέραν (περάω, &c.), and *ya*, εἶμι. The *Pelasgians* will be simply the "emigrants," like the Ionians (Ἰάϝονες, *Yavanas*) from *ya* (= i-re").

valuable material to the science, so far at least as Latin and Greek are concerned; but even here its supposed discoveries often turn out to be erroneous when investigated by the light of the comparative method, and can seldom be received without further examination, unless the facts are very plain and self-evident. The particular can only be understood in the light of the universal; and the empirical rules derived from a careful comparative study of some special language, indispensable as such data are to the scientific philologist, are still narrow, unexplained, and questionable. We are often told that a comparative philologist must be thoroughly acquainted with some of the principal languages with which he deals, otherwise the inner structure of the language will be concealed from him, and he will be obliged to take his facts at second-hand, and thus be often led into error. This is quite true; and the more numerous the typical languages that are thoroughly known, the better and more accurate will be the work of the scientific student. But it must be remembered, firstly, that if a specialist takes up Comparative Philology as a merely subsidiary matter, the minor details of his specialty, whether it be Greek, or Sanskrit, or Hebrew, will assume an unreal importance in his eyes, and the main phenomena be correspondingly dwarfed; and, secondly, that it is impossible for the student to have anything like a close acquaintance with the large number of languages with which he is obliged to deal. As in the other sciences, so here; division of labour is imperatively required, and much of the material has to be received on trust. Where this is done cautiously and scientifically, where the authorities are critically chosen and weighed, and where the comparisou of facts is large and wide-reaching, the chances of error are minimised, and the single wrong fact is neutralised by the many accurate ones. We do not require a linguist, but a philologist in the true sense of the word. As this sense, however, is unfortunately misunderstood, I should prefer to use the term Glottologist, and in the rest of these chapters I shall speak of Glottology rather than of Comparative Philology. Glottology will be the science of language which compares and classifies words and forms, and so arrives at the empirical and finally the primary laws which govern the development of speech and its varieties. The laws will be verified by an appeal to history, to psychology, to physiology, to ethnology; and inasmuch as words are but uttered thought, and language the reflection of society, the results of the science and the application of the laws we have discovered will be to reconstruct the past history of man and to determine the character of those long-forgotten strata of society which our fossil-like records reveal to us.[1] We shall thus be enabled to trace the gradual growth of the mind of man, whether displayed in the creation of language generally as an instrument of intercommunication and the embodiment of the conception of the relations between thought and the world, or in the triumph of the will over the mechanism of the bodily organs and the limitations imposed in turn by them upon it, or lastly, in the evolution of the religious idea—in other words, in Comparative Mythology and the Science of Religions.

[1] For an example of the way in which forgotten epochs and facts of history can be thus restored, see Appendix. Mangold (in Curtius' *Studien*, vi. 2), by tracing δῆμος to the root δα, "to divide" (Sansk. *dây*, *dâ*), has shown that private property in Attica (and elsewhere in Greece) originated in the allotment of land by the commune, which still prevails among the Slaves, and has been made familiar to us by Sir Henry Maine.

## CHAPTER II.

### THE IDOLA OF GLOTTOLOGY—THE LAWS OF THE SCIENCE DETERMINED FROM THE ARYAN FAMILY ALONE.

In every science we must advance from the known to the unknown. This can only be done by the aid of hypotheses. These bridge over the gulf, and are, as it were, so many imaginary circles, half of which is filled up by facts already known, while the remaining half is a purely mental conception, which will, however, turn out to correspond with objective phenomena should the hypotheses prove correct. The younger the science, the smaller will be the amount of known facts, and therefore the greater the number of hypotheses required. Now, in so far as these are the product of the imagination, it is clear that wide scope is given for subjective prejudices, false analogies, and a distorted view of the evidence. This tendency to error will increase with the increased meagreness of the facts, and can only be checked by enlarged knowledge and a critical comparison of the theory with what is actually known. Hence as a science grows older, its ascertained laws become more numerous, its provisional hypotheses either passing into laws by a process of verification, or being thrown aside for something that will better stand the test of facts. Even discarded hypotheses, however, have done a good work. In so far as they had any facts to support them, they helped to unify a string of isolated phenomena, and to set the student on a definite path of research. We cannot collect facts to any solid purpose, or compare them afterwards, without having some theory to guide us in our selection. But good care must be taken to place all such hypotheses upon their proper footing, to remember their provisional character, and to compare them again and again with the phenomena that come before us. Too often they become unverified assumptions, which we accept without questioning, and thus exalt into scientific laws, thereby vitiating our further investigations, and falling into numberless false conclusions. In this way what were intended to be mental landmarks become what Bacon expressively called *Idola*, empty assumptions and misconceptions, which take the place of the true conceptions that correspond with the order of existing things. Glottology, I think, like all other new studies, will be found to offer a plentiful crop of these Idola.

Partly the science is still overshadowed by the false associations connected with the word Philology, to which I alluded in the last chapter; partly the interest of special portions of the science—phonology, for example—are allowed to obscure the several interests of the whole; partly it has been forgotten how large is the mass of materials, and consequently the results obtained in one department have been supposed to be of universal application; partly opinions which were necessitated by the only evidence available when the science was in its infancy have been adopted without criticism, and regarded as so many first principles which no one would dream of disputing. It is time, however, that such questions should be fully discussed. We have now become accustomed to the idea of applying the scientific method to language; a large body of classified facts have been brought before our notice, which is being increased every day, and the sister sciences of ethnology, prehistoric archæology, and comparative law, not to speak of psychological and physiological discoveries, are ever throwing fresh light upon the problems of Glottology, and assisting us to verify the conclusions to which it comes. Hence we are in a position to examine anew the foundations of the science, and to determine what are to be accepted as really the principles of Comparative Philology, and what is of doubtful authority or altogether erroneous.

One of the first assumptions of the glottologist, either openly avowed or unconsciously implied, is that a scientific investigation of the Aryan family alone will give a full and complete solution of all the problems of the science of language, helped out perhaps by a few illustrations from non-Aryan dialects.[1] The causes of such an

[1] Mr Alexander J. Ellis, in his address to the London Philological Society, 1873 (p. 12), says, "Education in English schools was contrived when I was a boy—and though somewhat improved, I am glad to think, during the intervening forty years, yet, like the tree, it preserves its old bend, and may therefore be regarded as contrived, undesignedly, of course, and perhaps unconsciously (which makes amendment not particularly hopeful)—to bring up a boy's mind in the one Aryan faith of the one Aryan linguistic mode of thought. The instrument was mainly the Latin grammar, to which even all other Aryan heresies were made to succumb. Boswell reports a speech of Johnson which puts the feeling thus generated in a very strong light. 'I always said,' quoth the oracle, 'Shakespeare had Latin enough to grammaticise his English' (anno 1780, æt. 71). We know now what to conclude of Johnson's own knowledge of English grammar. Latin and Greek eternally ground in, with French as an 'extra,' and English merely as a medium for 'construing,' is the received English preparation for linguistic study. Well, we have got out of it a little. Thanks to Christianity, some people had to learn Hebrew, and the Semitic verb at least ought to have opened our eyes. But if any philologist wishes to see how truly all Aryanism and Semiticism are merely the favourite literary dialects of the world, how extremely remote they are from representing all logical connections of thought, to indicate which inflections and insertions, reduplication, guna, and umlaut and ablaut, conjugational forms and voices, and the other

assumption lie upon the surface. Not only did Comparative Philology begin with the Aryan family; not only are its students members for the most part of that family, and best and primarily acquainted with some one or more of its dialects; not only does the historical position of Europe give to this group of languages an immediate and practical interest; but still more it is here that the facts of language are most numerous, and its vicissitudes most accurately known, from the oldest hymns of the Rig-Veda down to the newspaper of to-day. When the great discovery of the affinities of this group dawned upon Schlegel and Bopp, and the commonest inflections of grammar were traced from dialect to dialect and from century to century, it was impossible not to believe that what held good of the Aryan would hold equally good of all other tongues. We can only work by means of analogy, and there seemed no reason for supposing that the phenomena would differ in the two cases. Moreover, there was the continual striving of the human mind after unity, which would tend towards the

paraphernalia developed by these systems of language in different proportions, are supposed to have been constructed, in ways which different scholars have wanted words laudatory enough to characterise; if any philologist wishes to see radicarianism and hereditary preservation of forms of words break utterly down, and find a system of language which preserves its individuality by its mere mode of grammatical construction, let him study the Basque."

belief, unless disproved by fact, that all languages have radiated from a single centre; and tradition and religious prepossessions had fixed that centre in the East. In the enthusiasm of a new discovery, bewildered by the vagueness of Indian chronology, it was hard not to fancy that the primeval language had been found in Sanskrit, or at least in the parent Indo-European speech. It is to this that we must ascribe the attempt of Bopp to attach the Polynesian idioms to the Aryan family. Already the world had been accustomed to derive all the languages of the earth from some common ancestor, whether that were Hebrew as orthodoxy ruled, or Basque with Erro, or Dutch with Goropius. It was the Christian spirit that saw the same blood, the same origin, and the same hope in all men, in contradistinction to the pagan spirit of classical antiquity, which localised its gods and its institutions, and could discover in a foreign language nothing but a "barbarous" jargon. Everything seemed to favour the belief that the new science had made its way back to the sources of all living speech, or at all events, to something very near those sources, at a single leap. Every day brought fresh proofs of the close affinities of Greek and Sanskrit, of Latin and Gaelic; while on the other hand, it became increasingly evident that many of the inflections, the origin of which had hitherto been ascribed to nature or convention, had primitively been independent words. Was it not clear, then, that Aryan speech itself had once been in a condition similar to Turkish, if not to Chinese? Here, therefore, the common starting-point of all languages had at last been reached, that plain of Shinar which ended in its Babel of confusion. The idea was strengthened by the fossilised antiquity of the Chinese Empire itself; it was like some pterodactyl or ichthyosaurus happily preserved in the rocks to tell us the character of animal life in the liassic period. Accordingly it was assumed without further debate that the Aryan group of languages was the model of every other; either they were all descended from a common source, or, at any rate, were subject to identical laws. Philology could offer no difficulty which a fuller knowledge of Aryan would not solve. Where, for example, was an explanation of the Etruscan inscriptions to be found? In some Aryan dialect, of course.[1] What was the original form

[1] So far as Etruscan is concerned, the influence of the belief still seems dominant. I will say nothing of the Earl of Crawford's book, in which the key to the inscriptions is discovered in German, in rivalry of Dr Donaldson, but confessedly without any knowledge of Philology. But even that splendid monument of German patience and industry, the first volume of Corssen's work, "Ueber die Sprache der Etrusker" (1874), in which he has collected and classified every scrap of inscription yet discovered, is another illustration of the distorting effect of special studies, even though carried

of all articulate speech? The verbal monosyllables to which the Sanskrit grammarians had reduced the lexicon. How was the idea of action first expressed? By attaching a pronoun to one of these verbal roots. These and such like were the answers readily given to the inquirer; and time was needed to learn that the inner mysteries of a science cannot be so easily penetrated; that it is not the first solution that comes to hand which is necessarily the true one; but that the truth is only to be gained by slow degrees, by the labours of many students, and by the orderly succession of hypothesis after hypothesis, until the right one is at length hit upon. We are still too far from seeing this. We inherit the opinions and idola of our predecessors along with their method, and it requires an effort to criticise what has been con-

on in a purely scientific spirit. In defiance of physiology and ethnology, an attempt is made to explain Etruscan as an Italic dialect. But a study of the book has convinced me that, whatever Etruscan might be, it was certainly not an Italic dialect, and Aufrecht's criticism, as embodied in papers read before the Philological Society of London, will make it clear that the key of the Etruscan problem has not yet been found. Aryan words certainly exist in the Etruscan inscriptions, but they were borrowed; the list of Etruscan numerals given by Corssen consists of the *Roman* proper nouns "Quartus," "Octavus," &c.; and a perusal of the inscriptions quoted by the great German philologist himself shows plainly that the words found on the famous dice of Toscanella are really numerals. (See the cogent criticism of Deecke: "Corssen und die Sprache der Etrusker," 1875.)

secrated by great names, and has become part and parcel of our belief. Above all, the glottologist has still to be trained for his work in the Aryan family. Here alone are the materials sufficiently large, clear, and certain; here alone have we the immense advantages offered by a preparatory knowledge of some of the languages to be studied, and by the possession of monuments at once so old and so perfect as the Rig-Veda; and here alone have the facts been classified, their conclusions drawn out in their full extent, and the whole brought into scientific shape. The Semitic family is at once too small and too compact; its branches do not differ more among themselves than do the Romance languages in Europe; and until its Sanskrit has been found, as it may yet be in the old Egyptian or the sub-Semitic idioms of Africa, we cannot get back beyond a parent speech which is philologically late, and which fails to offer that facility for comparison which is needed by the young glottologist. As for the other languages of the world, they are still, for the most part, awaiting their Bopp. Something has been done for the Ural-Altaic or Turanian family, which embraces Finnic, Tataric, and Mongolian, especially by Schott, and the cuneiform records from Babylonia and Susiana are likely to lead to important results by revealing the character of this group of tongues at an early date.[1] Bleek, too, has worked at the Ba-ntu of South Africa,[2] and Chinese has been more and more attracting attention to itself. As yet, however, but little has been done outside Aryan beyond the determination of the most general conclusions, and much of that little will probably have to be revised. Consequently, just as Latin and Greek are still the basis of popular education, it is in the Ayran family that the glottologist will have to receive his training for some time to come. Hence, when he begins to deal with other classes of languages, his mind is filled with certain prepossessions and beliefs, which are likely to colour his researches more or less. He naturally expects to find the same phenomena and obtain the same results in his new

[1] The study of Accadian and the closely related dialect of Sumerian has made great progress since it was worked at by myself in 1870 and Fr. Lenormant in 1873. Thanks to the labours of Delitzsch, Oppert, Hommel, Pinches, and more especially Haupt, the grammar of the old agglutinative language of Babylonia is now fairly well known, and considerable advance has been made with a knowledge of its vocabulary. Hommel has lately tried to show that it represents an early stage of the Turkic branch of the Altaic family of speech. For the cognate idioms of Susiana, see my paper on "The Languages of the Cuneiform Inscriptions of Elam and Media," in the *Transactions of the Society of Biblical Archæology*, vol. iii. part 1 (1874).

[2] See his admirable "Comparative Grammar of the South African Languages" (1862-69).

field of inquiry as those with which he is already familiar. It is only after considerable experience that he comes to see that the Aryan family is but one out of many, and that in several respects its character is altogether exceptional. The languages of civilisation are not numerous. The case is still worse if the student be unacquainted with any non-Aryan dialect, or, at all events, only uses these to illustrate the views he already holds. Unfortunately this is what is only too comman. Glottology has for the most part been confined to Aryan scholars, and consequently the laws they have formulated, however true they may be of the Aryan group itself, are not necessarily of universal validity.

Then, again, these laws are not always obtained from a survey even of the whole Aryan family. The modern languages of Europe, whether Romance or Teutonic, afford us the most numerous and the most certain data for our studies that we can find. It is these, moreover, that furnish us with the best means of verifying our theories. They have, therefore, especially attracted the notice of glottologists, and some of the most valuable results of the science have been gained from them. But it must never be forgotten that the phenomena they present are in large measure unlike any that have ever occurred before throughout the history of language. As we saw in the last chapter, the subject-matter of an historical science is continually incorporating fresh elements with the process of time, like some organic growth; and this is particularly the case with the languages we are now considering. These modern dialects have grown up in the midst of literature, and of the influences inspired by the Roman Empire and the Christian Church. The latter worked on the side both of law and of religion—the most potent influences to which society is open—and thus not only filled the vocabulary even of Teutonic tribes with Latin and Greek terms, but perpetuated a popular knowledge of the Latin tongue itself, and gave a Latin shape to the expression of popular thought. Literature kept up an artificial standard of linguistic purity and excellence, and to some extent prevented the natural progress of phonetic decay and the rank growth of dialects. Shakespeare and the Bible have stereotyped English not less than Dante has determined classical Italian, or than the railway, the telegraph, and the daily press will arrest the further development of European speech.

These considerations will explain how it has come to pass that eminent philologists have committed themselves to general theories which will not bear a very close examination. Every one can see the absurdity of supposing that the history of the Aryan family faithfully represents in all particulars the history of all other families of speech or of language generally. No one, for example, would argue that all civilised languages must be inflectional; but when the opinion is not stated in this broad way, it is very liable to escape notice, and to be unconsciously assumed and acted upon. I shall give two or three instances of this, in which theories have been put forward, and are still commonly held, which rest entirely upon the above assumption. No canon is so often laid down by glottologists as that the roots of all languages are monosyllabic. And yet this assertion rests simply upon the fact that such is the case in the Aryan family. It is true that Chinese may sometimes be called in to corroborate, or rather to illustrate, this belief; but then we are too little acquainted with the primitive form of Chinese to say what was the original nature of its radicals. And indeed, so far from confirming the canon, the present character of Chinese would rather tell against it, seeing that the tendency of all languages is towards phonetic decay and the loss of syllables; while Mr Edkins would lead us to infer that the existence of longer roots can still be detected in the living language.[1]

[1] Thus along the southern bank of the Yang-tsi-kiang, and through

The recovery of Accadian from the cuneiform records of Babylonia—the importance of which, for philological purposes, will make me often refer to it—enables us to go back to a very remote period of Turanian speech; and here, though the majority of roots are monosyllabic, dissyllables like *dugud*, "heavy," *dingir*, "god," are by no means unfrequent; and not only are there no data for reducing them to monosyllables, but their obedience to the law of vocal harmony would seem absolutely to prevent such an analysis. Bleek's investigations, again, into the Ba-ntu of South Africa have led him to the belief that polysyllabic roots are rather the rule than the exception, many combinations of sounds which seem to us most difficult being really the most primitive, while mimetic roots—those, for instance, which denote sneezing—would most naturally take a dissyllabic form.[1] These few facts are sufficient to show the worth of the attempt made to pare down the Semitic radicals to monosyllables in accordance with the supposed law of monosyllabic roots. The task

Chekiang to Fuh-kien, the old initials are all preserved, while in the northern provinces no less than three finals have been lost.

[1] Böhtlingk says ("Ueher die Sprache der Yakuten," p. xvii. *note*), "The commonly assumed view, that the words of a monosyllabic language are all roots, has little to say for itself. In Tibetan it can be shown that several words, which now seem monosyllabic, have grown out of a combination of two words."

is a hard one; and the disagreement among the many eminent scholars who have tried it as to the way in which the desired result is to be secured, would of itself indicate the worthlessness of the whole proceeding. One would slice off a letter at the end of the word, another in the middle, another at the beginning, while a fourth, with an arbitrary eclecticism, would cut out letters in all three places according to his fancy.[1] No one,

[1] The last and by far the most scientific endeavour to compare the Semitic and Aryan families, and to reduce Semitic roots to monosyllables, is Friedrich Delitzsch's "Studien über Indogermanisch-semitische Wurzelverwandschaft" (1873). The most valuable part of the work is a review and criticism of his predecessors, from Guichard (1606), Thomassin (1697), and de Gébelin (1774), to Ascoli, Von Raumer, Gesenius, Fürst, and Franz Delitzsch. The author bases his researches upon the fact that Indo-European roots may contain more than two consonants, while many Semitic roots seem to have only two, or even one. But he forgets to inquire what is the general and distinguishing character of the radicals in the two families. The fatal objection to his labours is, however, that he has begun them at the wrong end. If Aryan and Semitic are to be compared, we must commence with the structure and the grammar, not with the lexicon. Moreover, Assyrian and old Egyptian are deliberately ignored—indispensable as they would seem to be if we would find the oldest obtainable forms of the radicals; and the roots selected for comparison are all, on the one hand, more or less of an onomatopœic nature; and, on the other hand, contain three consonants, two of which may be pronounced together without the intervention of a vowel. Delitzsch does not say what he would do with a root like קטן. Minor difficulties, such as the great importance of vowels in Semitic, which would appear to be incompatible with a theory in which the vowels necessarily count for little, may be passed over.

Since the publication of this work, an article by J. Grill, "On

however, can enter into the spirit of the Semitic languages without seeing how entirely they are built upon the principle of triliteralism. It is implied in the whole theory of their grammar; and to imagine that it has grown out of something essentially unlike, is to admit the possibility of a change of mental view, which is inconsistent with all the experiences of psychology. Triliteralism is not the invention of Jewish-Arabic grammarians of the tenth century; long before this, it was recognised to the fullest by the literati of Assur-

the Relation of the Indogermanic and Semitic Radicals," has appeared in the *Journal of the German Oriental Society*, vol. xxvii. part 3. It contains several ingenious suggestions, and well contrasts what the author calls Indogermanic Vocalism and Formalism with Semitic Consonantalism and Materialism. As regards his main thesis, however, the writer falls behind Delitzsch. Semitic triliteralism is assumed to have developed out of a more primitive stage of biliteralism, on the ground that "the simpler forms of the root come first, the more complex and artificial being a later and organically developed product of these." What is *logically* first, however, is by no means necessarily *historically* so; and the modern dialects of the lower races show us, as a matter of fact, that in language the complex precedes the simple, and that simplicity and unity are the last result of reflection and culture. When Grill goes on to assume a prehistoric isolating stage of language, which lies behind the Aryan and Semitic roots, he steps beyond the data of philology, and calls in the aid of a theory which will be controverted in a later chapter. He lays down, moreover, that this primeval root-language was an "alpha-speech," that is, one in which *a* was the only vowel known! Roots like *i*, "to go," show how little this view is supported by the Aryan languages; and if, as Grill admits, Semitic roots take no account of vowels, it is difficult to understand how they can be said to presuppose this lost and vanished root-vowel *a*.

bani-pal, the son of Essar-haddon, whose lexical and grammatical tablets are now in the British Museum; and so clearly was the principle felt by the people, that foreign words of one syllable, which were borrowed by the Assyrians, had to be Semitised by the addition of a consonant or semi-consonant. The so-called biliterals are either the result of phonetic decay, or else, as I think we now have materials for proving, were loan-words.[1] The concave roots were really of triliteral origin, and are primarily used as triliterals in Assyrian, which possesses the inestimable advantage of a syllabary; while such few compounds as really exist go back to triliteral elements. The same holds good of quadriliterals, which for the most part have extended a vowel into a liquid;[2] and the occurrence of words of similar meaning which differ in having letters of cognate sound merely shows that certain letters interchange, not that the word was originally triliteral.[3] No argument

[1] See a paper of mine on "The Origin of Semitic Civilisation" in the *Transactions for the Society of Biblical Archæology*, vol. i. part 2 (1872).

[2] Thus דמשק has become דרמשק in 1 Chron. xviii. 5, 6, as in Syriac; and כסא (Assyrian *cússú*), "throne," is the Arabic *curs'ya*, and the Aramaic *corsai*. See my "Assyrian Grammar," p. 6. Damascus is *Dímasku* in Assyrian.

[3] In many cases it is difficult to decide whether two letters really interchange, and the two parallel roots are originally due to dialectic differences, or whether the several forms have sprung from the same mental type, which was never itself clothed in speech, but

can be drawn from old Egyptian, because, whatever may be the relationship of the grammar, the bulk of the lexicon is certainly non-Semitic, while those few archaic words, like *p'takh*, "to open," and *kh'tam*, "to close," which have Semitic analogues, are triliteral. This is one example of the false conclusions, the hasty neglect of evidence, and the wasted ingenuity that have resulted from the attempt to apply a law peculiar to Aryan to other families of speech.

We may take another example from what has been called the doctrine of roots. From an analysis of Aryan it has been inferred that all roots were originally verbal. This is certainly the case in the Indo-European family, so far as our facts allow us to see; and it seems to have psychology in its favour. Language is the expression of thought, but it is equally the expression of will; and this was true more especially at first, when it was used in the service of the primitive wants of mankind. Now will, as realised in action, is essentially of a verbal character; hence it might be supposed that the verbal nature of radicals was a fact which held good not only of Aryan, but of all other human languages. Not so, however. In

constituted a kind of generative centre for the productive energy of early language.

this case we cannot appeal to Turanian; for though Accadian seems to have nominal as well as verbal roots, our data do not carry us back to their original content and meaning, and they may have been a confused combination of nominal and verbal elements, in which neither of the two had the predominance. But, like the idioms of Polynesia the Semitic languages refer us to nominal roots as decidedly as the Aryan do to verbal ones.[1] The Semitic verb presupposes a noun just as much as the converse is the case in Aryan. Here, then, the conception of the *object* lay at the bottom of the language—an intuition in which the subject ignored, or rather absorbed into the object; subjective action and the development of will being left out of sight. A similar explanation seems necessary in regard to idioms that have few, if any, abstract general terms, like Tasmanian, which could express an abstract idea such as "round," only by saying, "like the moon," or some other round object.[2] The same

[1] What was the original content and purport of roots is not referred to here. All that is meant is the conception with which Aryan and Semitic grammar consciously started. The first clearly defined intuition which lies at the back of Aryan grammar is that of the verb, while the growing consciousness of the Semite fastened itself upon the noun.

[2] Milligan, "Vocabulary of the Dialects of some of the Aboriginal Tribes of Tasmania," p. 34. The whole passage is very instructive. "It has already been implied that the aborigines of Tasmania had acquired very limited powers of abstraction or generalisation. They

deficiency of abstract terms, that is, of words in which the subjective predominates over the objective element, marks many barbarous languages. The Malayans, for instance, have words to signify different sorts and parts of trees, but none to signify "tree" itself; while the Algonquin can localise special individual acts of loving, but cannot express the act regarded in the abstract, when it is removed from the category of space to that of time—in other words, becomes an action which can be repeated any moment, instead of being a definite objective fact.[1] Similarly the Cherokee possesses thirteen different verbs to denote particular kinds of "washing," but none to denote "washing" in a general sense.[2] Perhaps the verbal conception

possessed no words representing abstract ideas; for each variety of gum-tree and wattle-tree, &c., &c., they had a name, but they had no equivalent for the expression 'a tree;' neither could they express abstract qualities, such as hard, soft, warm, cold, long, short, round, &c.; for 'hard,' they would say 'like a stone;' for 'tall,' they would say 'long legs,' &c.; for 'round,' they said 'like a ball,' 'like the moon,' and so on, usually suiting the action to the word, and confirming by some sign the meaning to be understood." The latter words are especially noticeable, bearing as they do upon gesture-language, out of which the various *nuances* of grammar have been developed.

[1] See Du Ponceau, "Langues de l'Amérique," pp. 120, 200, 236, 237. The same holds good of the dialect of the Hurons, according to Charlevoix, quoted by Du Ponceau, p. 234.

[2] These verbs are as follows:—*kŭtŭwo*, "I am washing myself;" *kŭlēstūlā*, "my head;" *tsēstūlā*, "another's head;" *kŭkūsquō*, "my face;" *tsēkūsquō*, "another's face;" *tākàsūlā*, "my hands;" *tātseyàsula*, "another's hands;" *takōsūlā*, "my feet;" *tatseyàsūla*,

upon which the Aryan languages are built pointed out from the beginning the active, self-conscious, nature-subduing character of the Aryan race, just as we seem to trace the features of Judaism in the determinate objective Semitic root and the resignation of the subject which it implies.

The last example of the *Idolum*, or rather of its effects, which I shall select, is the expectation of finding elsewhere the same similarity of grammar, if not of vocabulary, that exists among the several members of the Aryan family. But the striking unity of form that meets us in this family is really exceptional, and will have to be explained hereafter. The rule is rather change and diversity.[1]

"another's feet;" *takŭngkalâ*, "my clothes;" *tatseyângkēlâ*, "another's clothes;" *takŭtēyā*, "dishes;" *tsēyŭwă*, "a child;" *kôwēlâ*, "meat." (Pickering: "Indian Languages," p 26.) It is the same in Cherokee with all verbs, the object being never named. This is also the case in Central and Southern America; thus in Tamanacan, *jucurù*="to eat bread;" *jemeri*="to eat fruit, honey," &c.; *janeri*="to eat meat."

[1] Sir Charles Lyell ("Antiquity of Man," 4th edit., p. 152) well observes that "if the numerous words, idioms, and phrases, many of them of ephemeral duration, which are thus invented by the young and old in various classes of society, in the nursery, the school, the camp, the fleet, the courts of law, and the study of the man of science or literature, could all be collected together and put on record, their number in one or two centuries might compare with the entire permanent vocabulary of the language." Further on he gives the following remarkable instance of the rapid changes which non-literary languages undergo:—"A German colony in Pennsylvania was cut off from frequent communication with Europe for about a quarter of a century, during the wars of the French

The dialects of barbarian tribes are perpetually altering. There is nothing to preserve them—neither traditions, nor ritual, nor literature. The savage has the delight of a child in uttering new sounds, and exhibiting his power and inventiveness in this manner, with none of the restraints by which civilisation confines the invention of slang to the schoolboy and the mob. In some cases, among the Caribes of the Antille Isles, for instance, where the wife was generally stolen from an alien tribe, the language of the women and the men is essentially different; and this, of course, exercises considerable influence upon the language spoken by the next generation.[1] Then, again, the barbarian is especially open to all the influences of external nature, climate, food, and so forth, with nothing to check the disintegrating effect these may have upon the combination of sounds;

Revolution, between 1792 and 1815. So marked had been the effect even of this brief and imperfect isolation, that when Prince Bernhard of Saxe-Weimar travelled among them a few years after the peace, he found the peasants speaking as they had done in Germany in the preceding century, and retaining a dialect which at home had already become obsolete. Even after the renewal of the German emigration from Europe, when I travelled in 1841 among the same people in the retired valley of the Alleghanies, I found the newspapers full of terms half-English and half-German, and many an Anglo-Saxon word which had assumed a Teutonic dress, as 'fencen,' to fence, instead of *umzaünen;* 'flauer' for flour, instead of *mehl*, and so on."

[1] Similarly we are told that the women in Greenland change *k* into *ng* and *t* into *n*.

hence we are not surprised at finding the same word, *orang*, "man," appearing in the Polynesian idioms under the various forms of *rang*, *olan*, *lan*, *ala*, *la*, *na*, *da* and *ra*.[1] Sometimes, moreover, the custom known under the name of *tapu* among the Pacific Islanders will have acted upon language, according to which every word which contains a syllable identical with that forming part of the name of the reigning chief has to be dropped or changed, and a new word adopted in its place. Thus *mi* has been substituted for *po*, "night," in Tahitian, since the reign of Queen Pomare; and a king with the name *Tu* caused *fetu*, "star," to be transformed into *fetia*. Professor Max Müller[2] points out that a similiar custom, called *ukuhlonipa*, prevails among the Kafir women, who are forbidden to pronounce a word

[1] Logan, "Journal in Indian Archipelago," iii. 665.

[2] Lectures, ii, 37-40. Sacred dialects, also, will little by little come to exercise an influence upon the current language. These are not unfrequent among barbarous nations. Thus in Greenland the sacred language of the conjurors is for the most part an arbitrary perversion of the significations of known words; *tak*, "darkness," for instance, being used in the sense of "the north," giving rise to two new words of this secret speech, *tarsoak* (earth) and *tarsoarmis* (roots). These sacred languages are the analogue of the slang of the schoolboy, the European representative of the barbarian. At Winchester, for example, a secret jargon has been handed down from generation to generation, and every newcomer, like a fresh member of the thieves' fraternity, has to be initiated in this school slang, as has lately been made unenviably notorious.

which happens to contain a sound similar to one in the names of their nearest relations. This usage, however, is but one phase of the way in which the barbarian will play with language, regarding it at once with superstitious awe, as though the word in itself had an ominous power, and as an opportunity for displaying his wit and imagination.[1] Nothing is really harder than to keep a language from changing where it is not protected by the habits of settled life, especially when men meet but seldom together, and when the transparent uninflectional character of the language allows every word, however formal, to retain its full force and independent meaning. The comparatively stationary nature of Eskimaux, which seems to have changed but slightly since

[1] According to Hale ("United States Exploring Expedition," vii. 290), "the manner of forming new words" among the Tahitians "seems to be arbitrary. In many cases, the substitutes are made by changing or dropping some letter or letters of the original word, as *hopoi* for *hepai*, . . . *au* for *tau*, . . . *vea* for *vera*, 'not,' &c. In other cases, the word substituted is one which had before a meaning nearly related to that of the term disused. . . . In some cases, the meaning or origin of the new word is unknown, and it may be a mere invention, as *ofai* for *ohatu*, 'stone;' *pape* for *vai*, 'water;' *pohe* for *mate*, 'dead.'" What a picture this is of the variability and living productiveness of savage languages; words invented and altered at will to supply the places of those which have been banished from the speech by superstitious fear!

Dr Hyde Clarke tells me that in China "the new Emperor's name taboos a character, but by compounding it is only clipped.'

the time of Egede, and the astonishing identity of dialect, more especially among the eastern tribes, may be ascribed to the long winters, which oblige the different communities to live closely packed together. At all events, we are told that since the institution of an annual fair among the Rocky Mountains, the idioms of the eastern and western portions of the nation, who at first were hardly understood by one another, have become more and more assimilated;[1] while the phenomenon noticed by Messerschmidt among the Ostiaks, where villages a mile or two apart are unintelligible to each other,[2] will be explained by the agglutinative framework of the language. Where the plural is expressed by an independent word signifying number, one word will do as well as another; for such a purpose we might use indifferently "many," or "multitude," or "company." Nor must we forget how rapid are the social changes that take place among savages, and language is the expression of an existing state of society. A tribe may be decimated by famine or disease, it may amalgamate with another, or still oftener it may be conquered and enslaved, and so forced in the course of a generation or two to adopt the dialect of its

[1] Gallatin's "Synopsis of the Indian Tribes of North America," in the *Archæologia Americana*, vol. ii.

[2] Max Müller, "Lectures," i. 56.

conquerors. The vocabulary of a savage is never very large; the strain upon the memory of the learner, therefore, is not great. All this is abundantly sufficient to show that the persistency of form which we observe in the Aryan family is altogether exceptional, due partly to the semi-civilised life attained before the first emigration set out, partly to a common stock of traditions, partly to the inflectional character of the language; and we cannot argue from this to other families of speech where the rule will be change and not fixity, variety and not similarity.[1]

[1] So greatly do the several Basque dialects differ from one another, even on the same side of the Pyrenees, that a servant girl of my acquaintance, who had been born and brought up at St Pée, and therefore spoke the Labourdin dialect, found the Souletin of Tardets, a place not forty miles distant, perfectly unintelligible.

The Rev. W. Webster writes to me: "One of the most curious cases of mingled dialects was Bayonne. Old people have frequently told me that there used to be three distinct dialects in what is now the modern town. North of the Adour, in S. Esprit, where the railway station is, they spoke the Landais patois; in Petit Bayonne, *i.e.*, between the Adour and the Nive, they spoke a peculiar patois, possibly influenced by the Jews, of whom Petit Bayonne was the compulsory 'quartier' before the Revolution; in Bayonne Proper, south of the Adour and the Nive, they spoke the Anglet patois. The difference between the Anglet patois and the Landais is considerable, in writing at least; between the Anglet and Petit Bayonne chiefly in pronunciation. All three would be called 'Gascoun.' So in the little basin of Bédous, in the Vallée d'Aspe, there are three distinct patois in a radius of three miles: one is nearly = the Bearnais of the Val d'Ossau; another much influenced by Spanish, the third more thoroughly Gascon. The difference in single words is as great as *hilhe*, *hilho*, for *maynatge* and *mainade*, 'boy' or 'girl,' 'son' or 'daughter,' *hemno* and *mougerre* for 'women.'"

Besides these negative instances of the misconceptions and erroneous generalisations which arise from too narrow a view of Glottology, and from the false belief that all its problems can be solved by a study of the Aryan languages alone, an affirmative instance will be needed to show how the converse holds good, how the particular can only be explained from the universal, the part from the whole. We cannot understand even the Aryan group aright, unless we put it in its proper place, and examine it in connection with the general facts of philology. The original form of verbal expression—that is, the representation of the carrying out of will into action in time—is ordinarily said to have been the immediate addition of a pronoun to a root. This would hardly be an adequate explanation, even were it true that all radicals were verbal; and this, as we have seen, is by no means the case. In Magyar *vár-t-am* is "I waited for it," and *kés-em* is "my knife," while in old Egyptian, *ran-i* means indifferently "my name" and "I name." What is it, then, that constitutes a verb? or rather, since Glottology is an historical science, what is the origin of the verbal idea? Now the different words and tenses of the Aryan verb have been created by suffixing various pronouns and verbal radicals, some of which belong to an older period than others. Those moods and tenses which have been formed by the help of another verb, such as the Romance futures, the Teutonic perfects, the Latin perfect passive, or the third person plural of the same tense in Greek, are clearly of secondary antiquity, and presuppose already existing verbal forms. The aorists, again, and presents with extended bases, can hardly go back to the first beginning of the verb. The reduplicated perfect affords room for doubt, and it may have been coeval with such simple presents as *ad-mi* or *as-mi*, in which the pronoun is attached to the root without any intervening syllable. Granting, however, that these simple presents are the oldest forms of a verb—and their rarity and simplicity of meaning point to this—we have not advanced towards a solution of our question, What was the original purport of the verbal idea? From the Aryan alone we should be inclined to conclude that it expressed present time, the most definite possible conception of action, however, and one which philosophy teaches us is among the latest arrived at. Present time, moreover, implies a knowledge at least of the past, if not of the future, with which it may be compared; and some of the lower races, like the New Caledonians, who cannot be made to understand the abstract notions of "yesterday" and "to-morrow," are equally unable to express the notion of "to-day." The primitive Aryan, therefore, if he began with the expression of present time, must have stood on a high level of culture. Here, then, the study of the Aryan family cannot give us the answer we require. With Semitic, however, it is altogether different. The Semite, who never had the sense of individual freedom of will and action which distinguished the Aryan, preserved with but little alteration the primitive vague conception which underlay the verb. The so-called future or imperfect of the Semitic languages is not a tense in the Aryan acceptation of the word. It does not express time at all, merely relation. Now, this was originally the sole Semitic verbal form. The other so-called Semitic tense is nothing else than the participle, the *nomen agentis*, from which the third person singular masculine can still be only artificially distinguished,[1] and it did not take its rise until what Ewald calls the Aramaic or second period in the growth of the Semitic family. In

[1] Ewald disputes this, but his arguments are not convincing. A parallel instance may be quoted from the Turkish, where the persons of the present are formed by postfixing the pronouns, the third person being (as in the Semitic languages) the bare form of the present participle. Thus *dogur* is "striking" and "he strikes;" *dogur-um*, "I strike" (literally "striking I"), and so on. In this way the present is distinguished from the aorist, which is an abstract substantive with the person-endings affixed. Thus from *dogd*, "a striking," is derived *dogd-um*, "I struck;" and with the plural suffix *dogdi-ler*, is at once "strikings" and "they struck," just as *dogur-lar* is "strikers" or "they strike."

time this perfect, as it is commonly termed, came to acquire a kind of present force; but though more verbal in character, according to our Aryan ideas, than the imperfect, it never was a tense in the true sense of the word.[1] Where intercourse

[1] Since the above was written, my friend the Rev. G. C. Geldart has been good enough to send me the following remarks, which seem to me to be extremely valuable, and to show that other nouns besides the *nomen agentis* went to form the Semitic perfect, although the latter came at last to preponderate. "In (the Assyrian) *dapsacu* (*acala*, 'I mature corn'), you have undoubtedly a very near approach to a verb; it seems to me to stand proportionally as near to one as *ristanacu* (I [am] eldest) is distant. In cases like the last there is no verb at all, it being supplied in the mind of the writer and reader. Although in Æthiopic *gabarcu* means 'I *did* make,' this is a further development which does not fully belong to the Assyrian stage of Semitic. Hence I should designate a word like *ristanacu* as a transitional form detected in a state wherein it very closely counterfeits the verb, and is seen to be passing in that direction, but not as a genuine verb. The value of such compounds, as affording an insight into the manner in which real verbs may arise from the combination of verbal and other conceptions with personal pronouns, and actually have done so, may be illustrated by the following example. In Professor Lee's 'Hebrew Grammar,' p. 214, § 13, I find cited from Jer. xxii. 23, the unique forms ישבתי, מקננתי, נחנתי, which consist of the second person of the pronoun combined with participles in Kal, Puhal, and Niphal respectively, into a sort of word which can hardly be called correctly a verb, and is, I believe, entirely without a parallel in the language. This form has been, I gather from Lee, a regular crux to grammarians; but it seems to me to stand on just the same footing as *tsabtacu* (I am taking), and so the two illustrate each other. I should speak of ישבתי as a tentative form which turned out abortive and unsuccessful; *tsabtacu* I should call one which did succeed, made good its appearance in the language, and in the later stages of Semitism became accepted as a

with a foreign people, as in the case of the Assyrians, and to a lesser degree of the Gheez, brought about something like a conception of verbal time and mood, the varying vocalic forms of the imperfect were appropriated for this purpose, but even here with no very great strictness. A similar device has been adopted in Arabic, helped out by the use of other words like *kad*, "now." In the Semitic family, accordingly the original purport

true and real verbal form, embodying the association of action in past time, *i.e.*, a genuine perfect tense. . . . Now my idea is, that of two views one is right, according as we may be able to settle the matter by the aid of chronology or not. Would it be possible to fix the relative historical dates of the inscriptions wherein these several *-cu* forms appear? and would not such a chronological arrangement of them bring out the fact that *ristanacu* stood among the earliest, *dapsacu* among the latest, of them? If so, then *ristanacu* will constitute the first, and *dapsacu* the last, term in the progress of the Assyrian compound towards that condition which its Æthiopic analogue (*gabarcu*) really has attained, viz., that of a genuine verbal inflection. Or if this cannot be done, then I should describe these *-cu's* as a cluster of instances wherein a pronominal affix was seen vacillating at random in its choice of a base to which it could most congenially attach itself; the one ultimately preferred being, as we know from other sources, exclusively a verbal one. But either way, my general impression is, that in our survey of these formations we are admitted to no less interesting a spectacle than the genesis of an inflection, and that we here obtain a deeper insight into the constructive processes of language than we have ever gained before. Hincks, I see, styled Assyrian the 'Semitic Sanskrit;' but I do not think that even Vaidik Sanskrit affords us any traces of the active origination of a tense. In order to have a Sanskrit equivalent to *dapsacu*, we ought to seek the suffix of the first personal pronoun, *-mi*, fastening itself promiscuously to the end of nouns and adjectives as well as verbs, and ought

of the verb was purely indefinite: it had no reference to any particular time or mode; it did not even denote action in general, but regarded the act of the will as an affection of the object, not as an exertion on the part of the subject. We may compare the use of the Greek aorist in similes, where it is a little remarkable that the verbal form which best exhibits the bare root should be set apart for this aoristic or indefinite purpose. More remarkable still is the usage of the polysyn-

indeed to find some pronoun of which *-mi* is a manifest abbreviation, as *-cu* is of *anacu;* but there is not, so far as I can discover in Professor Wilson's chapter on the grammar of the Vedas, anything of the kind. But the comparatively recent origin, in point of time, of this tense in Assyrian seems to me highly suggestive as regards the history of inflections. First, the perfect could have formed no part of the '*original* stock of the Semitic speech.' In Assyrian the *-cu* has not yet acquired any definite association with the idea of past time at all; and it is plain that this association, when connected with it, as in the Æthiopic *gabarcu,* was purely fortuitous and conventional. Also it is very surprising that so important an inflection should have been delayed so long in the social and intellectual existence of the Assyrians. They must be supposed to have felt the want of it as the need for precision of thought progressed among them; because I conceive it is not pretended that the aorist *iscun* (he made) was definitely a past tense. But it is quite beyond what one would have expected in the history of language, that a people should have possessed a well-organised literature before their system of inflections was completely settled; and we apparently learn what as a general truth I had long suspected, that even within historic ages the instability, and in consequence the expansibility and flexibility, of language was proportionately much greater than it became afterwards." The views here expressed have since been more fully worked out by the author, and embodied in a paper read before the Oriental Congress at London in 1874.

thetising languages of North America, where the idea of time or mode is altogether absent from the verb, and personal relations are alone indicated. For this purpose a most intricate and elaborate machinery has been devised, and according to the Baptist missionary, Edwin James, the Chippeway Indian possesses no less than from six to eight thousand verbal forms. So, too, in Eskimaux we have such monstrosities as *aglekkigiartorasuarnipok*, "he goes away hastily and exerts himself to write."[1]

Much the same phenomenon reappears in Basque, a different form being employed for addressing a superior, an equal, a child, or a woman, and in reference to an object in the first, second, or third person singular and plural. Thus *det* is "I have;" *ditet*, "I have them;" *dizut*, "I have it for thee;" *at*, "I have thee;" *zaitustet*, "I have you;" *dizquizutet*, "I have them for you;" *daunat* replacing the last when a woman is meant, and *dayat* when an equal. Here the forms originated in the incorporation of the objective and oblique cases of the personal pronouns, for the most part before the root, which is followed by the postfixed subject, a noun of number (*it*) being actually intercalated into the root itself when the plural has to be signified.

[1] See Gallatin, "Trans. Amer. Antiq. Soc.," vol. ii. p. 176; Crantz, "History of Greenland," vol. i. p. 224.

The same fact meets us again in Accadian. Here we have but two tenses, an aorist and a present. The first is formed by the immediate addition of the pronouns to the root; the second by a vocalic prolongation of the root; thus, *in-sum*, "he gave;" *in-summu*, "he gives;" *in-gar*, "he made;" *in-garra*, "he makes." The present is formed in the same way in the Tibetan dialects, and clearly points out the priority of the aorist, from which the idea of present time was obtained, with the growth of experience and civilisation, by dwelling upon the sound of the aorist.[1] With the creation of a present the aorist ceased to be aoristic, and became a past tense. Thus Turanian bears the same testimony as Semitic, and explains the original nature of the Aryan verb; while the observation of actually existing cases, like that of the New Caledonians mentioned above, supplies the historic verification of the theory, and throws a new light upon the development of mankind.

[1] Dr J. H. Trumbull writes to me:—"I observe the accordance of Algonkin with Accadian in the later formation of the *present* by an affix, the so-called present of the missionary-grammars being demonstrably an aorist. Eliot—who knew the Algonkin language better than any Anglo-American since his time has known it, and who was a good Hebraist—used throughout his version of the Bible the same form for present and "narrative" aorist, from which the immediate and *continuing* present is formed by a suffixed particle."

# CHAPTER III.

## THE IDOLUM OF PRIMEVAL CENTRES OF LANGUAGE.

PLATO has laid down that the end of science, as of philosophy, is unity; and he attempted to anticipate the slow processes of modern induction by discovering a master-science from which all the others radiate. It would seem nowadays as though the dream of the Greek thinker were in a fair way to be realised. The physical sciences are becoming more and more metaphysical with the increasing transcendentalism of their highest laws, while the historical sciences are growing more and more physical as the interdependence of the two is more clearly recognized. Science is beginning to deal almost exclusively with *force*, in itself a metaphysical conception; and the doctrine of the conservation of forces, that is, of one invariable whole which manifests itself under various interchanging forms, is the keynote of modern research. Whether, however, an ideal unity will ever be attained, is a question which admits of grave doubt in the face of the opposition and contradiction which lie at the foundation of the world, of the separation of our several senses, of the deficiency of our data and the limitation of our positive knowledge, and of the mysterious but impenetrable background which appears to lie beyond the highest and primary laws. Nevertheless, unity is the goal of every inquirer; it is necessitated by the very constitution of the mind; and in so far as thought is one, or rather, as the way in which we are compelled to regard the phenomenal world is the same, a certain kind of unity is not only attainable, but necessary. We cannot help believing that under all the variety that we see there lies a hidden unity, and that that variety is itself but a way of producing unity. If we are to think at all, we must sum up the isolated phenomena under general heads, we must discover some similarity and order in them; and the more nearly the mental order corresponds with objective sequence, the more fully shall we satisfy the requirements of science. But we must not forget that the so-called laws of science are, after all, only so many mental conceptions, the imaginative framework which we fill up with the results of our experience, or rather of the manner in which we are obliged to look at things. Now these conceptions are all alike in so far as they are thought, and we can ideally sum up one conception under another, until at last we reach the highest and most comprehensive unity. It is this that we call the world; and the day on which this general unifying conception was first struck out was a day of importance in the progress of the human race. The Greeks ascribed the discovery to Pythagoras; and whether or not it was really invented by the semi-mythical Samian, the Greek word was well worthy of a nation of philosophers. Κόσμος, or "order," is the best and truest conception of the universe that can be arrived at; it is the summing-up of civilisation and civilised reflection in contradistinction to the unreflective fetichism of the savage, who can see nothing except caprice and disorder around him. Unity must be found in order, if it is to be found anywhere; it is just that orderly arrangement of our conceptions, that successive sequence and co-ordination of thought which impresses itself upon the outside world, that enables us to detect and name an unity amid the everlasting flux of things. The Romans, in this, as in most other intellectual matters, the pupils of the Greeks, were content to translate κόσμος by *mundus*, in which, however, the reference to well-disciplined arrangement was lost, and replaced by an allusion to the neatness of personal adornment.[1] It was only for the needs of Cicero's

[1] In Sanskrit, also, *loka* means both "mundus" and "monde," as in the compound *sakala-loka-pujyah*, "venerated by all the world."

amateur philosophising, and under the subsequent pressure of a dry scholastic philosophy, that the Latin language yielded *universum*, *universe*; where all the vivid concrete metaphor of fresh Greek thought has had to make way for the barren abstraction which simply affirms that unity is "one." Our own *world* is of far humbler parentage. It is merely *wer-alt*, "generation of men," from *alt*, the Gothic *alds*, "age" or "generation,"[1] and the Old Saxon *wer*, "man," which appears as a Gentile suffix under the form *ware*, "men," in words like *Rôm-ware*, "Romans," and has its kindred in the Gothic *vair*, the Latin *vir*, the Greek ἥρ-ως, the Gælic *fear*, the Welsh *gŵr*, and the Sanskrit *vîr-as*. It is the same root, *vri*, that has produced *virago* and *virgin*, as well as *vires*, "strength," in Latin, and *vrîhi*, "rice," in Sanskrit, and whose primary meaning is simply "to grow." The same idea is contained in the word which is used instead of the representative of *wer-alt* in the Gothic of Ulfilas, *mana-sedhs*, "man's seed."[2] It is characteristic of the practical, domestic, conservative Teuton to have found *his* world in the past

[1] The word is equivalent to the Greek *αἰών*, as in *ald-ins*, *ald-e* *αἰῶνας αἰωνων*, or *ald bauan αἰῶνα διάγειν*.

[2] Ulfilas also has *fairwus* in the sense of "world," while οἰκουμενη is translated by *midjungards*, "the half-way house" between the celestial and infernal regions. We get the same idea in Scandinavian.

generations of mankind, just as the richly-gifted Greek, with his keen sense of the "golden mean" of proportion and beauty, found his in the unchanging order that underlies the whole course of nature.

This instinctive desire to discover unity has had its effect upon the science of language. Here, as elsewhere, the aim of science is to generalise, and to show that there is order, and not caprice, among the phenomena—classification, and not isolation. But in this search it is bound not to go beyond the facts and the strict inferences which may be drawn from them. However tempting an assumption may be, it must at once be set aside if our data fail to give it plausibility, much more if they actually tell against it. Now this, I think, is the condition of a very common philological hypothesis: that all languages are descended from one original centre, or at most from two or three centres. The assumption runs through a great deal of our modern glottological reasoning. It is implied in the ordinary classification of languages, which assume that families of speech analogous to the Aryan are to be found all the world over. Every idiom, ancient or modern, has to be brought, willing, nilling, under some "family;" the admission that a language may be *sui generis* is never even dreamt of. We have even had a "Turanian family" invented, into which everything that is not Aryan or Semitic has been thrust, from Turkish and Tamulian to Chinese and Red Indian. Now, however, that the term "Turanian" is more properly confined to the chain of dialects which extend from the North Cape to Tungusia, embracing Finnic, Tartar, and Mongolian, to which even Basque has been added by some, and which in some measure exhibit the same marks of resemblance as the members of the Aryan group, a new family has been brought into existence, to be called Agglutinative, or Allophylian, or heaven knows what. Scholars of the highest reputation have endeavoured to derive Aryan and Semitic from a common source; and, when all else failed, have had recourse to the desperate expedient of making them separate down the opposite slopes of the same chain of mountains shortly after the invention of a common tongue. Nay, attempts have been made to show at least the possibility of one primeval language, or embryonic language, on the basis of the theory that would make a language develop out of an isolating into an inflectional stage, through an intervening period of agglutination; and this, too, in a scientific spirit, and on professedly scientific grounds, and not after the manner of Mr Forster, who discovered the language of Eden in the combination of a modern Arabic lexicon with a rudimentary Chinese grammar. We are still too much under the influence of early prejudices; we remember that there was one speech before the confusion of Babel, and that in the old days of etymology nothing was easier than to derive any one language from any other according to fancy. A few such instances as the resemblance of *sanguis* to the Mongolian *sengui*, "blood," or *sex* to the Hebrew *shêsh*, "six," were sufficient to settle the question. Then, again, there is the analogy of the Aryan languages, which all emanate from one source; and, as we observed in the last chapter, the ordinary procedure of Glottology has hitherto been to predicate of language in general what has been found true of Aryan in particular. The other sciences have aided in the matter, tending as they do towards a common point of agreement, and returning to the primeval world-egg of Egyptian philosophy, out of which all things have been generated by a continuous process of differentiation. No utterance of science is clearer than this, that all which is now in being is the result of evolution or development; that look where we will, to the most distant horizon of space, or the dimmest antiquity of time, there is no break, no void, nothing but an unvarying, unchangeable continuity of progress. Darwinism is the most fashionable hypothesis of our day; and Darwinism is supposed to imply a common type and a single pair of ancestors. But some even of the most advanced supporters of the Darwinian theory have themselves been obliged to resign the homogeneity of the human race so far as origin is concerned. The very fact of the variation of species demands it, as different varieties would have the best chance of succeeding in the struggle for existence in different parts of the earth; and sexual selection alone cannot explain the black skin of the negro, whose brain also contains the colouring pigment, or the small stature of the Andamanner, or the curious fact that the population of a continent corresponds with the typical characteristics of its brute animals. We have all been cast in the same mould, or, as St Paul puts it, we have all the same blood; but it does not follow that we all come from the same ancestry, still less that all languages have radiated from the same centre. In fact, if we are to believe that articulate language began with the period of roots, remote as this period is in the history of the Aryan race, it is still not remote enough to allow for the vast changes that have taken place in the distribution of earth and water, in the fauna and flora that inhabit the land, and in man himself in all his variety of form and colour. The human remains found in the upper levels of the Seine near Abbeville, or the geological alterations that must have happened since the entrance of the Papuan race into their present habitat, supposing they had migrated from a common cradle of mankind, seem irreconcilable with the limited antiquity of the root-epoch of the Aryan languages. When they first become known to us in the hymns of the Rig-Veda, it is in the neighbourhood of the Punjab. Is it likely that the Dravidian races, the "Dasyus," whom their speakers encountered in India, or the tribes they found existing in India, in Asia Minor, and in Europe, could have once belonged to the same race with themselves? All things, of course, are possible in science, and we are often called upon to believe what is far stranger than the strangest fiction; but where this is not the case, where there are no facts to support the assumption, we must abide by the ordinary analogies and conclusions of experience. The class of languages nearest akin in appearance to the Aryan is the Semitic; and here, if anywhere, upon the received theory, we should expect to find the most convincing proofs of relationship. On the contrary, everything is against it: the structure of the language,[1] the phonology of the speech,[2] the

[1] What can be more unlike than the triliteral Semitic root, consisting wholly of consonants, and ignoring the vowels, and the monosyllabic Aryan radical, in which the vowel is dominant, with its capacity of infinite development and unlimited composition?

[2] Thus *qu* is essentially an Aryan sound, unknown to the pure and

conception of the grammar, the character of the lexicon, alike forbid the supposition, unless we can imagine a psychological miracle, by which the same mind was capable of originating two things so contrary as the Aryan and Semitic conception of the verb.[1] Add to this, that while Northern Europe seems to have been the first home of the Aryans, the earliest revelations of Semitic speech point unmistakably to the deserts of Northern Arabia. The theory of common primitive centres breaks down at the very threshold.

I have more than once said that, in studying Glottology, we must not go beyond our facts; and the statement, simple as it seems, cannot be too often repeated. Now our facts, scientifically considered, are, firstly, similarity of general structure in language; secondly, similarity of grammar both in form and meaning; and thirdly, a regular and

unadulterated Semite. Æthiopic seems to have borrowed the sound from its African neighbours, as the Himyaritic alphabet, the original of the Æthiopic syllabary, is without it, while the semi-vowel, which attaches itself solely to the gutturals in the Æthiopic, is found in Amariñña or Amharic after other consonants, *lua*, *mua*, *rua*, *sua* *shua*, *bua*, *tua*, *nua*, *zua*, *yua*, *dua*, *dhua*, *fua*, which M. d'Abbadie ("Catalogue raisonné de Manuscrits Éthiopiennes," p. vii.) tells us must be pronounced like the French *loi*, *moi*, *roi*. On the other hand, in what Aryan language can we find the *ayin* of the Semitic?

[1] I cannot do better than quote Schleicher's words on this subject:—"Bei den so tief in's innerste Wesen der Sprache eingreifenden Gegensätzen an eine Verwandtschaft der beiden Sprachstämme nicht im Entfernsten zu denken sei" ("Die Deutsche Sprache," 2d edit. 1869, p. 21).

uniform interchange of phonetic sounds between the languages we are comparing. When once a sufficient number of instances have shown that a certain letter in one dialect is replaced by a certain other letter in another dialect, we must never admit any violation of the rule unless it can be explained by the action of subordinate laws; and the explanation of these interchanges of sound and their mutual relationship is part of the duties of philology. In addition to these facts, which belong for the most part to the province of phonology, a fourth fact will be similarity of signification. Two words may conform to all the requirements of Grimm's law, and yet have nothing to do with each other. Ὀδὸς and ἕδος, *solea* and *sella*, for instance, both point back to a root, *sed*, but there is no common idea that will allow us to bring them together, or from which we can derive them; and the attempt to do so is as futile as to reduce the various incompatible meanings of a Semitic radical under one head, or to find some single fundamental conception for the numberless significations attached to the same sound in such languages as Chinese or old Egyptian, where *yu* means at once "me," "agree," "rejoice," "measure," "stupid," and "black ox;" or *ta*, "thou," "gift," "direction," "corn," "drop," "type," "tear," "heap," "stick," "health," "head," "throne," "man," "assembly," "wicked," "navigate," "steal," "burn," "carry," and "give an account." Such, then, are the facts with which Glottology begins, and the lower empirical generalisations so derived furnish the means for arriving at those higher and wider laws which are the ultimate object of the science. Beyond the facts we can never get, at least if we wish to obtain valid conclusions. But similarity, the comparison of the like with the like, is what lies at the bottom of them all; and hence, where he cannot find a similarity which can be scientifically proved, the glottologist must resign an opinion, however plausible. This is precisely the case with the subject of this chapter. The amount of likeness in sound, meaning, and relation which is sufficient to establish a common origin between various dialects is the exception and not the rule in language. A general likeness, of course, there must be, otherwise the science of Glottology would be impossible, since the subject-matter of each science must be of the same character; but this general likeness results from the fundamental identity of the human mind and human experience, and of the physical organs which determine the limitations of articulate speech.[1]

[1] I am glad to find that Professor Max Müller, in his recently published "Lectures on the Science of Religion," expresses himself

When we come to look into the facts, we find that, so far from supporting the hypothesis of a small number of primitive centres of speech, they are all, so far as they go, on the opposite side. We have already disposed of the alleged common origin of Aryan and Semitic in the last chapter; we need only add the significant fact, that a closer analysis, instead of confirming the belief in the original identity of the Aryan and Semitic numerals—one of the chief arguments in favour of the idolum we are now discussing—has shown that they are of wholly different origin. The coincidence of sound between the Hebrew *shêsh*, "six," and *shebà*, "seven," and the Sanskrit *shash* and *saptan*, had led to their being identified; and to the further attempt to compare the Heb. *êkhad*, "one," with the Sansk. *êkas*, and *kam-esh*, "five," with the Sansk. *pan-chan* (*quin-que*). But the Arabic

fully in accord with the views of this chapter. Thus he says (p. 154), "If we confine ourselves to the Asiatic continent, with its important peninsula of Europe, we find that, in the vast desert of drifting human speech, three, and only three, oases have been formed in which, before the beginning of all history, language became permanent and traditional; assumed, in fact, a new character—a character totally different from the original character of the floating and constantly varying speech of human beings." And again (p. 161), "Families of languages are very peculiar formations; they are, and they must be, the exception, not the rule, in the growth of language. There was always the possibility, but there never was, as far as I can judge, any necessity for human speech leaving its primitive stage of wild growth and wild decay."

*sittuñ* and Eth. *sedestu* prove that the primitive form of *shesh* contained a dental, derived probably from *sad-sad*, a by-form of *sal-sal*, which appears in *shalos*, "three," while the Zend *kshwas* points as clearly to an original initial guttural, justifying Professor Goldstücker's view that it stands for *ka-katwar*, "(two) and four." *Saptan* may be a participial form from the same root that gives us ἕπω in Greek and *sequor* in Latin, and thus to have signified "following," while no amount of reasoning can ever get rid of the final guttural of the Semitic numeral, which is best traced back to *arbá*, "four." *Ekhad*, I believe, is from a foreign (Accadian) source; at all events, the vowel at the beginning is prosthetic, and cannot be compared with the initial syllable of *e-ka*, which, when compared with *u-nus*, οἶνο-ς, Gothic *ái-n-s*, and the Sanskrit pron. *ê-na*, "that," would appear to be a principal part of the Aryan word. To connect *kamesh* and *panchan* is comparison run mad. The whole argument rests upon the same unscientific comparison of words superficially alike that was the staple of the etymologising of the last century, and the conclusions arrived at are equally valid. As well might we join the Basque *sei*, "six," with *sex*, or *bi*, "two," with *bini*.[1]

When we pass from the Semitic to other groups

[1] See my "Assyrian Grammar," pp. 132-138.

of languages, the difficulty of connecting these with Aryan becomes even greater. First of all they are lumped together in one mass, or at best divided into agglutinative and isolating, and then it is asserted that the parent Aryan language had passed through both these two stages before it reached the inflectional stage, and that it was during the first of these periods—in other words, during the epoch of roots—that it formed one with all the known languages of the world. But, passing by the assumption of this graduated development, which we shall examine in a future chapter, we may well ask how such a fact, if fact it is, can possibly be known? Nothing is more deceptive and dangerous, it is agreed on all hands, than the comparison of words only, unless we are guided by rules like Grimm's law, more especially when the original meaning of the words is vague and obscure. In order that our conclusions shall be sound, we must begin by the comparison of the grammar; and in the present instance, such a comparison is excluded by the nature of the case. In fact, the whole attempt rests upon air; its sole basis is the inherited prejudice in favour of a common primeval tongue. It cannot be urged that the readiness to change which distinguishes savage dialects, as we saw in the last chapter, gives any countenance to the maintenance of the theory. In the first place, the extent and nature of the changes are unknown, and science does not allow us to spin theories out of what *may be;* in the second place, however great may be the change in the vocabulary, the manner in which the mind views objects and their relations, that is to say, the structure and grammar of the language, remains unaltered; in the third place, war and pestilence, the chief instruments of change, do not introduce any new language, they only bring about the extension of one idiom and the destruction or diminution of another: and lastly, the peculiar language of the woman and of the nursery is at once conservative and confined to the lexicon. Where two Manipuran villages are unintelligible to one another, it is on account of changes in pronunciation, in idiom, and in vocabulary, not in the grammatical forms. It may be doubted, moreover, whether we should not always be able to recognise some, at least, of the ordinary terms of daily life in two dialects which were once closely united, however great their divergence may have been. In spite of the wide interval in time, space, and social relations, Dr Hommel believes himself able to point out many words of this sort which are common to Accadian and the modern Turkic languages of Central Asia. This is more especially the case with the numerals. Common roots have also been pointed out between Accadian and the Uralic idioms of Northern Russia and Finland; *pi*, "the ear," for example, reappears in the Votiak *pel*; *kats*, "two," is the Esthonian *kats*, like *dingir*, "god," the Turkish *tengri*, "heaven."

How far grammar is changeable, how far it may be affected from without, is a matter which we shall have to investigate hereafter. For the present, we may acquiesce in the received doctrine that the forms of grammar are never borrowed, even though the dictionary may almost entirely consist of foreign words.

However, it is not enough to overthrow the arguments brought forward by the homogenists; we require positive instances on the contrary side; and these, I think, we have. How else can we explain *consistently with the given facts*, such phenomena as the ancient languages of Etruria and Lykia? It is said that our inability to decipher the Etruscan inscriptions is a disgrace to philological science. So it would be if they fell within the province of Comparative Philology, if, namely, there were any other known language with which they could be compared. If such does not exist, the taunt is undeserved. And it seems to me that this is the conclusion to which every unprejudiced thinker must be driven after the vain attempts that have been made to find the key in every possible or impossible language. The latest decision is that they belong to the Indo-European family, because the language of them is inflectional; but surely the decision refutes itself. Were they Aryan, they would have been explained long ago. If any one thing distinguishes an Aryan language more than another, it is its persistency of type, its general fixity of grammatical form, its common residuum of roots, which allow us to determine its character at a glance, whether among the valleys of the Caucasus or on the shores of the Atlantic. As soon as the cuneiform inscriptions of Persia could be read, there was no doubt as to the Aryan affinities of their language, or its place in the Aryan family, and the Umbrian dialect of the Eugubine Tables, or the idioms concealed under the Runes of Northern Europe, offer equally little room for hesitation. The characteristics of the European portion of the family are even more distinct; and we may well ask, whence did the Etruscan acquire its peculiar features? We know that it descended into Italy from the north, and hence, if Aryan, could only be connected either with Keltic, Teutonic, Slavonic, or Thracian. With the three first every one allows that it has nothing in common, in spite of Sir W. Betham and Dr Donaldson; and little as we know of the last, we know enough to deny its kinship to

Etruscan. The Rhætian Alps are now inhabited by a population which speaks Romansch and Ladin; but these are Romance dialects, and in spite of many strange-sounding Etruscan-like local names—Velthins, and the like—all the researches of Dr Freund and Mr Ellis have failed to discover a single Etruscan word in the modern idioms. The Etruscans may have been the bronze-men of the Swiss lakes, or their predecessors of the Neolithic age, whose pile-dwellings in the north of Austria have yielded wheat and coral, evidences of Eastern intercourse; at any rate, except in Italy, where they had the good fortune to come into contact with Greek civilisation, they have passed away and left no trace behind them. Unlike the Aryans, they were unoriginative and receptive; and not only did they receive into their vocabulary Greek words like βροντή (in the *phrunt-ac* of the Pisaurum inscription) or αἰών (in *aiv-il*, "age"), but even the Latin inflections of a proper name, *Velthina, Velthinas,* in the late inscription of Perugia. The native inflections, however, were of a very different character; the patronymic *al*, the termination *isa* to express "the wife of," the verbal *c* and *ke*, and the nominal *l*, *ls*, *n*, *k*, are all non-Aryan either in form or use.[1]

[1] Dr Isaac Taylor's attempt to connect Etruscan with the Ugro-Altaic or Turanian class of languages (in his "Etruscan

Unlike the Etruscan, a few of the shorter Lykian inscriptions can be read, thanks to the Greek legends attached to them. Here again we have an inflected language; which has accordingly been added to the Aryan stock, with the support of such forms as *prinafatu*, "he made," by the side of *prinafūtu*, "they made." The nearest Aryan language fixed upon is Zend; but a certain admixture of Semitic has also been assumed![1]

Researches," 1874) cannot be judged more successful than the solutions of the problem proposed by his predecessors. The evidence which he brings forward from physiology, ethnology, and mythology upsets all endeavours to refer the Etruscans to an Aryan origin in agreement with craniologists who have long ago asserted that while the skulls of the lower classes found in Etruscan tombs belong to the Italic type, those of the upper and ruling class are of a wholly different character; but the philological portion of the book is not likely to convince any one.

Mommsen, in his "History of Rome" (*Engl. transl.*, pp. 189, 249, 495, &c.), has well pointed out how thoroughly the religion, art, and manners of the Etruscans contrast with all that characterises an Aryan people.

[1] See Daniel Sharpe's appendix to Fellows' "Account of Discoveries in Lycia," pp. 480 *sq.* Since Moriz Schmidt's great work, "Vorstudien zur Entzifferung der lykischen Spachforschung," with its sequel, the "Corpus of Lycian Inscriptions," Savelsberg has published the first part of "Beiträge zur Entzifferung der lykischen Sprachdenkmäler" (1874), in which he tries to explain the inscriptions by the help of Zend. Apart, however, from the question how an Iranian dialect came to be spoken in the far west at so early a date by tribes whose characteristics were but little Aryan, Fick has proved that the languages of Asia Minor, which are unquestionably Aryan, belong to the European and not to the Iranian branch of the family, and that the stream of Indo-European migration did not pass westward along the southern

The general character of Lykian, however, so far as we know it, as displayed in the nature of the vocabulary and grammar, is so clearly and widely removed from that of the Aryan family, that an endeavour has been made by Mr Ellis to attach it to certain of the Caucasian idioms, but with scant success. The language is inflectional, it is true; but the inflections are not those of the Indo-European group. If the supposition be hazarded that it branched off from this group, or rather from some remote ancestor of this group, long before the days to which Fick's dictionary and Schleicher's grammar of the parent-speech refer, we can only reply that there is not a single

shores of the Caspian until a very late period. (See Appendix.) After reading works like those of Corssen and Savelsberg, we cannot help feeling that the difficulty of modern philology is not to show that a language is Aryan, but that it is not Aryan. If our spectacles are coloured, everything that we see through them will assume the same tint; and when the Aryan languages are made the sole standard of philological inquiry, it will be as easy to find their characteristics in Etruscan or Lykian as it is to read a modern opinion into the writings of some ancient author. Surely the philologist will gain more credence for his study if, instead of forcing every new dialect he may come across into an "Aryan" mould, he frankly confess that he has met with a language which the strict application of the laws of his science will not allow him to compare with any other or bring into a pre-arranged scheme. Nothing would show more convincingly the scientific soundness of his method than the fact, that whereas a Runic or Persian cuneiform inscription has only to be deciphered to reveal its Aryan character, as soon as he has to deal with an Etruscan or Lykian legend which can be read without the

fact to support the belief. Behind that period we know only of the so-called period of roots, and an intermediate epoch during which the inflections of the parent-speech were being settled; but neither these roots nor these inflections are to be found in Lykian. The root-period must in any case have preceded the branching off of Lykian or its presumed ancestor: how is it, then, that the Lykian radicals are not Aryan? Besides, we may ask, as in the case of Etruscan, whence did Lykian come, and what are the genealogical links by which its affiliation to Aryan is to be established?

Another inflectional language not comprised in the Indo-European family is the Georgian.

slightest difficulty, he comes at once to what the geologist would call a fault.

Had our knowledge of Basque to be gleaned from a few inscriptions, I have little doubt that our Aryanising scholars would have claimed the language for our own family of speech. Surrounded as the Basque is by Aryan dialects, there would have been an *a priori* presumption in favour of comparing it with Keltic or Latin. Let us suppose that a bilingual inscription had informed us of the meaning of the following sentence: *etchea suakartu da* ("the house has taken fire"); and that further—which is granting a good deal —we knew which of these words were substantives and which were verbs. Then our Basque Corssen would demonstrate that *etchea* had the same root as *οἶκος*, but had lost (as in Greek) the initial digamma and the final *s* of the nominative; *sua* might be for *sura* from *swar* (*σείριος*, *σέλας*, &c.), and *kartu* is clearly the past participle (again with a final *s* dropped) of *kri* (*creo*, &c.), the two words together forming a very Aryan compound; *da* finally stands for *dat*, and so the whole sentence is easily explained. Evidently Basque has followed the example of Etruscan in dispensing with the terminal consonants of its flexions!

This is still spoken, and consequently we are not reduced to the allowance of forms and words that can be extracted from inscriptions. The language has a fair antiquity, if it can be shown, as M. Lenormant believes, that the cuneiform inscriptions of Van are written in a cognate dialect. However this may be, Georgian on its inflectional side differs remarkably from the Aryan in several particulars. Thus the sign of the plural, *bi* or *ni*, is inserted between the root and the case-endings, as *thavi*, "head," genitive *thavisa*, plural *thavebi*, *thavebisa*, assimilating the language to the Turanian family; the pronouns have a demonstrative and a copulative case; the ordinal numbers are formed from the cardinals by the prefix *me;* and the verbs incorporate the objective pronouns, and are able to lengthen themselves by the help of unmeaning letters. Like the grammar, the roots of the language show no affinity to the Aryan. Georgian, with its allied idioms, is *sui generis;* and if we abide by the simple facts, instead of following delusive analogies and prepossessions, we shall recognise here also a new independent class of languages. The same must be said of the Caucasian dialects. Anomalous groups of speech as distinct as Abkhasian and Mingrelian exist side by side with an Aryan dialect so nearly allied to Persian as the Ossetian of the Iron; and in spite of attempts to compare them with the dialects of Tibet, the Caucasian group remains a mixture of languages that bear no resemblance either to one another or to the other known idioms of the world. In the words of the homogenists, they are still "unclassified." The only inference that can be legitimately drawn from the facts, without stepping beyond them, is that the mountain fastnesses of the Caucasus—the "snow-white" peaks, as Isidore interprets the word—afforded refuge to the last relics of many old tongues which might have otherwise disappeared, just as Basque has preserved itself in Biscay and Gaelic in the Highlands. The social revolutions to which barbarous and semi-barbarous tribes are exposed, particularly through their limited numbers and the reverses of war, more than account for the entire loss of languages; and when we consider the great antiquity of man, as revealed by geology, by ethnology, by glottology itself, together with the vast extent of area over which he had spread himself at a remote period in scattered isolated bands, with no protection against the beasts of the forest except miserable chipped flints, no protection against the excessive cold of winter except the skins of wild animals and the shelter of a cave, our sole wonder must be, not at the diversity of languages, but at the paucity of the wrecks of ancient speech that still remain spread over the face of the earth. The modern races of mankind are but the selected residuum of the infinitely varied species that have passed away: the same surely will hold good of language; and we ought no longer to be surprised at the multitudinous variety of dialects found in North and South America, in Australia, in the islands of the ocean, or in the continents of the Old World, but be content to believe that they represent but a small part of the extinct essays and types of language which have gone to form the language-world of the present day, like the numberless types that nature has lavished since the first appearance of life upon the globe. Manifold must have been the earliest attempts to form articulate speech, to utilise the mouth for the purpose of supplying daily wants. Man is a social animal; comparative law and comparative ethnology first introduce him leading the communistic life of bees, out of which the idea of individualism grew up with the progress of civilisation. Intercourse by means of gestures and signs could not long have been adequate to the needs of the community; the hands were wanted for other purposes, even if, as Helvétius held, it was through them that man became man; and accordingly the natural powers of producing sound that lay in the voice would have been employed to procure what one man required from another. Whether or not, however, language was at first communistic, like everything else, and not individual, is a question which we have no means of determining. This much is clear, that at a certain period of social life, the impulse towards the expression of articulate speech must have become irresistible, and primitive man would have delighted in displaying his newly-found power, as much as the modern savage or the modern child, the best representatives we now have of primitive man. The child is never tired of repeating the words it has learned; the savage and the schoolboy of inventing new ones. Indeed the slang of the school is the reaction of the still unextinguished feelings of primeval barbarism against the restraints of civilisation, and the strange interjectional "tongues" of religious enthusiam are the return, under the pressure of strong emotion, to the original state of productive energy. After all, the barrier between interjectional utterance and articulate speech is very slight, and it must have been slighter when both were but the outburst of natural feelings and the expression of wants differing in degree only, and not in kind. Can the emotion that prompts the savage to shout be said really to differ from the sense of power and life that makes him turn his shout into a significant word? In both the object is the same; in both the means of attaining that object by the use of the lungs is the same. Surely language originated in the desire to speak, in the pleasure felt in the very act of inventing sounds; and to limit such invention, such desires, to a single body of men is as reasonable as to hold that the manifold songs of different species of birds have all developed out of some original one, or at most out of two or three.

If there is one lesson that modern savage life teaches more emphatically than another, it is that in a so-called natural state separation and hostility are the rule. Mankind live apart in numberless small groups or families, which have no connection, except perhaps a hostile one, with one another, and which continually tend, unless checked by other circumstances, to become narrower and smaller. We see them, too, in a constant state of flux and migration, exposed to all the dangers of famine, disease, and want of wives. Language, the product and mirror of society, faithfully reflects this state of things. In Colchis, Pliny says (vi. 5), there were more than 300 dialects. Sagard in 1631 states, that among the Hurons of North America, not only is the same language hardly to be found in two villages, but even in two families in the same village, while each of these multitudinous dialects is changing every day.[1] Waldeck asserts that a dictionary compiled by Jesuit missionaries in Central America became useless within ten years; while Captain Gordon tells us that "some" of the Manipuran dialects "are spoken by no more than thirty or forty families, yet [are] so different from the rest as to be unintelligible to the nearest neighbourhood." Spix and Martius bear the same testimony in regard to the languages of South America, in reference to which Humboldt[2] writes, that together with a great analogy of physical constitution, "a surprising variety of languages is observed among nations of the same origin, and which European travellers scarcely distinguished by their features."[3] Now we may

[1] Dr Trumbull points out, however ("On the Best Method of Studying the American Languages," p. 11), that Sagard describes the instability of language among the French as being nearly as great as among the Hurons; while "Sagard's very imperfect dictionary of this unstable language, 200 years or more after it was compiled, enabled Duponceau to make himself understood without apparent difficulty by the Wyandots, a remnant of the lost nation of the Hurons."

[2] "Travels in South America" (*Engl. transl.*, i. p. 298).

[3] A very instructive account is given by Washington Matthews, in his "Grammar and Dictionary of the Language of the Hidatsa" (1874), of four tribes of agricultural Indians, numerous and prosperous, found by Lewis and Clarke when they ascended the Missouri in 1804. The four tribes then inhabited eight permanent towns in the Upper Missouri Valley, west of the Dakota nation.

fairly take modern savage life as representing the condition of man when he first comes under the notice of philology, remembering, however, that all the traits we have just been alluding to must have been exaggerated at that early period, when the human race was on a lower level of culture than the most degraded barbarian of to-day, and necessarily existed in scantier numbers. But we need not even go to savage life to exemplify what is the normal condition of spoken language. Every dialect that we meet with gives us evidence against the actual reality of those ideal centres to which he would relegate the various languages of the world. Dialects and diversity are the natural order of things; and as soon as the coercive hand of a literary civilisation is taken off a language, it at once breaks out into a plentiful crop of dialects.

All now left of them is one small village of 2500 souls at Fort Berthold, Dakota. The four tribes are reduced to three, one having been so decimated by smallpox in 1838 that the survivors joined the Hidatsa, and adopted its chief, traditions, and customs. Though the three tribes inhabit one village and have been near neighbours for at least 100 years, in peace and intimacy, freely intermarrying, each has a distinct language. The languages do not tend to coalesce, and only a remote likeness can be traced between two of them, the third having *absolutely nothing* in common. To make the survival of these three tongues side by side more surprising, almost every member of each tribe understands the language of the others; so that "it is not an uncommon thing to hear a dialogue carried on in two languages, one person, for instance, questioning in Mandan, and the other answering back in Gros-ventre, and *vice versa*." Moreover, many of them are acquainted with the Dakota tongue, and all understand the language of signs.

Thus in Greece alone there are (or were a few years back) no less than seventy different dialects. Many of these, no doubt, were new creations; that is, they have originated among the isolated communities of Greece since the tenth century, testifying to the perpetual creativeness of language when left alone. But others will go back beyond the rise of the literary language, which is but one out of many dialects, though selected by circumstances as the standard of the rest. Dialects are the material out of which the idioms of the court and of the book-writer have been formed; they reach back as far as Comparative Philology allows us to carry our investigations. We may, indeed, conceive of a time when, in the Aryan family, for instance, they did not yet exist, and picture to ourselves some parent-speech which held them, as it were, in embryo; but we must not forget that such a parent-speech is altogether ideal; that, so far as our data go, they presuppose the existence of dialects, and that the attempt to explain the laws of *lautverschiebung* by original indeterminate sounds, out of which the various letters which correspond to each other in the several branches of our race were derived, although possible, is neither demonstrable nor satisfactory. In fact, as soon as a language ceases to be confined to a single household, it breaks out into varieties. Every family has its peculiar pronunciation, its favourite words. And the period in which language first becomes an object of study to Glottology is one of scattered and isolated communities. How these first acquired articulate speech is not for the glottologist to ascertain; for him the origin of language means the analysis of the words that we at present possess, the determination of the monuments that have come down to us. This much, however, is clear; that the beginning of articulate speech, the beginning of that language with which he has to deal, is not coeval with the physiological beginning of man; that it is a product of society; and that as society in those primitive times was infinitely numerous, so also were languages. To derive one language from another is to derive one community from another; and where we find all living at once separately and simultaneously, without any mark of priority or derivation, such a procedure can obtain no scientific sanction. We may make ideal centres, like the ideal types of natural history, to which to refer the different members of one or two so-called "families;" but these centres will ever remain ideal; for the philologist dialects exist from the beginning. Nor can we exclude the possibility that some at least of these dialects never had philologically any connection with each other; but that a common climate, common food, and common conditions of life produced similar linguistic phenomena among the isolated communities of a given area, and that a similarity of germ necessarily brought about a similarity of development. The physical descent of certain tribes from a single household must be kept carefully distinct from any philological descent, since, as far as Glottology is concerned, language is posterior to the physical beginnings of man. When we consider the immense multitude of savage idioms, and the changes which these are always undergoing, we may form some idea of the infinite number of tongues that have been spoken since the first epoch of language, and have left no trace behind them. Here and there a few have been stereotyped and preserved by a happy selection; here and there relics of others may be detected; but the large majority have perished more completely than the animals of geological antiquity. When mankind first awakened to linguistic consciousness, each isolated community had its own means of intercommunication, its own dialect, if you like; and from a combination of some of these which lived near one another, or were brought together by war or migration, the dialects which make up a "family" were originated. Instead of deriving the latter from a common ancestor, a common centre, the truer account would be that they were slowly evolved out of an amalgamation of pre-existing dialects. Even the hypothetical root-period of Aryan speech cannot disguise this; we need not go further than Greek to discover roots which exist in no other cognate dialect, or which, like *ῥάχις, σιγή, θεάομαι, τρέμω, νεφρός, τέμνω*, are found but in one or two. How can this be explained upon the hypothesis that all the linguistic material of the Indo-European tongues has been developed out of one original common stock-in-trade of radicals?

Indeed, if the history of language shows anything clearly, it is the exact converse of the theory usually maintained on this subject. The tendency of time is to unify what was originally separate, not to multiply what was originally one. Every war among savages which ends by the subjugation of a tribe and the extinction of its language justifies this assertion. But its full truth is not seen until we come to examine the records of civilisation—that is, until we pass beyond the period of barbarism in which language arose. Were the ordinary hypothesis correct, barbarism would show union, civilisation disunion. But the contrary is the case. All the social conditions of civilised life tend to break down dialects, to assimilate languages, and to create a common medium of intercourse. The Macedonian Empire spread a common language through the East; the Roman Empire still more effectually stamped out the various idioms of the West, until a second period of linguistic disunion was brought about by the return of barbarism with the invasion of the German nations. The Church alone, the sole representative of civilisation, continued to have a common language. In fact, the more intense and extended the civilisation, the more impossible is it to keep up a diversity of tongues. The one unites, the other disjoins. A common government, a common literature, a common history, a common law, all require a common language. The material triumphs of the present century—the railway, the steamer, and the telegraph, with increased facilities of travelling and intercommunication—all emphatically tend in the same direction. Above all, the same holds good of commerce, the mainstay of our modern civilisation, which is gradually absorbing the whole world, and carrying with it, wherever it goes, the languages of the chief trading nations. "One coinage and one language" is a cry now heard often enough. Small nations, like the Dutch, find it absolutely necessary to be bilingual, if not trilingual; and the children in the schools are regularly taught to speak some other language besides their own, commercial reasons making English especially favoured. Politics, too, look the same way. The desire of unification, which has been satisfied in Italy and Germany, aided by compulsory education, is fast destroying the local dialects of Europe; and already the vanguard of democratic socialism and sameness have disowned the distinctions of language, just as they have disowned the distinctions of race. Such is the end of that cry of nationalities which shook Europe so short a time ago: in the midst of their successes, the migration of his countrymen to America is practically disclaiming the words of Arndt, "So weit die Deutsche Zunge klingt;" and the Teutonic population of Alsace has preferred exile to reunion with Germany. In spite of the efforts of philologists Welsh is rapidly disappearing from Wales, and Gaelic from Scotland; while German alone is heard in the schools of the Engadine, and French in the schools of Brittany. The fact that the revival of Flemish has been the work of the literary classes shows its artificial and hollow character, and is of itself a proof how thoroughly the attempt is contrary to the spirit of the age when the language is preserved, not on account of its utility—the sole foundation of the continuance of a language—but because it is regarded as a literary curiosity, a philological plaything. The cry of nationalities was really a backward step: it was the reaction against the bourgeoisie of the French revolution, and a revolt against the old-world diplomacy that parcelled out anew the empire of Napoleon.

To sum up: Instead of maintaining the existence of a few original centres of speech, the truer view would be that languages at first were infinitely numerous and diversified, being the natural and spontaneous outcome of the powers, the feelings, and the needs of primitive man, just as much as the formation of flint tools or the ornamentation of sun-baked pottery, and that they have gradually diminished and disappeared through the course of ages by a long process of natural selection, civilisation finally threatening them with utter extinction, and tending to reduce their number to the smallest possible cipher, if not finally to one universal medium of intercourse between man and man.

## CHAPTER IV.

### THE THEORY OF THREE STAGES OF DEVELOPMENT IN THE HISTORY OF LANGUAGE.

WE are often told that one of the chief results of the science of language has been to show a continuous and regular development in the history of speech: first an isolating stage, or period of roots, when the position of the word alone denoted the meaning of a sentence without the assistance of any (auxiliary) signs of relationship; then an agglutinative stage, when these auxiliary marks were added, each, however, remaining a fully significant, independent word; and lastly, an inflectional stage, when the auxiliary marks have lost all independent meaning, and have become so many inseparable signs. The final stage has a further tendency to analysis: the inflections are broken down, and the decayed compounds are used, as in English, to express singly and independently, by the aid of position, the various relations into which a sentence may be resolved. The analytical period differs from the isolating, in that in the latter each root is a sort of germ which contains within itself every kind of mode and relation, while in the former the germs have been broken up into their elements, and these are represented by words each of which is a relic of a preceding era of inflection.[1] The three stages have been supposed to answer to the solitary individual life the first men are imagined to have led — contrary, however, to the communistic beginnings which comparative inquiries now assign to them—to the family and tribal life of nomads, and to the social life of the civilised citizen. Chinese is taken as an illustration of the first, Turkish of the second, and Sanskrit of the third.

I have said, in a former chapter, that the starting-point of Glottology, the ultimate fact with which it has to deal, is thought expressed in speech. This is more accurate than the ordinary view, which makes philological science begin with

[1] The difference between the analytical and isolating forms of language is well exemplified by Schleicher's illustration in his "Languages of Europe" (p. 51). A sentence which in English runs thus, "The king spoke: O sage! since thou dost not count a thousand miles far to come, wilt thou not also have brought something for the welfare of my kingdom?" when expressed in Chinese presents the following unintelligible form: "King speak: Sage! not for a thousand mile and come; also will have use gain me kingdom, hey?" Pigeon-English is a good instance of an attempt on the part of a Chinaman to enter into the mysteries of Europea thought.

the word. We may ask, "What is a word?" and the only answer we shall get which will cover all words alike is, "Meaning combined with form." This is nearly the same as saying that it is thought expressed in speech; but then what becomes of such words as auxiliaries and conjunctions? It is certainly difficult to detect much meaning in such particles as "and" and "or;" and logic tells us that the copula "is" represents simply the act of mental comparison. Again, are interjections to be considered words? In this case it would be very hard to define the significations of "oh!" or "alas!" By a word, therefore, a definite conception must be intended to be understood; and a conception must be subject to the relations of time and space. Now every conception is the result of a judgment, the decision that such and such particulars are compatible with one another: when expressed in language, it is the shorthand form of a sentence or proposition. A difficulty, however, arises in the case of the verb. The verb, as its name implies, is pre-eminently the subject of philology: it is emphatically *the word;* and yet we cannot say that we have any very definite conception of its meaning in the sense that we have of the noun. The fact is, that the idea we form to ourselves of a verb is an idea of *action*, whether that is restricted to a definite single act or extended to an indefinite succession of acts. But in either case the conception of action implies the conception also of a subject and of an object; and neuter verbs, which throw the object into the background, or even seem to obscure it altogether, are as rare in an early period of language as verbs of a purely abstract signification. Hence we find the middle voice, where the subject is also an object, preceding the passive; while languages of a more primitive type than the Aryan, such as the Accadian, the Basque, or the Mordvinian, insert the object-pronoun between the subject-pronoun and the verb, even in cases where it seems to us superfluous; just as the Algonquin has no verbs to express "to be" and "to have,"[1] or the Semitic languages preferred to denote existence by the paraphrase, "something is an object to him." Analysis, again, is leading us to the conclusion that the prepositions are, for the most part, old substantives, while even the conjunctions, such as *and*, the Greek ἔτι, and Sanskrit *ati*,[2] or *que* (Greek τε, καί, Sanskrit *cha*), were originally demonstratives. Thought must have a beginning and an end as well as a middle, and to seize upon one of these alone apart from the rest as the

[1] See Trumbull "On Some Mistaken Notions of Algonquin Grammar," p. 9.

[2] According to Weber, from the root *at*, "to go;" hence originally "a going further."

starting-point of Glottology is manifestly absurd. It would be as if geology were to concern itself with the individual pebbles of a sea-beach, and endeavour to draw conclusions from them, instead of comparing them one with the other, and with the texture of the neighbouring rocks. Language is based upon the sentence, not upon the isolated word, for the latter can mean nothing except interjectional vagueness. It is merely a bundle of syllables and letters, or rather of animal sounds; merely the creation of the grammarian and the lexicographer. To become language it must embody thought and emotion; it must express a judgment.[1]

[1] Waitz has arrived at the same conclusion, as far back as 1858, in his "Anthropologie der Naturvölker," vol. i. He says (*Engl. transl.*, p. 241), "We do not think in words, but in sentences; hence we may assert that a living language consists of sentences, not of words. But a sentence is formed not of single independent words, but of words which refer to one another in a particular manner, like the corresponding thought, which does not consist of single independent ideas, but of such as, connected, form a whole, and determine one another mutually." He goes on to point out that a sentence is conceived of as a whole (or complete picture) by the mind, the sensible image of an action being immediately reproduced in thought, and that consequently the words by which it is expressed, if unconnected with one another, would convey but little meaning. Such unconnected words are arrived at by a process of conscious analysis. May we not say, then, that the incorporating languages of America, in which an individual action is represented by a single sentence, the component parts of which have not been isolated and assigned an abstract sense, exhibit a lower grade of consciousness than the more analytic, agglutinative

It is the conception of the sentence, therefore, wherein languages will resemble or differ from one another. In Chinese the sentence is summed up in a single word; the mind has not yet clearly marked off its several parts, and analysed what we may call the early communism of speech. This is done in Turanian; but here the sentence is of the most simple character, each portion being of the same hue and force. It is not till we come to the inflectional stage that the parts are duly subordinated; co-ordination of function gives place to a fitting correlation, and makes possible the long compounds of Sanskrit or the exquisite periods of a Greek writer. In the terms of the Hegelian philosophy thought first lies implicit, indetermined, and confused, in a kind of rough block; then it becomes determined, but by means of an opposition which equalises the contradictory elements; and the opposition is finally removed by making each term supplement

languages? From this point of view flection would belong to an earlier stage of development than agglutination, and a transition from the agglutinative to the inflectional conception of the sentence would be a retrograde movement wholly inconceivable in the races which speak inflected languages. We can thus explain how it is on the one side that agglutinative dialects, though often adopting inflectional forms, never become inflectional (*i.e.*, never express an idea by an inflected sentence), and on the other side that inflectional dialects, though presenting numberless specimens of agglutination, yet end by assimilating these to the general inflective character of the language.

the other, according to the laws of a relative subordination. But the conception which underlies each form of the sentence, each stage in the development of language, is as essentially different as the idea or principle which lay at the bottom of the national life of those races who, according to Hegel, have successively worked out the problem of history. Regarding them from the point of view of science or philosophy, we can see how these stages stand related to each other in the order of thought; but we do not see how the gulf between them could practically have been bridged over, or how it is psychologically possible that the same race which conceived its sentence as consisting of co-ordinate elements could also have been potentially able to conceive it as consisting of subordinate elements. There is no question here of growth or evolution. The Aryan languages may or may not have originally been in a state not very unlike that of agglutination, the Finnic group may or may not have come to offer many of the phenomena of inflection: the agglutinative idioms are still agglutinative, and the Aryan family, so far as Glottology has cognisance of it, has always been inflective. We may resolve the Aryan verb into root, or base, and pronoun, but we can never point out a time when the two were of full, equal, independent power; we may show that the suffix *ter*, whence we get *father*, *mother*, and numberless other words of agency, is the root which means "to cross" or "get through" (with a thing), as in *trans* and *through*, but we prove no more than when we demonstrate that the last syllable of *kingdom* is the same word that we get in our *doom* and the Greek *θέμα*, or that *knowledge* and *wedlock* are compounded with the old English *lác*, "sport," "gift," the Gothic *láiks*. The Teutonic languages were inflective before these suffixes were added, and they remained so even while these suffixes still retained their original independent power. In fact, had they not already been inflectional, the suffixes would not have become so, but have continued agglutinative and independent, since mere outward phonetic change cannot produce an internal mental change, and, without the inflectional instinct to precede it, cannot alter the manner in which the sentence and its several parts are regarded by the mind. In the same way, however nearly some of the Turanian dialects may approach to the perfection of inflectional speech, the character of the language still remains fundamentally agglutinative. The wearing of time may, indeed, have wasted away the personal terminations of the Votiak verb *adzo*, "I see," *adzi*, "I have seen," or even have acted upon the earliest known Accadian, so that the origin of the participial affix *á* is obscured, and the termination of the third person plural of the past tense in *-es* and *-us* exhibits but slight trace of the primitive *mes*, "many," out of which it arose; but the example thus accidentally set has not been followed, and the most "Europeanised" of the Turanian tongues keeps true to its original conception of objects and actions. Time will do much, but it will not bring about an entire change in the mode of thought, in the whole constitution of the mind through the external accident of phonetic decay. We, whose idea of language and manner of viewing things in thought belong altogether to the inflectional stage, naturally fancy that it will be with other races as it is with us, and that when certain antecedents are given, the phenomena of inflection will necessarily follow. But how is it possible for one to whom objects and actions and relations are all equally concrete and important to be brought to regard them otherwise, at all events without the help of education? Can we expect a "Principia" from the Negro, or an "Organon" from the Arab? The Ethiopian cannot change his skin, nor the leopard his spots.[1]

[1] Böhtlingk says ("Ueber die Sprache der Jakuten," p. xvii. *note*), "I cannot understand how, with such views on the origin of flexion, any one could remain in doubt for a moment as to whether

The advocates of this theory of development, who would cast all men in exactly the same mould, instead of admitting that different races have started in history with different tendencies, different potentialities, are obliged to lay down that each successive stage in the evolution of language marks a successive progress in civilisation, and that as men became more civilised, so did they approach more nearly to the inflectional level. But this is to ignore the facts. Chinese civilisation is the oldest now existing in the world; its origin is lost in myth, and its continuity is unbroken. And yet its founders spoke an isolating language, while their barbarian neighbours on the West were in the more advanced and civilised stage of agglutination; and not only so, but all their long unbroken civilisation, all the meditations of Confucius or Mencius, all the desperate contrivances of writing, all the intercourse with an Aryan population that Buddhism introduced, have not made the Chinese language advance one step beyond its first isolating stage. Phonetic decay has been at work in the vocabulary, dialects have sprung up in the empire,

a monosyllabic language like Chinese and Sanskrit *could* have one and the same origin. I say 'could have' and not 'had,' since all efforts to make such a common origin in any way probable must be regarded from the outset as idle and fruitless, and consequently unscientific."

new words have been applied to denote the relations of grammar (more especially in writing), and yet the sentence is still confined to the individual vocable, and position and tone must determine the meaning of the speaker.[1] It is the same with the other Taic languages in the south, where the late King of Siam, at all events, is said to have been the most learned monarch in the world. Nor is it otherwise when we look at the western side of Asia. Civilisation there began in the valley of the Tigris and Euphrates; and the cuneiform monuments have informed us that the first known inhabitants of the country, the inventors of writing and arithmetic, the builders of cities and temples, the observers of the phenomena of the sky; nay, it

[1] Professor Whitney ("Language and the Study of Language," 3d edit., p. 336) writes as follows about the Chinese :—"The power which the human mind has over its instruments, and its independence of their imperfections, is strikingly illustrated by the history of this form of speech, which has successfully answered all the purposes of a cultivated, reflecting, studious, and ingenious people throughout a career of unequalled duration; which has been put to far higher and more varied uses than most of the multitude of highly-organised dialects spoken among men—dialects rich in flexibility, adaptiveness, and power of expansion, but poor in all the mental poverty and weakness of those who wield them. In the domain of language, as in some departments of art and industry, no race has been comparable with the Chinese for capacity to accomplish wonderful things with rude and uncouth instruments." Before building the huge inverted pyramid of the development theory upon a few one-sided inferences and hasty assumptions, derived from the phenomena of Aryan flection, it would be well had the advocates of the theory considered this single fact of the fossilisation of the Chinese language side by side with a progressive society and civilization.

would also seem, the instructors of the "inflectional" Semites in the rudiments of civilisation, were a people whose language was agglutinative in the highest degree. Is it not strange that throughout their long career, in spite of the example given them by their Semitic neighbours, the Accadians should not have improved upon the original character of their language in the slightest, although their Elamite kindred, less advanced in culture, it would appear, than themselves, had reached just that amount of semi-inflection in the verbs which strikes us in the Finnic dialects? It is equally remarkable that the latter, which show a very close parallelism to this Elamite idiom, should have made no further progress in the direction of inflection, notwithstanding their longer period of existence and their contact with the Aryans. All goes to show that an isolating or agglutinative stage does not imply civilisation or the reverse, and that no amount of culture, no amount of years, and no amount of foreign intercourse has been able to change the radical character of a language. Surely, if the three stages of language mean mental progress, that progress would have been attained more or less by those who were capable of originating civilisation; and if the circumstances of civilised life are able to alter the conception of the world and its expression in language, Chinese and Accadian would have afforded marked illustration of the power. To say that Chinese is artificially fossilised is not only to beg the question, but also to assume that civilisation stereotypes an early expression of thought; an assumption contrary to facts, as well as to the theory of continuous development itself; and then what becomes of a *barbarous* isolating language like that of the Ainos? The Aryans were not very highly civilised when they herded together among the snows of Northern Europe; yet, according to the common hypothesis, they had already passed through the stages of isolation and agglutination which their more civilised cotemporaries in China and Babylonia were never able to transcend. Nothing can show more clearly the baselessness of a theory which asserts that every language, with sufficient time and civilisation, must pass through the three epochs of development. What was sufficient for the Aryan or Semite was surely sufficient for the Chinaman or Accadian. The civilisation of the latter may have been defective and inferior, but it has the merit of origination; and the superiority of our own shows only the superior intellectual capacities of the race, that is, that the mind of the primitive Aryan was potentially superior to that of the Chinaman, and accordingly potentially conceived of things and their relations and embodied its conceptions in speech in a superior way. We are apt to underrate the extent of the psychological change that is implied in the passage from one of these modes of expressing thought to the other. It is little short of a radical metamorphosis of the mind. And when we think of the impossibility which the Jew of Alexandria, and afterwards the Arab of Spain, had in understanding the primary truths of Greek philosophy, in spite of education and culture, as well as the fact of their all using inflected languages, we may gain some idea of the impossibility the unassisted primitive savage would have found in changing his mental point of view in the concerns of everyday life. What Philo and Averrhoes could not do on a small scale, could the early Aryan or Semite have done upon a large scale?

The theory, moreover, does not take account of the forms of speech which do not strictly fall under one of the three heads. The so-called polysynthetic languages of North America, for instance, are extremely important, characterising as they do a whole continent. Here the sentence is fused together into a sort of long compound, the several words of which it is composed being cut down to bare themes or roots by the same kind of accentual instinct that makes the French drop their final letters in pronunciation, though each fragment still remains an independent word of equal force with the rest. Thus in Mexican a priest is addressed as *notlazomahuizteopixcatâtzin*, compounded of *no* "my;" *tlazontli*, "esteemed;" *mahuiztic*, "revered;" *teo-pixqui*, "god-keeper;" and *tatli*, "father:"[1] and in Delaware, *kuligatchis* signifies "give me your pretty little paw," from *k*, the inseparable particle-pronoun of the second person; *wulit*, "pretty;" *wichgat*, "paw; and *shiss*, "littleness." Compound words are, of course, formed in the same way, like the Delaware *pilápc*, "a youth," literally "new" or "untried man," from *ápe*, "vir," and *pil*, "acting." Are we to class these languages under the isolating, since the sentence is reduced to one long word pronounced at a breath; or under the agglutinative, since the elements continue coequal and independent; or under the inflectional, since they have been subjected to a species of phonetic decay? Again, if we consider the incorporating languages, those, namely, which insert the objective pronoun into the verbal form, we shall have to admit two possible ramifications of the agglutinative group. Incorporation appears in its simplest form in Accadian: thus *in-bat*, "he opened;" *in-nin-bat*, "he opened it;" and various particles, indicative of conjugation and tense, may be inserted between the pronoun and the verbal root, as *in-ta-*

[1] Humboldt, "Essai Polit. sur le Royaume de Nouv. Espagne," p. 81.

*an-ê* "he causes to depart." The same phenomena show themselves in Basque, where the endless forms of the two auxiliary verbs are due to the wearing of time, which has amalgamated the incorporated pronouns, and sometimes even (as in Accadian) an incorporated noun. *Didac*, "you have it for me," for instance is decomposed into the acc. *d*, the dat. *id*, the root *a* or *au*,[1] and the nom. *c*; *dizut*, "I have it for you," into the acc. *d*, the dat. *iz*, the root *au*, and the nom. *t*; while the characteristic of the pl., *it*, is intercalated into the root, thus cutting it in two. Certain verbal forms in Magyar, again, enclose the objective pronoun; and the Finnic Mordvinian of North Russia, where *m* + *ak* = "me + thou," or *m* + *am* = "me + he," sets the contrivance before us as plainly as Accadian and Basque. When, therefore, we are told that language must pass through an agglutinative stage, we may inquire whether that means incorporation or not, or whether it is necessary that every agglutinative language should once have been incorporating?

[1] Mr Van Eys ("Le Verbe Auxiliaire Basque," 1874) has shown that this *au*, which has been further weakened into *ei* and *i* in the Souletin dialect, is a worn-away form of *eroa(n)*, "to make go." *R* between two vowels falls away in Basque, and the Biscayan dialect still preserves the full form *eroa*. *Eroan* is itself contracted from *erazo-joan* or *erazo-yoan*, the causative of *erazo*, "to go." A verb which signifies "to go" may easily become a simple auxiliary, as in Italian, where *se va dicendo* represents the French "*on dit*."

Of course, polysynthetic and incorporating are to be kept carefully apart: in the one the words of a whole sentence are reduced to their unmodified roots and fused into a kind of long word; in the other a few words are loosely attached to the verbal root, unimpaired and independent. There is much more difference between incorporation and polysynthetism than between incorporation and inflection. In some respects, indeed, Basque might almost be considered to have entered upon the road of inflection.

This leads us to what first suggested, and has since been the chief support of, the theory under discussion. An analysis of the Aryan inflections seems to take us back to a period when the primitive language was purely agglutinative, and to a still earlier period when it consisted of rough isolated roots alone. The inflections of the verb in Aryan as well as in Semitic have been traced to the attachment of the objective cases of the personal pronouns to the root or base, and certain verbal forms seem to some to be the result of a combination of the root with other verbs, *ye*, "to go;" *dhe*, "to place;" or the substantive verbs *as* and *bhu*.[1]

[1] Westphal and Merguet deny this, and Westphal's view, as expressed in his "Vergleichende Grammatik d. indogermanischen Sprachen," vol. i. pp. xxiii. *sq.*, is at first sight very plausible. He urges that, just as science has shown that the earth goes round the sun, and not the sun round the earth, so the person-endings of the

Other forms, however, such as the reduplicated perfect or the optative (Sanskrit *bhavey-am* = φύοιμι), have had a different origin, not unlike that of the Teutonic *ablaut,* which represents unmeaning vowel changes (caused by the accents) in Sanskrit, or of the use of the vowels in Semitic to distinguish

verb are the originals out of which the personal pronouns have been afterwards elaborated by a process of analysis and differentiation. His arguments against the ordinary agglutination theory of the origin of verbal flection are, (1) that none of the existing forms of the third pers. sing., for example, numerous as they are, represent what the agglutination theory assumes as the primitive pronoun-termination—*ti* in the present, *t* in the first preterite, and *tu* in the imperative instead of the hypothetical *ta*—and we are not justified in assuming the existence of a form which is never found in any of the many Aryan dialects, and must, on the contrary, have branched off into three distinct varieties; (2) that the change of the hypothetical *tata* into the deviating *tai, ta,* and *tau* of the Atmane-pada present, first preterite, and imperative is unparalleled and unwarrantable; (3) that no sign of the third person can be discovered in the *n* of the third pers. pl. (*nti, nt*); (4) that the explanation of the fulcrum vowel (as in *bhav-a-ti*) as a demonstrative is absurd, since a demonstrative would have no sense in such a position; and (5) that if the pronouns had been prior to the verbal endings, the latter would have been formed by means of the nominative and not the objective case of the pronouns, whereas as a matter of fact the nominative case of the pronouns (*aham, ego,* for instance) is later than the oblique cases and posterior to the flection of the verb. Prof. Curtius's answer to the last objection ("Das Verbum der Griechischen Sprache," pp. 21, 22) is not wholly satisfactory, and Westphal's third and fourth arguments cannot well be controverted; but an analysis of verbal flection in Semitic (so different in this respect from that of nominal flection) is convincing as to the truth of the "agglutination theory" so far as the verb is concerned, and I confess to feeling as unable as Prof. Curtius to understand Westphal's "logical categories of the organism of flection," or to admit the assumption of "pleonastic" letters.

different parts of the verb. The modern languages of Europe have returned to the simplicity of the primitive Aryan verb, though the pronoun has become subject instead of being semi-objective. All this would apparently tend to show that flection did not originally belong to the verb, and that there was a time when its several relations of time and mode and person were each expressed by independent words. The analysis thus successfully carried out in the verb has been applied to the noun, but the results here have not been so decisive. One or two of the case-endings have been identified with prepositions, or in this case postpositions, the locative (primarily *-in*, as in Sanskrit *tasmin*, "in that") with *in*, and the instrumental with *bhi*, "by," and an attempt has been made to compare the sibilant of the genitive and of the dual and plural with the adverbial *sa* (*sam*, *sahá*), and that again with the demonstrative pronoun. The other cases are referred to pronominal roots; but however well a demonstrative may suit the nominative, it is difficult to see how it could express the other cases, or how the other cases could have arisen out of it. How, for instance, could the third personal reflexive pronoun *swa*, *se*, produce the plural locative, or the idea of the accusative be obtained from *mâm*, *má*, "me," or *ama*, "that," used to denote "a suffering object"? Moreover, the pronominal *ta*, which plays so important a part in the ordinary analysis of flection, is, as Ludwig[1] points out, a nonentity, since *t* is always followed by the vowel *i*. In fact, the whole pronominal theory rests upon a very narrow basis, as we shall see further on; and the primitive Aryan must have been at once supernaturally clever and supernaturally stupid to extract the various cases of the noun by ringing the changes on a row of demonstrative suffixes.[2] Against the whole assump-

[1] "Agglutination oder Adaptation," p. 18.

[2] Professor Curtius ("Zur Chronologie d. indog. Sprachforschung") endeavours to set aside the objection that two such different cases as the nominative and the genitive could hardly have been formed by the same demonstrative suffix by the assumption that they belong to two different periods of linguistic growth. I think there can be little doubt that the idea of the genitive was later than that of the nominative or accusative; but the difficulty in the present case is this: either the suffix out of which the genitive relation was to grow was affixed to the nominative (*swana-sa-sa*), which is contrary to fact, or the genitive suffix was attached at the same time to what afterwards became distinguished into nominative and genitive, which is contrary to the hypothesis. The eminent German philologist further urges the two following arguments in behalf of the originally isolating character of Aryan speech. First of all, he instances compound tenses like *a-dik-sa-t* (ἔδειξε), in which I agree with him in seeing the substantive verb. But the statement that if cases had already existed the root *dik* ought to have had the plural affix in the plural and the accusative affix in the singular, like the Latin *amatum iri*, is met partly by Scherer's answer ("Zur Gesch. d. d. Spr.," p. 343 *sq.*), that *dik* is a *nomen actionis*, like the later Sanskrit *chôrayâm âsa*, and would therefore not require the plural sign; partly by the consideration that just as *sa* has lost its initial *a*, so *dik* may have lost its final *m*, while we find later compound tenses, like the Latin imperfect or the Teutonic preterite, which certainly

tion lies the fact that no such vague generality, such clumsy confusion, appears in the attachment of the pronouns to the verb. Can we suppose that the same people who so distinctly marked out the meaning of *mi* in the verb can have employed it to express the sense of the accusative? If it be replied that the pronouns were all of indefinite signification, and might be attached to the roots at haphazard to express the various relations of the sentence, out of which the different cases gradually grew in some unex-

came into existence after the flection of the noun was fully formed, equally using, if not the pure root, at all events the thematic one. Such verbs as *cale-fio*, again, bear the same testimony. Professor Curtius's second and strongest argument is derived from the existence of compounds which might be regarded as survivals from an uninflected stage of language. A word like *ῥοδοδάκτυλος*, for instance, might seem to be a witness of a time when the special suffixes of the plural and the genitive were altogether unknown. But I think a different explanation of the phenomenon will be suggested as soon as we remember that philology does not start from the isolated written word, but from the sentence. Mr. Sweet (*Academy*, January 17, 1874) says very truly—"The antiquarian philologist, having the written symbols constantly before his eyes, gradually comes to abstract them entirely from the sounds they stand for, and at last regards them as *the* language. . . . If a spoken sentence from some African language is submitted to him, with a request to point out the word-divisions, he will ask to see the sentence written down, and then, if told that the language has no alphabet, and has never been committed to writing, will have to confess that he is utterly ignorant of the real nature of a word." A word is really a complete conception; and a compound word, accordingly, is but one whole, one word, the component parts of which exist only for the analyst. Δύσπαρις and *tyrranicide* are as

plained way and appropriated the several pronominal roots to themselves; we must answer, firstly, that the whole hypothesis is unsupported by facts, and therefore beyond the range of Glottology; secondly, that even the communistic inhabitants of a bee-hive would find it hard to be mutually intelligible with such conversational machinery; thirdly, that the growth of the idea of the several cases out of such a chaos, much less their selection, is inexplicable, since the accidental terminations would have

truly single words as Πάρις and *tyrannus*, and it was but the living instinct of language that separated between the radical idea and the relational suffix, and when closely subordinating one idea to another, so as to weld them into one new whole, left only the bare root or theme to the first. The vocative and imperative were abiding monuments of the flectionless type-stem. I cannot conceive a period in which men talked to one another in roots; the roots must have had many suffixes of little meaning attached to them—even the anti-inflectionists admit this—but behind all these uttered suffixes lay the root-type firmly though obscurely fixed in the consciousness of the savage. The instinct which still strips the subordinated word of its flection in a compound is the representative of this early feeling of language, not the imitation of a pattern set in a preflectional age. Indeed, in this case all the words of a sentence must have stood in the same flectionless relation to each other; and it is hard to see how some could have remained in their old condition while the rest followed the new analogy and law of inflection. But the evidence of the Semitic tongues seems to me conclusive upon this point. In Assyrian the construct case is marked by the loss of the case-vowel, but not of the feminine termination; thus *sar sarri* (for *sarru sarri*), "king of kings," but *sarrat mati*, "queen of the land." Surely it will not be said that the case flection is older than feminine flection, or that a compound can more readily dispense with the one than with the other.

confused the mind, not led it towards analysis; fourthly, that there was no difference between the nominative, the genitive, and the dual and plural, so far as suffixes go, and yet these are among the most important distinctions; and fifthly and chiefly, that even supposing we grant all that is required of us, we shall still be no nearer to an agglutinative condition of the primitive Aryan, since the agglutinative languages do not form their oblique cases by the help of pronouns, but of postpositions, or rather verbal and nominal roots.[1] The relation of cases, like all other relations, is with them an independent word; and from the Accadian down to the latest and most barbarous dialect, we find words like *lal*, "filling," *ge*, "deep," *da*, "the side of," employed to express the several cases. In fact, to represent these by indefinite pronouns is the characteristic of a language inflectional from the beginning, in which the suffix is weakened and subordinated to the radical. It points to a primary inflectional instinct, which shaped the sentence accordingly as soon as the period of conscious speech

[1] What are "apparently" demonstrative pronouns (like *wa* and *wo* in Japanese, or *ano*, *inu* in Mongol) may be loosely attached to mark the nominative and accusative. Analogy would lead us to infer that these demonstratives, like the other pronouns, had a substantival origin; and Accadian, the oldest example of agglutinative speech that we possess, distinguishes the nominative and accusative by position only, forming all its "cases" by means of verbs (participles) and substantives.

arrived. When the conception of the locative case, for example, first arose in the mind of the Aryan, he selected some formally existing but hitherto meaningless suffixes to express the new relation, and so turned a mere phonetic complement, a mere formal sound, into a grammatical inflection. It is the same with Semitic. Here the original machinery of cases was elaborated by the adaptation of the three primary vowels *u*, *i*, and *a*, though *a* might have been the earliest sound, shading off into *u*, the sign of the nominative, by slowly closing the lips, and into *i*, the sign of the genitive, by raising the tongue towards the palate. It was not until later times, that the case-terminations were confused together, and replaced, as in English or Persian, by prepositions. It is plain that before the setting apart of the three primary vowels the Semites had no cases; as soon as they became conscious of the want of them, the cases came into existence, and this by purely inflectional means, in which there can be no question of agglutination with pronouns or aught else. In Aryan, likewise, we must believe that case and flection—whatever may be the origin of the latter—are co-existent. As far back as the Aryan had any conception of the relations of a sentence, he expressed them by subordinate suffixes, not by the help of independent agglutinations. More complex nominal relations might be represented, as in the Latin *gratiâ*, or the Greek *χάριν*, or the German *wegen*, by a kind of postposition; but whenever the latter ceased to be a separate word which could receive inflections of its own, and became simply the sign of a case, it was forthwith assimilated to the other merely flectional cases, and its individuality lost. The clear flectional growth of the verb shows only that it took place during the historic period, when the structure and tendency of the language were already inflectional, and that it was of later origin than the noun.[1]

[1] Prof. Curtius, indeed, has endeavoured to prove the converse —that the inflections of the verb are older than those of the noun. I have already tried to meet his arguments in my note on p. 149, and Prof. Max Müller, in his lecture on "Chronology as Applied to the Development of Language," has, as it seems to me, demonstrated the untenability of the great German philologist's view. Indeed, Prof. Curtius himself ("Das Verbum d. Griechischen Sprache," vol. i. pp. 8, 9) has pointed out a fact which is hardly consistent with his theory. "While the system of the cases," he says, "not only had no addition made to it during the period of which we have documentary evidence, but, on the contrary, were reduced in number, and even in the language of Homer had already suffered very considerable losses, in the case of the verb the creative impulse of language continued far longer active and living." The weak future passive is altogether wanting in the Homeric poems, while the only certain example of the strong future passive is *μιγήσεσθαι* (Il. x. 365), and the future optative is equally unknown. Such is also the case with the aspirated perfect, and the extended use of the perfect in *κ* is still a matter of the future. Surely it would have been in the forms of the verb and not of the noun that "the creative impulse of language" first died out, had verbal flection been older than nominal flection.

But even so this flectional growth of the verb refers only to the verb as we have it in our grammars, with all its moods and tenses and persons fully worked out. There was a time when the verb simply signified *action* in general, and the suffixes which it then possessed were sufficient to denote this general idea. It was not until the conception of personal relation had been struck out that any necessity for the employment of the personal pronouns arose; though Ludwig cannot be right in referring the *-sti* of the second person of the Latin perfect to an old infinitive termination, *σθαι*, now utilised for a new purpose, like *-mini* in the second person plural of the passive. Flection, it must be remembered, is constituted by a combination of meaning and form; it is meaning that gives it existence and content, and until this is furnished the form remains a mere phonetic sound. Now, meaning cannot be separated from the sentence out of which each *nuance* of grammar has been elaborated, and not out of lifeless sounds, which the prevalent glottological theory would assume to be the immediate parent of the inward and spiritual. The idea of the instrumental case, for instance, must have been obtained from a deeper analysis of the sentence, which all along implicitly contained it; and then some already existing ending or suffix was set apart to express it. In this way we are able to explain how it is that the same sound is not appropriated to the same case, to the same grammatical relation, in each and all of the Aryan languages, but that *i* and *bhis* stand for the locative singular and instrumental plural in Sanskrit, and for the dative singular and plural in Greek and Latin. Still more significant is the change of meaning of a form in the same language, as in the case of *tar*, which characterises the present tense in the Veda and the future in the later epic. That such unmeaning terminations existed in the period which lies immediately behind that in which Comparative Philology properly begins has been made sufficiently clear by the Prague professor to whom I have already alluded.[1] Although to the analytical lexicographer of the nineteenth century the ultimate germ of a group of words is a monosyllabic root, yet when we come to regard these germs as beginning to be endowed with life and meaning, as capable of being employed in living, actual speech by the addition of suffixes, we find that they are for the most part no longer monosyllabic, but are, in the jargon of

[1] A child whom I know, though learning to speak at a later age than her elder brothers and sisters, generally adds an ŏ to see her words, as "dog-ŏ," "come-ŏ," &c. May we not see in this a reversion to that primitive tendency of men to round off their words with merely euphonic suffixes which appears so plainly in the case-endings of the Semitic tongues?

the grammar, become bases. Thus the Sanskrit *vodhavai*, the Latin *vectu* ( = *vectuī*), the Slavonic *vésti*, must be regarded as independent unless a root. *vaghi-tavai*, be presupposed. The same fact appears still more unmistakably in varying forms with identical meanings, such as *rat* and *râjan*, *bhûs* and *bhûmi*, *uś-* and *uśaś*, *sthât* and *sthâtar*, *triś* and *triśâ*, where phonetic difference is not accompanied by difference of function, that is, where the material outward elements of flection exist, but there is no flection as yet, because the inward signification which makes flection still lies implicit and unrealised in the sentence; or, again, in roots of similar meaning and similar sound, but which differ either in the initial or the final consonant. *Sthâ*, *stabh*, *stav* (σταυρός), *star* (στερεός) in Sanskrit, or στεγ and τεγ in Greek, for example, like the Semitic לָהַע, לָעַ, לָעַט, לחט, לחם, all go back to the same ultimate analytical origin; but no one would think of discovering any diversity of signification in the several varying forms. Each was a form of the same unconsciously felt type, which lay at the bottom of the consciously-spoken word. But the word, as conveying sense and meaning, as filled with content and life, could not exist apart from the sentence; of this it formed a portion; and the relation which it expressed in this was determined by the other words with which it was joined. Now, it was just this determination, and nothing else, which created flection. The unmeaning terminations of the several words were used as the external signs and channels of this determination, and thereby flection, both on its internal and its external side, became perfect. What the primitive flections were and whether any of them have survived to later times, we cannot say. It may be that all the inflections of Schleicher's parent-speech will yet be traced back to independent vocables; but this, improbable as it is in the highest degree, will only show that the new suffixes, as soon as they became grammatical signs, were modelled after a fore-existing pattern; they imply that the language was already inflectional, and inclined to assimilate everything which modified the meaning of a sentence to the prevailing inflectional type. In the agglutinative dialects they would have remained independent or semi-independent words. There is little to be gained on the opposite side by bringing forward instances in which, during historical times, an independent vocable has gradually grown into a flectional suffix. Thus it may be alleged that the stem of *fero* has produced *candela-bru-m,* though even here the flectional suffix properly so called is distinct from the agglutinated word, and has to be added in order to express the relation of the whole compound to the rest of the sentence. But, in the first place, the very possibility of thus turning an agglutinated affix into an inflection shows that inflection was already the characteristic and rule of the language. Then, in the second place, we must bear in mind that Glottology is an historical science, and the historical sciences imply change and progress with the change and progress of time. Consequently what holds good of a late period in the history of a language does not necessarily hold good of an early period. The Coptic, which once formed its words by means of affixes, now employs prefixes instead; and the rich creativeness, the varied mobility, which distinguishes the older Aryan dialects disappears more and more the nearer we approach our own day and our own stereotyped mother-tongue. Just as civilisation blunts the keenness of our senses and the quick perception of the influences of nature, it tends to dry up the springs of speech and to confine us to a conventional round of already existing words. We can no more argue from the analogy of modern Aryan languages to their early condition than we can from the linguistic phenomena of the Aryan family to those of other families. To do so is to repeat in another form the error that would make the laws deduced from an examination of this family alone of universal validity. The last objection that may be produced against this appeal to historical instances of agglutination passing into flection is, that the later meaning of the case-suffixes, properly so called, could not be theirs if they were independent words; and how, then can we tell if they ever were independent words? As I have so often said before, we must not go beyond our data in Glottology, and these present to us the case-suffixes, for example, already in existence as inflections or modifying affixes. When Comparative Philology first becomes cognisant of an Aryan language, these affixes are simply grammatical forms; there is no trace, so far as meaning goes, of their ever having been separate or agglutinated particles. Now their meaning expresses the relation of the several parts of the sentence to one another; and we may well wonder how it could come about that, when the primitive Aryan first awoke to a consciousness of these relations, and began to distinguish between them, he denoted them by independent words, and yet, when his consciousness became clearer and more distinct, all vestiges of their original nature were lost, and a backward step was made in the analysis of the sentences. This, of course, grants the assumption that the independent origin of the case-suffixes has been made out, which is very far indeed from being the case; and that, as independent vocables, they were actual words, with real meaning and expressiveness, not the vague and indeterminate "pronominal" elements to which the modern school of philologists would refer them. Indeed when once this useful but impalpable "pronominal root" is introduced, the whole question is virtually decided. Every tittle of evidence for the theory derived from analogy is abandoned. The agglutinative languages do not express the relations of grammar by pronominal suffixes—indeed, it is hard to see how they *could* do so—but by the help of postfixed substantives and verbs or participles, each with a definite signification of its own. Thus the postposition *kyda* in Ostiak is *kyt*, "the middle;" the locative *pir* in Samoiedic Jurakish is "height;" the possessive *lal* in Accadian is "to fill." So, again, the Bornu of Africa says "side" for "with," "head" for "on," "place" for "to;" and the Vei would express "it is within the house" by *á be keneburo*, "in the house's belly." It is the same in the isolating languages. The "empty words" or determinative particles of Chinese mean "interior" (*chung*, *nei*, *li*, the signs of the locative), "to use" (*y̌*, which marks the instrumental), and so on.[1] Nor is it different in the Aryan

[1] Mr Edkins writes to me—"My inquiries have led me to the conclusion that the Turanian case-suffixes are always pronouns when the possessive and objective are in question. In

family itself, wherever we can historically trace the passage of an independent word into a semi-flection. Either it is a personal pronoun, as in the person-endings of the verb, or a substantive like *-dom* and *-head;* never an imaginary "pronominal root." But these semi-flections all belong to the later epoch of Indo-European speech, when the fresh period of youth and creativeness had passed away; and to assert that because the High German *taubheit* is compounded with *heit,* the A.-S. *hâd,* "character" or "rank,"

such instances the case-particles never differ in form from common demonstrative roots, *e.g.*, Tibetan and Mongol locative, instrumental and dative particles, can only be substantives and verbs, just as possessives and objectives can only be demonstratives. In Chinese we have a clear and instructive example of the identity of the demonstrative, the objective, and the possessive in *che*, old form *ti*, which has all three of these uses." Böhtlingk, in the Introduction to his great work, "Ueber die Sprache der Jakuten," upholds the same view against Schott in the case of the Turkish-Tatar languages; and Castrén identifies the termination of the Zyrianian accusative with the affixed first personal pronoun, while he assigns the ending *et* or *t*, which is sometimes attached to the Ostiak accusative, to the affixed third personal pronoun ("Versuch einer ostjakischen Sprachlehre," p. 28). In Accadian, however, the accusative has no distinctive mark, while none of the case-endings has a pronominal origin. It is safer to abide by the evidence of this oldest specimen of agglutinative speech than to assume the pronominal origin of those case-endings in modern dialects of whose real derivation we are ignorant. The cases of the old Semitic noun are formed by a mere change of the final vowel, and the machinery by which grammatical relations have been denoted in one language may just as well have been employed in another. *See above*, note on p. 151.

its earlier representative, *daubitha* must be similarly compounded with a "pronominal" element, is to defy all the principles of scientific inquiry. The pronominal root is a philological myth, which owes its origin to the supposed necessity of developing an inflectional language out of an agglutinative one. Such forms as *daubitha* will have been flectional from the first. The formal element existed before the significant element was added to make it a flection; and *this* genesis of inflection, *this* rise of new flections, can be tested and confirmed by historical instances. Thus the Teutonic idioms have adapted the *ablaut*, or change in the vowel of the root to the expression of the distinction between the tenses of the verb, thus making it inflectional; while it remains in Sanskrit a mere phonetic unmeaning modification of the vowel, the mechanical result of the accent. So, again, the Sanskrit verbal termination *-ayâmi* confounds together the three Greek endings -αω, -οω, and -εω, and these have been utilised in many instances to set forth different shades of meaning, -οω being appropriated to a transitive signification, -εω to an intransitive one, and -αω floating between the two. Πολεμέω, for instance, is to "wage war;" πολεμόω, "to make enemies." Such cases are more instructive than pages of indefinite discourse on the pronominal *ta* or *ya*, and they display the inextinguishable instinct of inflection working in Aryan speech late down into the historical period. If we are to listen to the testimony of facts, the agglutinative stage is a baseless dream, however convenient it may be for the purposes of provisional classification.[1]

[1] Professor Whitney, in his interesting "Oriental and Linguistic Studies" (p. 284), flies off into the following tirade against a misunderstood theory:—"There is here and there an ultra-conservative who will believe only so far as he is forced by unequivocal testimony, and, while he confesses the later formative elements of speech to be wrought out of independent words, refuses to infer that the older are of the same character, preferring to hold that there was some mysterious and inscrutable difference between the ancient and modern tongues as regards their principle of growth; and we even meet occasionally with a man who has done good service and won repute in some department of philology, and who yet commits the anachronism of believing that endings and suffixes sprouted out of roots by an internal force. But these are men with whom it is vain to reason; they must be left to their idiosyncrasies, and not counted in as bearing a share in the progress of modern linguistic science. There are also, of course, many whose studies in language have not gone far enough to show them the logical necessity of the views we have described [viz., the development theory]; but they too are to be reckoned as in the rear of the present movement." Hard words, however, are not arguments; and I, for one, hold the development theory to be a false though attractive assumption, simply because all science must rest on the law of the uniformity of nature, and consequently the formative *principle* at work in modern times must be of the same character as that at work in the earliest period. To infer that because the later formative *elements* are of a certain nature, the older formative elements must therefore be of the same nature, is in the highest degree illogical; indeed, it directly contradicts the very hypothesis Professor Whitney is maintaining, since the formative elements of an agglutinative language are wholly different from those of an

The Ayran languages have always been inflectional, so far as Glottology has any cognisance of them. Beyond that, the Ayran must be dealt with by physical science; and whatever the latter may demonstrate, even that he was the eldest-born of a gorilla, we feel sure of this much, that his brain could produce only an inflectional language, that is, could view things and their rela-

inflectional language. To say that an agglutinative suffix is identical with a flection is to confound two very different and unlike things. Now the principle in an inflectional speech which turns such words as *lic*, *ly*, into flections is one which must have been at work from the beginning; such words only become flections through the analogy and structure of the rest of the language, and of the instinct which underlies it. They would never have become flections had the language not been inflectional already. To imagine that mere phonetic change can produce mental and formative change is to confuse material and form, and to ignore the fact that the relations of grammar are purely intellectual. We see instances in plenty of the synthetic passing into the analytic, but the reverse process is contrary to experience. Cases like *aimerai* and *amavi* are not to the point. The synthetic comes first, the analytic, last; such is the general conclusion of modern science, and this principle of differentiation has been traced by Mr Herbert Spencer through the organic and moral world. The most primitive grammars, such as that of the Eskimaux, show us the greatest synthetic complexity. In fact, the development theory commits the old mistake of assuming that what is logically first and simplest is historically so, whereas the converse is really the case. We begin with the jelly-fish, we end with man. I need hardly refer to the grotesque misrepresentation which speaks of "endings and suffixes sprouting out of roots by an internal force." Material and form are co-ordinate and co-existent; we cannot have one without the other; and the idea that form is posterior to material is the fallacy which lies at the bottom of the development theory, and of the inability of its advocates to understand the arguments which are urged against it.

tions only in a particular way as soon as he came to speak consciously, and to be a subject for Comparative Philology. What animal-like sounds he may have uttered before that time we do not know; it is sufficient that his first endeavours to form a language took the direction of inflection.

What has been said of the hypothetical agglutinative stage of Ayran speech applies with still greater force to the so-called isolating stage. It is true that we can trace the lexicon back to a certain number of roots; and it is assumed that these roots, in which substantive, adjective, and verb lay implicit in an equally vague and chaotic state, once formed a language. Unfortunately we are not acquainted with the exact nature of these roots. We know them only in so far as they are the ultimate elements of later words. But to assert that there was a time when men conversed by means of these roots alone is altogether unwarranted.[1] For

[1] The development theory will be found stated in its most extreme form in Whitney's "Language and the Study of Language," p. 256. He there says—"Indo-European language, with all its fulness and inflective suppleness, is descended from an original monosyllabic tongue; our ancestors talked with one another in single syllables, indicative of the ideas of prime importance, but wanting all designation of their relations; and . . . out of these, by processes not differing in their nature from those which are still in operation in our own tongue, was elaborated the marvellous and varied structure of all the Indo-European dialects. Such is, in fact, the belief which the students of language have reached, and now hold with full confidence."

anything we know, the roots might have received flections, long since worn away; indeed, Pott and his school have endeavoured to make out that a large number of our radicals are really compounds, though with imperfect success. Nor do we know whether the roots ever existed except as so many unconscious types, after which inflectional words were fashioned, and which were first extracted from these by the grammarians, just as nowadays we might take some foreign vocable and fit it to numberless suffixes without ever using the vocable itself. It seems clear that we must account in this way for the numerous roots, or rather verbs, in Semitic with similar meanings and cognate

We can only say that their confidence is easily gained, and betrays a strange lack of logical insight. How *could* men talk with one another in single isolated syllables which wanted "all designation of their relations?" Such a jargon would do very well for an excited meeting of religious enthusiasts, who would express their feelings by unintelligible outcries, but such a disconnected series of exclamations could not be employed for conversation. Gestures alone could not be a substitute for all designation of relations. And the belief must indeed be large which can imagine that out of this antithesis of all that is meant by language, language could take its rise, much less that it *was* language, and the basis and beginning of the inflectional group of tongues. Language cannot contain its antithesis, not-language, at its bottom, nor disclose it to the researches of the inquirer. When Professor Whitney goes on to compare Chinese with this "rudimentary" state of things, he virtually gives up his own cause. Chinese *does* denote relations, and the words of Chinese are not roots.

letters, which cannot be derived either from one another or from some common root. In any case, we must not suppose that the imaginary isolating stage of Aryan really resembled the phenomena of actually existing isolating languages. In these the word is a sentence, and the reading of the sentence is determined by the relation which it bears to other sentence-words. Thus the Chinese *fú tzé*, "son of the father," or *ngó tá ni*, "I beat thee," are as truly analytical and determinate as their English or Latin equivalents.

The "root-language" of the Ayrans, however, as discovered by grammatical analysis, did not contain any sentences at all. A sentence implies a mental judgment, a limitation of one idea by another; and the vague, indefinite nature of the root excludes a judgment altogether. As soon as a judgment was arrived at, it was expressed by means of inflections, or, as the advocates of the development theory would say, of pronominal agglutinations. Thus in Chinese, just as in English, the same word may be either a verb or a substantive or an adverb, but not at the same time and in the same place; but this is exactly what the Aryan root was—a kind of phonetic germ, which contained within itself the potentiality of becoming any one of the several parts of speech. But until this was realised there was no language, since Glottology begins with the sentence; there was only an embryonic chaos of unconscious thought. When first we find this thought becoming conscious and embodying itself in language, we find also the phenomena of inflection.

It is because the fact that language is the outward expression of conscious thought has been forgotten that it has been supposed that the ultimate analysis of phonetic sounds is identical with the first beginnings of speech. It really gives us only the beginnings of the mechanical part of speech, the instruments of language. It is like the analysis of colours in painting. The whole misconception depends upon the false view that makes the bare word the starting-point of philology, and the belief that the history of the Aryan family is the history of language generally. Language is an art as well as a science; it is historical, not physical; and in studying it, therefore, we must not put out of sight the conscious effort exercised on its growth by the mind of man. It is not an organic product merely, any more than society; and since language is the reflection of society, whatever has influenced and determined the development of the one will similarly have affected the development of the other. This is the side upon which the hypothesis of a threefold evolution has chiefly been assailed by Pott. We may call language an organism metaphorically, but the metaphor must not be pressed too far. There is no inner necessity in language to expand like the seed into the tree, or the caterpillar into the chrysalis and the butterfly, any more than there is in thought and in society. An isolating dialect does not necessarily become agglutinative, or an agglutinative one inflectional; nor, conversely, must an inflectional dialect necessarily have passed through the stages of isolation and agglutination. The society of modern Europe is not the descendant of the society of ancient Babylonia or China: we can trace its ancestry back through the Middle Ages to Christian Rome and Periklean Greece, and far beyond that to the huntsmen of Scandinavia; but its general complexion, its fundamental principles, its innate tendencies, have always been the same, and must always continue to be so. External circumstances will modify and alter; but large as their influence may be, yet there remains an insoluble, unchangeable residuum, which we call the character or instincts of race. The intellectual growth of the negro stops at fourteen; and although he has been brought into close contact with the civilisations of the ancient and the modern world—with old Egypt and Carthage, with Greece, Alexandria, and Rome, with the Arab, the Latin, and the Teuton—he is still, in form and colour and nature, what he was when he first appears in the sepulchral chambers of the Pharaohs. For racial change we need a period of time far exceeding the miserable six thousand years of history and civilisation; we must go back to those incalculably distant centuries when our earliest progenitors trembled before the mammoth and the cave-bear, and their animal-like condition allowed the full play of natural selection. But with this semi-human epoch of mankind Glottology has nothing to do. With language consciousness begins, and the several families of humanity have their characters already formed, their modes of thought already determined, in an earlier period. Without doubt the three stages of language mark successive levels of civilisation: this much is proved by the subversion of the one civilisation by the other; but each was the highest effort and expression of the race which carried it out, and the form which, by the constitution of the mind of the race, each was necessitated to assume. Mankind progresses as a whole, but the several steps of advance are made by the appearance of different races on the scene, each with his mission, each with his predetermined method of accomplishing it. The infusoria which to-day cover the bottom of the Atlantic have not changed since the era of the chalk; but, for all that, the world of life on the globe has been steadily improving and growing, although the lion has always been a lion, and the dog a dog.

## CHAPTER V.

### THE POSSIBILITY OF MIXTURE IN THE GRAMMAR AND VOCABULARY OF A LANGUAGE.

THE fallacy of imagining that language is a sure index of race still crops up occasionally, especially in second and third-hand writers, who undertake to acquaint the general public with the results of comparative Philology. We still not unfrequently hear that we have to claim kindred with the black Hindu of Southern India, not on the ground of a common tongue, but of a common descent. A very little consideration is sufficient to dispel the illusion. The Aryan tribes of the Rig-Veda who invaded India could not have been very numerous, and it was long before they spread beyond the north-western corner of the peninsula. Consequently the chances are that a modern Hindu will be altogether, or in great part, of aboriginal blood, unless he be a Brahmin; and even the Brahmin is to be found, according to Dr Hunter, among the lowest castes, showing that his purity of parentage was not always regarded during the disintegrating period of Buddhist democracy. Who, again, can say how far the blood of our own ancestors was contaminated during their distant migrations before they entered this country? We have only to look at su·h cases as the Kelts of Cornwall, who speak English, or the Jews of Southern Austria, who believe Spanish to be their sacred language, to see how little we can argue from language to race. Like the Lapps and Finns in Europe, the Melanesians and Papuans have the same tongue, but physiologically are essentially different; and the only question that we can ask in regard to them is, To whom did the language first belong, and which of the two races borrowed it from the other? Language is the mirror of society, and accordingly will reflect every social change. Wherever the social pressure is strong enough, either through conquest or personal interests, or other causes, the inferior people will adopt the idiom of the superior. Thus Keltic disappeared before Latin in Gaul and Spain, and social disadvantages have driven Welsh into the mountains and the cottages. Thus, too, Slavonic became extinct in Prussia in 1683, although five hundred years before this date German was unknown in the country.[1] Where the conquerors themselves

[1] On the island of Rügen, Frau Gülzin, who died in 1404, was

are not numerous, or where they are less civilised than the conquered nation, the necessities of everyday life and the influence of literature will cause them to adopt the language of the latter. Thus it was with the Normans in France and England, the Warings in Russia, and the Franks in Gaul. In fact, we may lay it down as a general rule, that whenever two nations equally advanced in civilisation, are brought into close contact, the language of the most numerous will prevail. Where, however, a small body of invaders bring a higher civilisation with them, the converse is the more likely to happen.[1] Visigothic was soon extirpated in

the last person who spoke Wendish, according to Andree, in his "Wendische Wanderstudien" (1874). Pott ("Ungleichheit menschlicher Rassen," p. 169) quotes from Chateaubriand that a "Prussian poet," who sang the deeds of the ancient heroes of his land about 1400, was not understood, and a hundred nutshells were given him as a guerdon.

[1] Not always, however. Physical disadvantages, such as climate or want of intercommunication, may cause the lower race to be totally unaffected by the arrival of a small body of more cultivated settlers. Thus Scandinavian colonies existed in Greenland for more than five hundred years, and left numerous relics in the shape of ruined houses and other material objects. But when Greenland was again colonised by the Danes in the eighteenth century, the only indisputable Norwegian word that had made its way into the language of the Eskimaux was *kona*, "woman," suggesting that a few women alone were spared when the colonists were extirpated. The migratory habits of the Eskimaux and the long dark winter of the north will sufficiently explain the little influence of the higher race and language upon the lower.

Spain, but English flourishes in India, and Dutch at the Cape. Conquest, however, is not the sole agent in producing social revolutions extensive enough to cause a total change of language. Before the Christian era, Hebrew, Assyrian, and Babylonian had been supplanted by Aramaic, which was fast tending to become the common dialect of the Semitic world, like Arabic in later times. It was the language of commerce and diplomacy, and this was sufficiently strong to outweigh the conservative influence of a sacred literature.[1]

In all the instances just given, with one or two exceptions, it will be noticed that a thoroughgoing exchange of language has taken place only among members of the inflectional family. There is hardly an example of an inflectional dialect being exchanged for an isolating or agglutinative one, or

[1] Several examples of the adoption of a foreign language will be found given in Waitz, "Anthropologie der Naturvölker," vol. i. (*Engl. transl.*, pp. 249-252). Thus the Bosnian soldiers sent by the Sultan Selim in 1420 into Lower Nubia have lost their mother-tongue, and the Negroes of Haiti have adopted French. Various American tribes have exchanged their own idioms for Spanish and Portuguese; the natives of S. Salvador, Nicaragua, Costa Rica, S. Margaretha, Baradéro, Quilmos, Calchaguy, and Chiloe taking to Spanish, and the Indians of Rio Janeiro to Portuguese (Latham, Jrl. R.G.S., xx. p. 189; Humboldt and Bonpland, i. p. 467; Azara, "Voy. dans. l'Am. mérid" ii. p. 217; King and Fitzroy, i. p. 278; Von Eschwege, "Jrl. v. Brasil," ii. p. 16). According to Humboldt and Bonpland (v. p. 774), "a million of the aborigines of America have exchanged their native for an European language."

*vice versâ.* The question accordingly arises, whether such an occurrence is possible. Can an individual or a nation, whose mind has been accustomed to regard the nature of things from a particular point of view, be taught to express himself under altogether different forms of thought? Here we have nothing to do with the possibility of an isolating speech developing of its own accord into an agglutinative or inflectional one. The settlement of this question is not affected either way by an artificial education, in which the mental faculties of one people are domesticated, as it were, into the ways of thought of another, to revert, like the domesticated animal, when again left to itself, into its old nature, its original expression of psychological habits. A child can learn as readily the vernacular of Canton as the language of London. The Japanese show a singular aptitude in imitating the externals of European civilisation. They may yet produce a satisfactory copy of the philosophy of Aristotle and Hegel, but I much doubt whether they will ever be anything more than imitations and copies; at any rate, experience is all against it. Not to speak of the Jewish and Arabic reproductions of Plato and the Stagirite, to which I alluded in the last chapter, we have facts like that of pigeon-English at Canton, where the Chinaman has endeavoured to assimilate English, or the

Chinook jargon of Oregon,[1] or the grammarless English of the Negro—all cases in which one race has read its modes of thought into the grammar of another, where it has not been able to resist the encroachment and victory of the latter. And yet English is, of all inflectional languages, not even excluding Persian, the easiest to acquire; and the extent to which it has pushed the clear probing of analysis, and shaken off the trammels of unpractical flection, make it deserve to be, what Grimm prophesied it would become, the language of the civilised world. Not less striking, on the other hand, is the preservation of the Basque; although driven by a Keltic invasion into the extreme corner of Spain, it has yet lasted out all the vicissitudes of Roman, Gothic, and Moorish domination, instead of yielding, like its Keltic neighbour, to the influence of the Latin tongue. The attempt to make one race of men think according to the forms of another is forced and unnatural; and however much we may seem for a time to have succeeded, yet, when the pressure of superiority is once removed, our pupils return to the conceptions of their ancestors, as the dog on the prairies to his howling. Where the race has not reached a high enough level of culture to

[1] A dictionary of this curious *lingua Franca* has been published by Gibbs (Smithson. Collect., No. 161).

appropriate the language of its superior, it is a sign that the race has done its part, and must pass away before the coming of civilised man. The Tasmanian and his language, in spite of every effort to save them on the part of the Government, have become extinct. Climate may save a tribe and its dialect by making it impossible for the European to settle in the country, but in that case the dialect is preserved only because the social conditions of which it is the expression are also preserved through the maintenance of the original state of nature. Civilisation inevitably kills the natural, unless the latter is favoured by external circumstances. Compatibility of existence on the part of two races depends upon their being more or less nearly matched in culture. The greater the distance between them the greater will be the influence, socially and linguistically, exercised by the superior, until a point is reached at which it will be impossible for the lower to live in the presence of its higher neighbour.

Linguistically, the influence will show itself in the shape of borrowing. We have already glanced at the cases in which this borrowing extends to the whole language, and have suggested the extreme improbability of its taking place where the ground principles of the languages are essentially different; that is, where two civilisations, with wholly different pasts, confront one another on equal terms, or where the interval between two races is morally and mentally too great to be spanned. Borrowing, however, by no means necessarily extends to the whole language. More often it applies only to the vocabulary, and loan-words are common to all dialects. No people can have near neighbours without receiving something from them in the shape of inventions, products, or social institutions, and these, almost inevitably, are adopted under their foreign names. The French have taken *meeting* and *turf* from us, together with the ideas which they denote; we have had in return *naive* and *verve.* Where the general condition of two nations is very unequal, the loan-words will be extremely numerous; in Basque, for instance, more than one-half the dictionary is from a foreign source. So, again, according to Campbell,[1] one-half the words in Telugu, as spoken in the higher regions, come from abroad. The same is asserted of Maráthá by Ballantine;[2] and some writers tell us that nine-tenths of the Hindi language is Sanskrit. It is clear, however, that the borrowing will not be entirely upon the side of the inferior; whatever the latter is able to contribute to the superior, whether

[1] Teloogoo Gram., p. xix.

[2] *Jour. of Amer. Orient. Soc.*, iii.

it be a human invention or a natural product, will generally carry its old name along with it. Thus the Latin *petorritum*, "the four-wheeled," is of Gallic origin, and has been supposed to be of some importance in settling the Cymric affinities of the Gauls;[1] *glæsum*, "amber," came from Northern Germany; and our own *tomahawk* and *boomerang* have been furnished by the Red Indians and the savages of Australia. *Maize*, *mangle*, *hammock*, *canoe*, *tobacco*, are all derived, through the medium of the Spanish, from the Haytian *mahiz*, *mangle*, *hamaca*, *canoa*, and *tabaco*.[2] Indeed, these loan-words are of the greatest use in tracing the history of languages by revealing the geographical and social relationships of the past.

Now, it has been much questioned whether it is possible for a people to mix its grammar in the same way that it can mix its lexicon, and adopt some of the inflections or grammatical contrivances of another speech. Before the rise of Comparative

[1] In the same way an Irish settlement in the west of Britain can be proved by a careful examination of the Welsh and other ogmic inscriptions, dating from the third to the ninth centuries. The *qu* (*c*), for example, found in them (as in *maqui*, "son") must belong to a Gaelic element in Wales, since Gaelic *qu* (*c*) answers to a Cymric *p*. Besides *petorritum*, *pempedula* is given as the Gallic word for "cinqfoil," where *pempe* would answer to the modern Welsh *pump*, "five," and not to the Gaelic *cing*.

[2] "Humboldt's Travels" (*Engl. transl.*, i. 329).

Philology, grammatical differences went for very little; and we still hear "philologists" of the old school talking about borrowed grammatical forms. Glottology, in which grammar forms the chief *fundamentum divisionis* of languages, meets this belief with a decided negative; and one of the primary articles of faith held by the scientific student of language at the present time is, that if grammatical inflection be borrowed at all, it must be borrowed throughout—we cannot have a mixed grammar. The whole of the vocabulary may be derived from abroad, and yet, if the foreign grammar be not learned at the same time *in extenso,* no part of it will be adopted, and the new words will be cast in the old moulds of thought and expression. This is pretty much what has happened in the case of the Negroes; though here, of course, an attempt has also been made to learn the English grammar artificially, with what success, however, is shown by the Negro jargon of the United States. It is hard at first to see what inducements there could be for one dialect to incorporate fragments of the grammar of another, as the causes which have acted upon a borrowed dictionary—inventions, products, social advantages—are here not applicable; and the psychological impossibility which we were considering in the last chapter, of forcing a race to regard the world with the mental eyes of its neighbour, would prevent the attempt if carried on spontaneously, and not as the result of artificial education. Nevertheless, the proximity of two languages implies that a certain number of the population are bilingual, and where this is the case to any large extent, the idioms of the two dialects will often be exchanged, and along with the idioms an opening is made for the introduction of new grammatical forms. Words like *avenir* and *contrée* in French are the result of an endeavour to express German idioms (*zukunft*, *gegend*) in the Romance of the conquered provincials; and it does not seem very difficult to stretch this process a little further, and adapt foreign grammatical conceptions to the contents of a native grammar. Thus it has been asserted that the great extension of the plural formation in *-s* in English was due to Norman-French influence, though undoubtedly the tendency had already been felt before; and certainly the use of the genitive and dative of the personal pronouns in English, "of me," "to me," in the place of the Anglo-Saxon *min* and *me*, appears to be modelled after the pattern of the French.[1] So, again, Bulgarian has imi-

[1] Professor Max Müller, in Bunsen's "Philosophy of Universal History," vol. i. p. 265, refers to phrases like "Zour honourable lettres conten*and*," and "brek*and* the trewis" (Letter of Gawin Douglas to Richard II., 1385), where the French participial ter-

tated the Wallachian usage, which attaches the article to the end of the word (*e.g.*, *domnul* = *dominus-ille*), as in Danish and Swedish, where *dag-en* = "the day," *guld-et*, "the gold," or in the emphatic *aleph* of Aramaic, which is probably the postfixed article. And still more strikingly, Persian has adopted the Semitic order of words so repugnant to the general structure of the Aryan group, saying, for instance, *dil-i-măn*, "heart of me," for "my heart;" *dăst-i-'Umăr*, "hand of Omer." Conversely, the Hararite is able to reverse the Semitic order, and adopt the idiom of its non-Semitic neighbours by writing *ámir askar*, instead of *askar ámir*, "the Emir's army." The so-called sub-Semitic dialects of Africa present us with the further phenomenon of a grammar which is decidedly Semitic in its main features, and which yet makes use of postpositions. The natives of Harar, for example, regularly employ these, except with the personal pronouns,[1] and use a postfixed

mination was no doubt assisted by the likeness of the Anglo-Saxon termination of the gerunds in *ende*. He also compares the Greek case-endings (*Ænean*, *heroa*, &c.) introduced into the Latin declension (like the *velthina*, *velthinas*, *velthinam* of the Etruscan Cippus Perusinus), as well as North Indian languages of Aryan origin like Assamese, which yet decline their nouns by the aid of postpositions, and insert words indicative of plurality like *bilak*, *hont*, or *bur* between the root and the affixes.

[1] See Prätorius, "Ueber d. Sprache d. Harar," in "Zeitschrift d. Deutschen Morgenländischen Gesellschaft," 1869.

*-n*, which seems a relic of a primitive nunnation, to denote the accusative.[1]

Here one of the fundamental principles of Semitic thought seems to be violated, and the attention drawn to the derivation, the ultimate elements of an object instead of to the immediate presence of the object itself. In the same way a close connection with a foreign race seems to have suggested to the Assyrians at one extremity of the Semitic world, and to the Ethiopians at the other, the utilisation of existing materials to denote more exactly the temporal relations of the verb; and Persian, which has filled its dictionary with Arabic since the days of Firdusi and his purely Aryan "Shahnameh" or "Book of Kings," has even gone so far as to form one of its plurals by means of the Arabic feminine plural in *āt*, *jāt*, as in *niwāzĭshât*, "favours," from *niwâzish*; *kăla-'jāt*, "castles," from *kăl'ăh*. Practically, however, this plural is confined to Arabic words; consequently it will no more be an importation of a foreign grammatical form than our own use of the Latin plural-ending in such words as *termini*. A better instance would be the Latin and English

[1] According to Charencey (*Revue de Linguistique*, 1873, vol. i. pt. 1, p. 57), the invariable rule of the ancient Maya of placing the adjective after its substantive is sometimes violated in the modern language through the influence of Castilian.

factitive suffix in *isso* (*izo*) and *-ise*, from the Greek ιζω. But this, after all, is only a suffix, not an inflection, and belongs, therefore, rather to the dictionary than to the grammar; the *nuances* of grammar require the true inflections of Latin and English to be affixed or prefixed to this exotic *-ise*; *patrissi-t*, *civilise-s*, TO *civilise*, and so forth. On the whole, therefore, the evidence before us will confirm the absolute denial which Glottology gives to the old notion of a mixture of grammatical forms. Idiom may be imitated, even also the conception of the relation of subject and attribute, for this, as logic teaches, may be looked at in two ways at the same time; but beyond this language does not seem able to go. No amount of intercourse and familiarity seems able to transmute the inflections of a dialect into the inflections of a foreign one, any more than the alchemist was able to change iron or lead into gold. He could gild them over, but they remained iron and lead still. The forms of grammar are the expression of the mental life and history of a people; they imply, therefore, the summing-up of all that history; and accordingly, although two nations may have started from the same source with a common stock of ideas and a common psychological tendency, yet in so far as their experiences have been different, the formative elements of their languages will be different, and not interchangeable. How much more will this be the case when the two nations did not start from the same source! The grammar of pigeon-English is not English but Chinese; the grammar of Persian remains Aryan. The formative part of language must ever be the surest *differentia* of linguistic kinsmanship.[1]

Of late years, however, the attention of European scholars has been attracted to a case of great difficulty which apparently contradicts our conclusions. Inscriptions of the Sassanian era have been found in Persia, written in what seem to be two dialects, now generally termed Chaldæo-Pehlevi and Sassanian-Pehlevi. Greek transcripts

[1] Spiegel, in his "Arische Studien," pt. 1, Nr. ii. pp. 45-61, has endeavoured to point out that the Zend of the Avesta has been influenced by the proximity of Semitic languages both grammatically and lexically. He traces this influence in the Zend use of the feminine to denote a neuter (or abstract), and of the dual to denote pairs, in the employment of the verb in the plural or singular after a dual, and of collective plurals (though Greek, too, has τὰ θήρια τρέχεται) in the accusative which expresses the condition, in the verbal nouns which govern the cases of their verbs, in the use of the imperfect and infinitive, and of words like *zaçta*, "hand," for "might" (after the fashion of Semitic), as well as in the occurrence of purely Semitic terms such as *tanûra*, the Heb. *tannur*, or *naçka*, the Aram. *noskha*. Prof. Rhŷs, again, in his Presidential Address to the Liverpool Gordovic Eisteddfod of 1874, stated the results of his examination of the idiomatic peculiarities of the Keltic languages, which throw a new light on the early fortunes of that branch of the Aryan family, and give a fresh illustration of the way in which

are added in a few instances; and we are thus enabled to discover that the unknown dialects closely resemble the language of books still preserved among the Parsis of Bombay, to which the name of Huzwaresh or Pehlevi is ordinarily given. The writing of these is extremely hard to decipher, owing to the corruption of the characters; and a comparison with the inscriptions and coin-legends on the one hand, and the old Pazend dictionaries on the other, shows that the traditional reading is often very far from the truth. Now, this Sassanian-Pehlevi is a most heterogeneous mixture of Aryan and Semitic, and the mixture is not confined to the lexicon alone; it dominates equally in the grammar. Thus the great inscription of Sháhpur I. (A.D. 240 - 273) at Nakish - i - Rajab,

idioms may be borrowed. Traces of Basque influence, he believed, were to be found in the incorporation of the pronouns between the Irish verb and its prefixes, a phenomenon which exceptionally appeared in Welsh (as in *rhy-'m-dorai*, "it would concern me," *Dofydd rhy-'n-digones*, "the Lord made us"), as well as in the Breton verb *to have*. So, too, the differentiation of the verb and noun, which had been effected at an early time in Aryan, has been partly effaced in Welsh, as though the latter language had come into contact with one in which the verb and nonu were not distinguished; thus the infinitive is always a noun, and the common construction *myfi a'ch gwelais*, "I saw you," is literally "I your saw." The inflection of the Welsh prepositions (*erof*, "for me," *erot*, "for thee," *erddo*, "for him," &c.), and of the substantive *yr eiddof*, "my property" ("mine"), finds its analogue in Magyár, suggesting that the Kelts had once held intercourse with a race which formed the link between the Basques and Finns.

which has a Greek translation attached to it, has in the first line the following representatives of the Greek *βασιλεως*. *βασιλεων*, מלכא מלכין and מלכאן מלכא, while the termination of the third person plural imperfect of the Semitic verb in *-un* is used as a verbal ending for all persons and numbers. Here we have not only a fusion of the Aryan and Semitic order of words, but also a fusion of their inflections. If the language were one ever spoken by the people, the decision of Glottology would have to be modified, and we should be compelled to admit the possibility of a mixture of different grammars under favourable circumstances. But everything goes to indicate that the dialect was never a spoken one, at all events, not outside the literary coterie of the court. How else could it have so entirely passed away, without leaving a trace behind it, that the language of Firdusi in the tenth century is the purest Aryan?—Semitic influence, notwithstanding the Mohammedan conquest, being as little discernible in the outward form as in the subject-matter of the "Shahnameh." It was not until after this date that Semitic began to penetrate into Persia, and even then, for the most part, into the vocabulary alone. Many of the grammatical forms, moreover, which are borrowed by the Pehlevi from the Semitic are used without any sense of their proper force and meaning: thus the verbal form quoted above could never have been taken from a living Semitic dialect or such curious hybrids as the prepositions in *man* like *levatman,* "with," which Dr Haug connects with לות (לוה).

On the whole, then, we must consider this anomalous Sassanian as an artificial court-language, invented for literary purposes from reasons now unknown to us, but which never did, and never could, make its way into conversation. We cannot adduce modern Persian by way of support, since the Semitic order of words, which it seems to have imitated by placing the governing noun before the governed, as in *rah-i-bāghbān,* "path of the gardener;" *rah-i-dānā,* "path of the sage," may be explained by regarding it as an analysis of the genitive conception, as in English. This is borne out by the fact that the qualifying word may be left out, and that the connecting vowel *i* is seldom used in familiar conversation. If, however, Schott is right in considering *rā,* the affix of the dative and accusative, to be borrowed from the Altaic postposition which we get in the Mongol *dotora,* "inwards," *abu-ra,* "to take," Turkish *szongra,* "to the end," a more serious difficulty arises. But Schott's suggestion is by no means proved, and we have to set against it the otherwise uniform experience of Glottology. The formation of a case in Persian by a suffix has its parallel in the poetic vocative, which affixes *ā* instead of using the preposition *yā* or *ai*, just as *rā* in the dative takes the place of the preposition *ba*. Until, therefore, some more convincing example can be brought forward, we must abide by the belief that the grammar of a nation will always remain pure and native, unless supplanted wholly by another through a kind of natural selection, although under certain circumstances foreign influences may occasion the adaptation of existing formative machinery to new uses. It is probably to this principle of adaptation that we must ascribe the phenomena which have been already mentioned as met with in the languages of Northern India—the Bengali, the Assamese, the Hindi, the Khasiya, and others. In these, the verbs and pronouns are unmistakably Aryan, while the nouns seem, on the other hand, to connect themselves with the agglutinative idioms. Just as the Tamil plural affix *gaḷ* or *kar*, the Telugu *lu*, has been traced by Dr Caldwell to the common Dravidian *taḷa* or *daḷa*, "a crowd," so the plural suffixes of these languages, *jâti gaṇa*, *dig*, *varga*, *bilak*, *daḷa*, are separate and independent words, which take the place of the usual Indo-European plural flection. Indeed, Professor Max Müller suggests that *daḷa* is nothing more than the Dravidian *dala*, which would thus have provided exactly the same grammatical machinery for Bengáli as for Tamil and Telugu. But the non-Aryan character of the nominal flection in these North Indian languages does not stop here. The plural affix is intercalated between the noun and the case-ending, which thus becomes a veritable postposition, separable from the base, and still preserving vestiges of its original co-ordinate relation to the noun. In this respect it resembles the Georgian, where the plural suffix *bi* is inserted between the root and the case-termination. In Assamese, for instance, *manuh* is "man," *manuh-bilak*, "men," and from this we get the genitive *manuh-bilak-or*, the dative *manuh-bilak-oloi*, the accusative *manuh-bilak-ok*, the locative *manuh-bilak-ot*, and the ablative *manuh-bilak-e*. Not the least striking part of the matter is that the suffixes are none of them Aryan. It is this which creates the chief difficulty of the case. Otherwise we might compare such plurals as our own *man-kind*, which, joined with words like *-wards*, as in *man-kind-wards*, are precisely analogous to the Indian forms of which we are speaking, and which only bear witness to the late analytic character of the language, and its loss of inflectional creativeness. It is this view of the matter that makes Professor Max Müller write: "We can easily imagine how people speaking the modern Sanskrit dialects, in which the old terminations by which the plural was distinguished from the singular had been worn off almost entirely, should, when again feeling a want to express the idea of plurality more distinctly, have fixed upon a grammatical expedient which, from their daily intercourse with their aboriginal neighbours, had long been familiar to their ears and to their minds. The words which they used as the exponents of plurality were, of course, taken from the resources of their own language; but the idea of using such words for such a purpose seems to have been suggested by a foreign example." Now, this very passage admits a non-Aryan influence upon the grammar; and when we consider the remarkable fact that the case-endings are not Indo-European, it is hard not to allow that something more than mere influence has been at work. Indeed, if it should turn out that the idioms we are discussing are at bottom not Aryan but Dravidian, this conclusion, in view of the verbs and pronouns, is absolutely necessary. Unfortunately this question is by no means settled as yet, and its determination will depend upon whether we find that the fundamental part of the dictionary containing the words of everyday life belongs to Sanskrit or to an aboriginal speech. But such a determination cannot be made until the vocabularies of these dialects are better known.

Meanwhile we may compare the somewhat parallel instance of the so-called sub-Semitic tongues. If we take the Berber, the Semitic affinities of which are unmistakable, we yet find the verbal conjugation admitting tense distinctions, not formed, as in Assyrian and Ethiopic, by a modification of the vowel, but by affixes and prefixes. Thus *edh* prefixed to the aorist makes the present and the future, *ere* the future and potential, while the affix *-ed* forms a perfect, and *-an* the participle. The suffixed pronoun is inserted between the verb and these prefixes and affixes, and consequently precedes the verb in many cases. This is always its position in the case of the participle, as in *ey-izran*, "seeing me," *eth-izran*, "seeing him." The definite tense-determination of these prefixes assimilates them rather to the old Egyptian, with its innumerable compound verbal forms, than to the Arabic use of *cāna* and *kad;* but their employment is not contrary to the spirit and usage of the Semitic languages: on the contrary, the affixes *ed* and *an* are altogether foreign to the genius of these tongues. Not less so is the prefixing of the suffixed pronouns, and we can scarcely help seeing in it the influence not only of the allied Coptic with its developed system of prefixes, such as *nen* for the plural, *mad* for abstracts, or *ref* for agents, but also of the once neighbouring Kafir tribes, which always prefix, never affix. Here, therefore, will be another example of the way in which the grammar of a people may be affected and modified from without. We fail to see, however, anything like the phenomenon which meets us in the North Indian dialects, where the case-endings appear to have been imported, as well as the manner in which they are applied; and it is not until we come to the postpositions of the Hararite that we discover any analogy to this. But the language of Harar, like that of Assam, is as yet too little known to permit us to come to any certain decision in so difficult a question. It is noticeable, however, that in both cases it is the nominal declension which presents the grammatical anomaly; and when we consider that we have in English such words as *fungi*, *prospectus*, and *termini*, while German can form from *Christus* both *Christi* and *Christo*, we may perhaps conclude that the noun does not always offer that sure criterion of the character and position of a language which the verbs and pronouns do, and that in certain stages of linguistic growth, when a speech has become more or less analytic, it is able to borrow from its neighbours, not only the form of the declension, but even the words which compose this form. The analytic period means the resolution of the sentence and its grammatical relations into separate vocables, and these can be borrowed freely by one idiom from another.

Intimately connected with grammar is the phonology of a language. It is a question of some interest how far the pronunciation of a dialect may be affected in the lapse of years by the contiguity of another. That such an influence can be exercised is certain. A familiar example, which will occur to the mind of every one, is the adoption of the Hottentot clicks by the Kafirs. This is a very remarkable case, as the sounds are difficult, and the superiority of the borrowing race is very marked.[1] So, too, the so-called "cerebral" letters in Sanskrit, which are not found in any of the other Aryan dialects, are commonly thought to be borrowed from the Dravidian; and the Norman Conquest appears to have had much to do with the softening of the gutturals in the southern part of England, the Gallicised invaders finding their pronunciation difficult, and accordingly setting the

[1] According to Bleek ("Comp. Gramm. of South African Lang.," i. p. 13), "the occurrence of clicks in the Kafir dialects decreases almost in proportion to their distance from the Hottentot border." Only the easier, and not the harder clicks have been borrowed by the Kafirs, and whereas the Kafir clicks are only found in the place of other consonants, and are used like consonants at the beginning of syllables, in Hottentot, *k*, *kh*, *g*, *h*, or *n* can be immediately preceded by a click, and form with it the initial element of a syllable. In the Bushman language even labial (and probably also dental) consonants are pronounced with clicks.

example of breaking them down. The retention of the gutturals in Spain, again, may be ascribed to the long settlement of the Moors; and I remember a Basque girl, to whom French had become the language of every-day life, when giving me my first lesson in Euskuara calling *egoitz* ("a house") *egoi'*. Of the same nature is the change of *i* to *g* in Anglo-Saxon, contrary to the usual softening of consonants to vowels, of which Professor March[1] remarks, that "the movement (of consonants to vowels) is sometimes reversed, as when a nation moves northward, or northern peoples mix with a vowel-speaking race." It must be remembered, however, that climate, food, and custom have much influence upon phonology, and that where these are similar, we may expect to find a general similarity in the pronunciation of two languages. We are all well acquainted with the hoarseness and roughness that exposure to the atmosphere lends to the voice; and the exercise and strength that a mountainous country gives to the lungs produce a corresponding effect in the vigour with which sounds are emitted.[2] Food, of course, will have an

[1] "Comparative Grammar of the Anglo-Saxon Language," p. 28.

[2] It is remarkable that just as a Latin *h* answers to a Greek χ (as in *hortus* and χόρτος), the modern Italian Greek spoken in the eight small towns in the neighbourhood of Otranto and Lecce

equal influence. The vocal organs are under the command of the muscles and the nerves, and these depend upon the health and robustness of the body. A mixed race will inherit the phonetic capabilities of its parents, and the preponderance will lie upon the side of the stronger parent. Particular fashions are not without their influence; thus the loss and confusion of the labials, and the excessive nasalisation in the languages of the savages of the Pacific coast of America, must be traced to the rings that are worn through the nostrils and the lips of the people.[1] So again we find from Bleek that the pronunciation of the *O Tyi-herero* in South Africa is lisping, and is due to the custom of extracting the four lower teeth, and partly filing away the upper teeth.[2] Imitation will also come into play: we acquire our pronunciation in the mimetic days of childhood, while the vocal organs are still plastic; and here, again, the preference will be given to the pronunciation which, for any reason, is the best fitted for success. Social superiority has much to do with this; we attempt, in school and out of school, to reflect

changes χ into *h* (*e.g.*, *homa* or *huma* for χῶμα) according to Morosi's "Studij sui dialetti greci della terra a' Otranto" (1870).

[1] Daa "On the Languages of the Northern Tribes of the Old and New Continents," in the *Trans. of the Philological Soc.*, 1856, p. 256.

[2] "Sir George Grey's Library," i. 167.

the prounciation of the higher circles of society; and just as the court dialect of Chaucer became the universal model in England, or Parisian French is extirpating the Languedocian patois, so a dissimilar pronunciation becomes the mark of vulgarity or provincialism. And when once a particular pronunciation has become prevalent, it reacts upon all words that still remain exceptions: thus in English, *balcony*, *retinue*, and *contemplate* have, after a long struggle, followed the rule which throws the accent back as far as possible. If we cross to America, we find a similar phenomenon taking place there. It is seldom that we cannot detect a born and bred American by his pronunciation. English seems in the mouths of them all to be diverging into a sharp quick nasalisation, which can hardly have originated in the twang of the New England Puritan or the commixture of European races, but which seems due to the influences of a dry, extreme climate, like the hatchet-face of the aboriginal, which is being reproduced in his white successor. Perhaps, however, one of the best countries in which to study this question of phonological borrowing is Germany, with its numerous dialects and various phases of guttural-pronunciation. Here the population has come into contact with Slavs, Finns, Magyars, and Latins; and Mr Howorth has endeavoured to trace the sibilants of South Germany to a Slavonic influence.[1] However this may be, imitation lies at the bottom of all pronunciation; and it will be one of the future tasks of the glottologist to determine how far the phonology of a language has been modified by intercourse with another, and how far the similarity of each is only the result of a similarity of external conditions. No psychological difficulty interferes here: we have to deal only with the outward mechanism of speech, and borrowed sounds are as natural and as possible as borrowed words.

The latter are of immense importance in tracing the growth and progress of the human mind. If Glottology is the science which ascertains the laws and successive history of that development as embodied in the fossils of language, not the least part of its work will be to detect the debts owed by one race and civilisation to another.[2]

[1] Mr Murray, in his valuable work on "The Dialect of the Southern Counties of Scotland," points out that the confusion of *ai* and *a*, *oi* and *o*, &c., in the same words, the change of *wh* into *f* in the north-eastern dialects, and the dropping of the initial *th* in *that*, are due to Keltic influence.

[2] We must be on our guard against drawing too wide an inference from such cases of borrowing. They prove two things, and two things only,—the social contact of one language with another, and the superior civilisation of the language borrowed from, where the loan-words are numerous or used for common things. But they do not prove a negative; they do not imply that the objects denoted

Nor is the work so easy as it seems to be at first sight. We must find out general laws which will

by the loan-words were previously unknown, and had no native names. The Basque terms for "knife," for instance, *ganibeta* (Fr. *canif*) and *nabala* (Sp. *nabaja*, Lat. *novacula*), are foreign importations; yet it would be absurd to suppose that the Basques were ignorant of such an instrument until it was introduced to them by their more cultivated neighbours: the flint-makers of Abbeville would have been in a more highly civilised condition. But in fact, Prince Lucien Bonaparte has found the original and native Basque word for a "knife" in a single obscure village. This is *haistoa*, from a root which means "to cut," and is the source of many derivatives. To infer a negative from the absence of a home term for any object in a language is parallel to the mistake sometimes made of denying the knowledge of certain things to the primitive Aryans, because the words which may have denoted them have left no traces in the derived dialects. Just as the modern geologist insists on the imperfection of the geological record, so ought the glottologist to remember that only the wrecks and fragments of ancient speech have been preserved to us by happy accident. Countless words and forms have perished altogether; and though Pictet can show that an object designated by the same name in both Eastern and Western Aryan dialects must have been known to our remote ancestors of the prehistoric period,—that the *birch*, for example, which is *bhurja* in Sanskrit, and *birca* in old German, grew on the slopes of their primitive settlement, or that they fed on the spelt, which is called *yavas* in Sanskrit and *ζεία* in Greek,—yet the converse of this does not hold good. The ancient Aryan may have been acquainted with the oyster, for all that language can tell us, although the word by which we denote it is now met with in the dialects of Europe only, and does not occur in those of Persia and Hindustan. It is to be regretted that Fick in his epoch-making book, "Die ehemalige Spracheinheit der Indogermanen Europas," has not been on his guard against this logical fallacy, but has ventured to describe the progress in civilisation made by the European Aryans after their separation from their Eastern brethren without considering that the want of a common name for the same object in Eastern and Western Aryan may be

allow us to determine whether words are really borrowed, or merely exhibit that accidental resemblance which the circumscribed number of articulate sounds sometimes brings about, as in the

explained by the loss of the word, as well as by ignorance of the object itself.

Another fallacy committed by the same scholar may be noticed here, as it illustrates one of the difficulties we meet with in determining where a word has been borrowed or not. In the work above cited (p. 290), he says that though the Latin *cannabis* and the old Slavonic *konop-l-ya* are undoubtedly borrowed from the Greek *κάνναβις*, the Teutonic *hanpa-*, *hanf*, seems to show that the cultivation of hemp was known to the European Aryans before their separation, since it has undergone the action of Grimm's law. But this assumes that the action of this law ceased at a definite period, and was not observed at the time when the Germans were brought into contact with the Romans. As a matter of fact, however, we are altogether unable to determine the epoch at which the influence of analogy ceased to be felt in Teutonic, and when loan-words were no longer reduced to the shape which the analogy of the language, and the instinctive requirements of ear and voice demanded for them. Indeed we should naturally infer that this epoch was considerably later than the introduction of a native literature, and the inference is strengthened by what we observe in other languages. Thus in Gaelic, *pascha* and *purpura* have had to become *caisg* and *corcur* in accordance with the general phonetic law which substitutes *c* for *p* in that branch of Keltic, and these words must have been borrowed subsequently to the establishment of Christianity in Britain. It will be shown in chap. ix. that the action of analogy upon phonology is still powerful even in the most civilised and stereotyped languages, and it is not an unheard of thing for a foreign word to be "Anglicised," even in this age of railways and travelling. It is plain, however, that if once we admit the possibility of a naturalisation of loan-words, and the subjection of them to the action of the regular "lautverschiebung," we lose one of our criteria for an offhand decision as to whether a word is native or not.

North American *potomac*, "river," and the Greek *πόταμος*; or whether, again, they are both taken from a common source, or one of them from the other. Then we must have rules for knowing whether a word is of foreign origin or really of native growth; and above all, when we have actually ascertained that two words stand in the relation of lent and borrowed, we must find out on which side the debt lies. In the case of the Semitic *keren* and the Greek *κέρας*, Latin *cornu*, for instance, we may ask, Are these words of independent origin, or are they loan-words; and if the latter, by whom were they lent? Or again, is the Greek *χρυσός* derived from the Semitic *khârûts*, "gold"? If we could learn that these were really loan-words, much light would be thrown on the history of early civilisation, and the relation of Semites and Aryans under this aspect. Now, the comparative laws of language inform us that while, on the one hand, the final nasal of the Semitic *keren* is a part of the root, the final *-nu* of the Latin is a mere formative, and that the same word appears in the Sanskrit *śringam*, "horn," (perhaps allied to *śiras*, "head," the Greek *κάρα*) as well as in the Latin *cervus*, and our own *hart*. The East Aryans of India had no such close intercourse with the Semites as would have given the latter so common and non-technical a word as *keren*, while among the West Aryans the nasal is found only in Latin, from which it could not have been borrowed by Assyrians and Hebrews. On the other hand, χρυσός offers no satisfactory Aryan etymology, the words for "gold" in the other Aryan languages (Sanskrit *hiranyam*, Zend. *zaranya*, Slavonic *zlato*, and Phrygian γλοῦρος) being related to χλουνὸς which is given by Hesykhios as a synonym of χρυσός. It is therefore reasonable to regard the latter as borrowed from *khârûts*, which, on its side, comes from a Semitic root meaning "to grave" or "dig." Let us select another example from Basque. A large proportion of the dictionary of the latter language has been taken from Spanish or Latin, and to this M. Bladé would add the Basque numerals *bi*, "two," and *sei*, "six." But the laws of phonology forbid this. The labial which we see in *bini* is nothing more than the *v* of *duo* which has lost its dental, as in *viginti*; and out of the distributive the Basques could never have got a cardinal. The only Latin form of the numeral with which the Biscayans could have come into contact was *duo* through the Spanish *dos*, as is again shown by glottological laws. And in fact, there is no need of connecting *bi* with any Latin word at all. The comparative study of the Basque numerals has relegated them to the Finnic family, and here both *bi* and *sei* are possible forms for "two" and "six."[1] Thus the laws which have been obtained from the comparison of phonetic sounds in different groups of speech, by enabling us to reach back to the earliest forms of a word in each group, or to dialects which are removed from the line of contact, allow us to determine whether or not we are dealing with loan-words. In the same way, other laws may come into play when we are doubtful about the priority of borrowing in any case. Thus in Accadian, *'eri* meant "a city," which at once reminds us of the Semitic עיר (Assyrian, *'uru*); and we ask, Supposing they are loan-words, on which side did the debt lie? Now, I believe I have shown[2] that a large number of Semitic words which denote the first elements of a higher civilisation are derived from Accadian, and this at once raises the presumption that עיר is borrowed, and borrowed from the Turanian neighbours of the Semitic nomads. When we find, however, that not only other words which signify settled habitations, like *hêcâl*

[1] In Accadian, *sei* seems a modification of the old numeral of "three," like the Japanese *mitsu*, "three," and *mutsu*, "six." It would then show itself in the Esthonian *sei-tze*, "seven" (3-10), as well as the Accadian *sussu*, "sixty."

[2] "Origin of Semitic Civilisation," in *Trans. Soc. Biblic. Archæol.*, i. 1872.

(Accadian, *ê-gal*, "great house"), are derived from Babylonia, while the ordinary Assyrian word for "city," *âlu*, is really the Hebrew *ôhel*, "tent," the tent having formed the original habitation of the primitive Semitic nomad, we are induced to conclude that it was from the old Turanian civilisation in Babylonia, which the last few years have revealed to us, that the early Semite obtained his first lessons in culture. It is a contribution of the highest importance to the mental history of mankind. From the beginning the Semite seems to have stood between the old and the new, between Asia and Europe—the trader not in material wares only, but in the far more precious merchandise of thought and invention. I cannot do better than conclude this chapter with two striking instances of this.

The Greeks derived their weights and measures, as well as their alphabet, from the Semitic East. The standard of these was the *μνᾶ*, which was handed on to the Romans, and so to the Western world, under the name of the *mina*. The *μνᾶ* is the Hebrew *maneh*, and the final *a* proves that it was immediately borrowed, like the letters of the alphabet, not from the Phœnicians of Tyre and Sidon, but from the Aramaic population further to the north. Böckh has shown that Pheidôn, the great king of Argos, arranged his scale of weights upon a Babylonian model; and clay contract-tablets in the British Museum, written in Assyrian cuneiform with Aramaic dockets, indicate that from the reign of Tiglath-Pileser (B.C. 745) downwards Aramaic was the language of commerce throughout the Assyrian world. And not only so, but the *mana* was the standard weight by which gold and silver were weighed, and all trade transactions carried out. There was the *mana*, or "maund," of Carchemish, whose position near the fords of the Euphrates, on the high road to the Mediterranean, had made it take the commercial place of Tyre after the destruction of the latter city by the Assyrians, as well as the *mana* of "the country" (of Assyria), or "of the king." Thus we find Nergal-sarra-nacir (B.C. 667) lending "four manehs of silver according to the maneh of Carchemish," at five shekels of silver interest per month; and in the Eponymy of Zazai (B.C. 692), a house in Nineveh, "with its shrubbery and gates," was sold for one maneh of silver according to the "royal standard."

Now the *mana* might seem at first sight of Semitic origin. We have the Semitic root מנה, "to number," from which comes the Hebrew *mânâh*, "a portion," and with which the Aramaic *mene*, that Daniel read on the walls of Belshazzar's palace, is connected, and it would seem to yield a good enough meaning for the *mana.* But this is put out of the question by the fact that *mana* in Assyrian is indeclinable when strictly used, not even admitting of a plural, whereas, were it a Semitic word, the nominative and ordinary form would be *manu.* It must, therefore, be a loan-word and the similarity of the Aryan root *ma,* "to measure," which has given us "moon" and "month," might incline us to seek its origin here. The Greek *μνᾶ,* however, comes from the Semitic; and the Semites could not have taken a foreign *root,* as distinguished from a derivative, and formed a technical word out of it; consequently we must look elsewhere for the home of the *mana.* This has generally been supposed to be Egypt, as the *mn* is found there also at an early date; not, however, before the times when the Egyptians borrowed freely from Palestine, not only words like *sus,* "horse," and *sar,* "prince," but even *marcabutha,* "chariot," and *sepet,* "lip." But a new light has of late been unexpectedly thrown upon the matter. An old table of Accadian laws, which has an Assyrian translation attached, orders the man who divorces his wife to pay "half a maneh of silver;" a mild penalty, by the way, compared with that of the wife, who was condemned to be thrown into the river for repudiating her husband. Now the word *mana* is found in the Accadian column, and the vowel harmony thoroughly suits the structure of the language. Here, then, we seem to have lighted upon the parentage of the word, which, after all, would have come from Babylonia in a truer sense than the Greek antiquary had any idea of, along with many other Semitic names of weights and measures, not excluding even some of the numerals. It is interesting thus to trace the beginning and growth of that idea of measure which lies at the bottom of science as well as of trade; to learn that Babylonia was its cradle, and a Turanian race its first discoverers; that the Semites have been imitators and mediators in the great work of civilisation, and that the Western nations have through them inherited the seeds of the culture which they alone have known how to bring to its fullest perfection.

The second instance to which I referred points in the same direction. In Semitic, the root חלף means "to change" or "exchange," and the derivative *khâleph*, "exchange" or "agio." From this the Greeks got their κόλλυβος which, like ἀῤῥαβών (Lat. *arrhabo* and *arrha*, from the Heb. *'êrâbôn*), bears witness to the ancient commercial activity of the Semite, from whom the Greek derived both his idea and his name of the relations of trade. It was trade, however, of a particular sort; and the very fact that the words denoting money-dealing are of foreign origin, is sufficient to show, without the testimony of Aristotle, that the whole business was originally distasteful to the Greek mind. It was the same at Rome. Money-lenders were never in good repute there; and Cicero's *collybus* is again borrowed from the borrowed Greek κόλλυβος. Here again, therefore, the Semitic race appears as the pioneer of commerce in the West, the mediator between Europe and Asia. But this is not all the history connected with the root חלף. From it the Khalifs of Mohammedanism obtained their name. They were "the deputies" and successors" of the Prophet,—those who, in a regular order of change, have been the Commanders of the Faithful in their struggle against the infidels of this world. Amid the uncertainties of succession, however, the divided Khalifate of Bagdad and Spain, and the vicissitudes of fortune, the name of Khalif gradually ceased to have that definite meaning which it originally bore. But it was reserved for the European and the unbeliever to borrow and misuse it as the proper title of any Mohammedan sovereign, and then to extend it to any ruler whatsoever, whether Turk or Christian, Eastern or Western. Far indeed has it departed from its original meaning when we find one of the few compositions left us by the disappointed life of Prince Charles Edward turning the Hanoverian king of England into a successor of the Arabian Mohammed—

> "I hate all kings, and the thrones they sit on,
> From the King of France to the Caliph of Britain."

## CHAPTER VI.

### THE DOCTRINE OF ROOTS.

ALL the sciences that bear upon the origin and early history of man are beginning to point out more and more clearly that he is a ζῶον πολιτικὸν in a much wider sense than Aristotle ever imagined. Instead of starting with atomistic individuals, we must start with the converse, the community. The individual is the last growth and result of time; and society, as composed of individuals, has arisen out of a sort of beehive existence, by a process of differentiation which holds good, as Mr Herbert Spencer has shown, throughout the organic world. The primitive savage was but a part of a tribe, with no ideas beyond those which the tribe possessed in common. Even the wives and children were common property, thus realising Plato's Republic in a practical manner; and special property in a wife appears to have originated in the acquisition of the women of another tribe in war. The captive was at the mercy of her captor; he might kill her or make her his slave—in other words, his peculiar wife—just as he chose. It was the same with other property; the commune preceded individual possession everywhere, thus bringing the gregarious period of human history down to a late epoch of development. All this throws much light upon the earlier stage of language. Judging from analogy, we should conclude that language also, the artificial link between the several units of a tribe or community, would have a communistic origin. We must go back to the beehive era in order to discover its beginnings. In other words, language ought first to have been common property, full of vague, instinctively felt signification, but not yet differentiated into individual words with special sounds and meanings. In fact, we ought to start not with the word, but with a wider indefinite whole, out of which the word, or rather the sentence, has been elaborated; and that whole would have conveyed the same general indeterminate sense to the several units of the community, whose wants and means of expressing them were the same.

Now we have already found that this is actually the case. If we wish to get at the primary facts of Glottology, we have to begin with the sentence, and not with the isolated word. It can never be too often repeated, that words have grown out of the sentence, though each race has carried out this process differently, in accordance with its primitive tendency. Everywhere, however, the general character of the process has been identical. Everywhere sounds, forms, and meanings have been differentiated; the indistinct sound, for instance, that stood for *r* and *l* in the parent Aryan branched off into those two consonants, just as the obscure sound which serves for *c* and *t* in the Sandwich Islands has become the first of these letters, and the vowel changes of the verb, which have no meaning in Sanskrit, have become the Teutonic *ablaut*, serving to distinguish the relations of time. The compound word is pre-eminently an example of this differentiation: two words must be so clearly marked off and defined already as to be able to be connected together to form a third with determinate form and signification. It is merely a matter of further progress in the differentiating direction when the idea contained in the compound has become so far fixed and definite as to lose all reference to its original factors, so that one or both of these are deprived of all independent force, and convey no meaning except when united together. Hence the existence of compounds in a language may be considered a mark of lateness; before it has acquired them the language will have advanced far beyond its period of childhood; the vagueness of infancy, when subject and object are blended in inextricable confusion, will have passed away, and the judgments that lay implicit in those first semi-conscious expressions which I have called sentences, will have been made explicit and precise by being summed up in an ever-increasing number of what I have called words. The number of words, in fact, with distinct and separate meanings, measures the progress of a language and the culture of those who speak it. Now it is evident that if language continually tends to enrich itself more and more with different words and sounds, in order to get at its beginnings we must reverse the process of differentiation, and discover those rude chaotic combinations of sound and sense out of which the manifold wealth of articulate speech has sprung. We must go to work in the same way as the chemist, who obtains his elemental substances by analysing the different products of nature. Infinitely various as these are, they have all been obtained from about sixty simple elements, which, by combining with one another in different proportions, have thus differentiated the manifold properties which each separate combination possesses. So in Glottology, we must throw our words into the retort of the comparative method, break up the compounds, analyse the grammar, simplify the signification, and trace the growth of phonetic distinctions. It is in this manner that we shall arrive at our simple elements, beyond which it is impossible for Glottology—at all events without the aid of other sciences—to proceed, just as it is impossible for chemistry pure and simple to advance beyond its primary substances.

The roots of language, then, must be reached by comparison. The truth is of old standing, though the scientific use of it is of such recent date. The grammarians of India, long before the Christian era, had reduced the Sanskrit lexicon to a certain number of primitive roots, by referring to one monosyllable all those words the non-formative part of which agreed in sound; and the Jewish doctors of the tenth century had resolved the language of the Old Testament into triliteral radicals through a comparison of Hebrew with Arabic. Every one could see that this or that series of words presupposed the same combination of letters; it was the root out of which the whole series seemed to have grown, like the tree out of the ground. But the discovery remained barren. The Greeks contented themselves with discussing whether language had originated by convention or by nature, and Christian writers took it for granted that the Semitic radicals formed the language of Paradise. It is only since the rise of Glottology that it has been asked what these roots are, and what is their relation to the words derived from them? Now here it is necessary to bear in mind two things, which have been too often overlooked in the discussion of this subject. One is, that Glottology cannot go beyond its facts; and as these are sentence-words and the ultimate analysis of such sentence-words, it cannot go beyond the Root-period and speculate as to what roots themselves grew out of. The bow-wow theory, or the pooh-pooh theory, or the ding-dong theory, all lie equally outside the proper province of Glottology. If we want to decide upon this matter, we must call in the aid of other sciences. The other thing to be remembered is the loose use of the phrase "roots of language." There was no one primeval language, as I have endeavoured to show, at least so far as our data allow us to believe; on the contrary, languages were infinitely numerous, as numerous as the communities which spoke them; and it by no means follows that the roots of all these languages were of a similar kind, or that words have been derived from them in a similar way. Indeed, I have tried to show that, so far is this from being true, that the chief modern races of the world have each followed a separate and independent direction in reflecting their thoughts in speech. Consequently to talk of finding the roots of language or of investigating the origin of language is highly misleading. What we have to deal with are the roots of *languages.* The results obtained from the study of the Aryan group are not to be applied universally, and be made the rule for Semitic and Turanian also. What we can do, however, is to investigate the roots of the various families of speech so far as is possible, and then to compare the conclusions drawn from each. Among the many one-sided theories produced by an exclusive regard to the Aryan family, none is so common as that which ascribes to roots a general abstract meaning, as if our ancestors of the Root-period employed nothing except abstract terms in conversing with one another. We have only to state the proposition, however, to see how absurd it is. How could savages, whose vocabulary consisted entirely of such words as "bringing," "shining," "defending," be mutually intelligible? There is no common bond of intelligibility between such universal ideas; language must begin with the objects of sense, if we are to communicate our meaning to others, and rise from these by the help of metaphor to abstract supersensuous conceptions. Moreover, these abstract ideas must either be the last result of reflection, the universals arrived at after a long course of education, or else must be of the vaguest and most unmeaning character. In the first case, we are ascribing to the primitive barbarian the mind of the civilised man; in the second case, any language at all would be out of the question. Two persons could not talk together in vague generalities, more especially when their conversation would be mostly confined to the bare necessities of life. Even with us, the same general term bears very different meanings to two different persons. It is what Locke called a "mixed mode;" and with all our culture and scientific definition, it is impossible to make such epithets as "good" or "noble" convey exactly the same signification and the same associations to two minds. In fact, the notion is absolutely contradicted by what we observe among modern savages. Here the individual objects of sense have names enough, while general terms are very rare. Thus the Mohicans have words for cutting various objects, but none to signify cutting simply; and the Society Islanders can talk of a dog's tail, a sheep's tail, or a man's tail, but not of tail itself. "The dialect of the Zulus is rich in nouns denoting different objects of the same genus, according to some variety of colour, redundancy or deficiency of members, or some other peculiarity," such as "red cow," "white cow," "brown cow;"[1] and the Sechuana has no less than ten words to express horned cattle.[2] The Tasmanians were so utterly deficient in the power of forming abstract ideas, that they were obliged to say "like the moon," or some other round object, when they wanted to express the conception of roundness. The theory in question has originated in a too exclusive attention to the phenomena of the Aryan lexicon. Here all the roots seem to bear a general meaning only, out of which the names of individual things have been obtained by means of suffixes. Thus *daughter* (*duhitâ*) is merely "the milker," from the root which has the general signification of "milking;" *father* (*pater, pitâ*) is "the defender," from *pâ; brother* (*bhrâtâ*) is "the bearer," from *bhar.* In the same way, a large proportion of the words we use turn out, when analysed, to be simply general epithets which have come to be set apart to denote some special object. Hence the conclusion to which the Sanskritists jumped, that the general precedes the particular, and their triumphant refutation of the onomatopœic hypothesis of the origin of language. But they have forgotten that their induction has been made from a single in-

[1] *Jour. of Amer. Orient. Soc.*, vol. i., No. 4, p. 402.

[2] Casalis Gram., p. 7.

stance only, and that instance altogether exceptional in the history of speech. The parent-Aryan, if it ever existed, was the language of comparatively civilised men. Such examples as *duhitâ* would of themselves show this, and point to a pastoral life; and the persistency with which the several members of the original stock have remained true to the primitive language can only be explained by supposing our ancestors to have advanced considerably beyond the degree of civilisation at present possessed by the Ostiak or Burmese tribes. The Aryan scholar, therefore, is dealing with a language in which we may well expect to find general epithetic terms; but he cannot conclude from this that there were no individual words originally which denoted some particular object.[1] Beyond the parent-Aryan lies a vast unknown period, upon which Glottology casts but little light; and the fact that in so many unallied languages the names of *father* and *mother* are formed by means of the labials, would seem to imply that *pitar* and *mâtar* were chosen not without a purpose; and although the lexicographer

[1] Buschmann, after an exhaustive comparison of words used by different peoples for "father" and "mother," in his paper "On Natural Sounds," says, "I am glad that the process which I have developed presents a simple proof of the independent formation of substantives; for a certain systematising philology has of late years, with absolute exclusiveness, set up the theory that the roots of all language must have been verbs."

must derive these words themselves from *pâ* and *mâ*, "fashioning,"[1] they yet point to a time when the names given to the parents were merely the first cries of infancy. "Father" and "mother" must have had names before the root *tar* was compounded with the roots *pa* and *ma* to denote them.[2] But the error of the Sanskritists goes deeper than this. They raise into a sort of pigeon-English language the residuum of sounds which lies at the bottom of the dictionary. Because a certain number of vocables presuppose a common monosyllable with a common vague meaning, it does not at all follow that this monosyllable ever formed part of an actual language. For anything we know, it may be merely an archetype of phonetic sound, presupposed by the derivatives, but never consciously expressed in speech. Still less can we assert that the vague general signification given to the root was originally expressed

[1] *Mâtâ* in the Rig-Veda is masculine, just as in Georgian and the (Athapascan) Tlatskanai, *mama* is "father." We can hardly identify this root *mâ* with *mâ*, "to measure:" it has produced the Greek *μαία*, and probably the Latin *manus*, *manes*.

[2] There is a truth, however, which lies at the bottom of this strangely-expressed theory of the abstract character of roots. Objects must have been named from their qualities. It was by these alone that they could be known; and though the qualities were necessarily external and superficial, such as the bleating of the sheep or the bellowing of the bull, they must still have arisen out of the impressions made by outward phenomena upon the senses and the mind.

by it. The root may have originally denoted an individual object or action, which was afterwards lost when the progress of composition and phonetic decay had supplied the vocabulary with other terms. There is, however, a truth in the prevailing theory, though thus faultily expressed. The sentence comes before the word, the indefinite before the definite; and the root-period, as we have seen, is characterised by the want of differentiation. The Aryan root, consequently, while primarily denoting an individual object, would have done so in a very different way from that in which we should denote the same. The individual can only be properly understood in relation to the general; when, therefore, the idea of the general has not yet been arrived at, the idea of the particular is at once vague and sensuous. The word which denotes it is merely a mark, nothing more; just as much as a proper name, and with no more subjective reference than the proper name has. So long as the object can be pointed out sensibly, the meaning and reference of the word is unmistakable. We know exactly, for instance, who a particular John or Henry are when they are indicated by the finger; but when the object is not present, the signification and content of the word is wholly vague and uncertain. The judgment which is summed up in it is not determined by immediate reference to such and such a thing: we cannot think "this is a tree;" and accordingly each person forms his own judgment, and attaches a different interpretation to the vocable. The term is not defined by its external object, and language has not yet arrived at the explication of its words by other means. In this way the Aryan roots might easily have come to have those vague general significations which are ascribed to them, although they properly represented individual objects and actions.

But we must not forget that the so-called root-stage of Aryan speech is very questionable in the shape in which it is usually set before us. So far as our data go, there is no reason for believing that the Aryan was ever otherwise than inflectional, however unlike the primitive inflections may have been to those with which we are familiar. We can only be certain of this much, that there was a time when the primitive Aryan spoke a language far simpler than that with which we are acquainted, in which the words were for the most part short, few, and of indefinite meaning, and that this earlier and barbarous condition was succeeded by what I would call the Epithet-stage. To identify this epithet-stage, however, with inflection is altogether unwarranted, and (as I hope I have shown) contrary to the facts. The root-period is not inconsistent with a rudimentary inflection, and the epithet-period points to a vast series of bygone ages, to an advanced civilisation, and to the development of the higher poetical faculties. When the moon could be called "the measurer," the tribe must have left barbarism far behind. It was still a tribe, however, and we may perhaps assign to this communism the general adoption of particular epithets for special objects, and the tenacity with which they were preserved and handed down when once adopted, At any rate, the individual had not yet emerged from the community; but this was inevitable when the imaginative faculty had once made its appearance, and the era of the Rishis could not be long delayed.

What I have called the epithet-stage is of great importance in the history of our group of languages, since it supplies in great measure the answer to the question which came before us in an earlier chapter, why it is that the Aryan family presents such a singular exception to the usual rule of rapid change in language in the fixity of its grammar and lexicon. Before the parent-tribe had broken up, it had already entered upon the later period of linguistic growth, in which conventional custom sets its stamp upon spoken speech, and consecrates its form and expression. Language loses its early creativeness; the very fact that new words have to be coined out of old material by a metaphorical use of the latter shows that settled habits and the enlarged sphere of imagination have to a great extent put an end to the invention of fresh "roots," while the common adoption of one of these metaphors to express an object of sense demonstrates the extinction of the creative faculty and the stereotyped conservatism of the speaker. Men have become at once too highly imaginative and too narrowly conventional to waste their energies in the pastime of the savage, the coining of new words. In fact, language has entered upon its ceremonial stage when the sounds which we utter have been made the subject of a conscious exercise of thought, and the mind has been called upon to compare some new object with one whose name has already been furnished by the ancient heirlooms of speech. Sound and sense are no longer commingled in chaotic confusion; sense becomes distinct and clear, and sound is made subordinate to it. A so-called "ceremonial language," such as the *Bhasa Krama* of Java, is but a further development of the epithet-stage, by definitely confining the epithets to persons and not things. Ceremonial languages and idioms are found all over the world, as in the larger islands of Polynesia, or in the ceremonial conjugation of the Basque, or in the women's language of South America; and they testify everywhere to an incipient fixity of language, and the beginning of a settled state of society. Closely akin to these ceremonial languages is the phenomenon which meets us in several of the South American dialects, where the words which denote "head," "body," "eye," or other parts of the person, cannot be named without personal relation being indicated by a prefixed possessive pronoun, or denied by a negative or privative prefix. Thus "head" is in Mbaya *na-guilo*, in Abiponian *na-maiat*, in Moxa *nu-ciuti;* "eye" in Mbaya is *ni-gecoge*, in Abiponian *na-toele*, in Moxa *nu-chi*, and in Mokobi *ni-cote*, where *na*, *ni*, and *nu* signify "my," reminding us of the Continental *milord.* The ceremonial or epithet-period of language is that in which I would place the origin of the personal pronouns. Bleek has shown that these were originally substantives, meaning "servant," "lord," "reverence," and the like, at least so far as the Ba-ntu idioms of South Africa are concerned; and the same fact appears in those languages of Asia, such as Chinese, Malay, and Japanese, in which the transparent character of the language allows us to penetrate to their primary signification. Thus the Malay *ulun*, "I," is still in Lampong "a man;" and the Kawi *ngwang*, "I," cannot be separated from *nwang*, "a man." To assert that this transmutation of expressions like "your reverence," or ὅδε ὁ ἀνήρ, into personal pronouns belongs to a late epoch of linguistic development, is to re-state my own position in other words; while the attempt to resolve the nominative of the Aryan first personal pronoun (*aham*, *ego*), for instance, into two "pronominal elements," *ma* + *ga*, breaks down at the very threshold. Initial *m* is never lost in the Aryan languages generally, although it may disappear in Greek through the medium of the digamma, as in μάλευρον by the side of ἄλευρον, *i.e.*, √Ϝαλευρον from √αλέω or μί-τος by the side of ἰτέα, the Latin *viere vimen*; while *ga*, the Greek -γε, is still found in the Rig-Veda as the aspirated *gha*. To metamorphose the singular *ma* into the plural *nas*, as has been attempted by some over-hasty adherents of the pronominal theory, does violence to all the phonological laws of Indo-European speech. In my "Assyrian Grammar," I have suggested that a comparison of the cognate dialects would lead us to infer that the original form of the first two personal pronouns in Semitic was the same, *'ecet*, which reminds us of the Ethiopic *acata*, "to honour" or "thank;" while the third personal pronoun can be proved to have originally been *su'u*, which may be akin to שׁוה, "like," and hence "companion."

The epithet-stage, therefore, would have been the closing portion of the root-period, or the commencement of the secondary period of analysis (*not* of flection), according to the point of view which we prefer to take. Its determination can no more settle the nature of roots or the existence of flection during the root-period than those falsely-called flections like *-dom* and *-head*, which I discussed in a former chapter. The root remains where it was before,—the residuum of a group of words in which the lexicographer has discovered a common combination of sounds and a common meaning, but which could never have formed part of a spoken language, and which, from the first, while denoting the individual and the concrete, was yet vague in meaning and indefinite in pronunciation, and capable of being used for all the parts of speech. This, however, was owing to the fact that language begins with the sentence and not with the individual word; the latter is the last growth of time, the last result of simplification and reflection. Of itself, the radical was as purely the mark of a single object of sense as any of the words which denote various sorts of tails in the idioms of the Sandwich Islanders; but this signification was extended by its use as a sentence-word or judgment; for, properly speaking, the primitive Aryan had no conception of a single object apart from the universal; such a distinction requires comparison, and as yet individual and general were blended into one, the general being an extended individual, and the individual a specialised universal. Without a world there can be no individual. Now the naming of each thing according to its momentary impression upon the senses would necessarily give rise to an infinite multitude of names, not only for objects which seemed to differ in some small particular, but also for the same object according to the time or circumstances under which it struck the senses. This, coupled with the early creativeness of language, which we still see exemplified among the lower races of mankind, would produce an endless number of words. The vocables, which at different times or at the same time served to point out the same thing, would have been as multitudinous as the dialects which I have endeavoured in a preceding chapter to show were the real primitive centres of spoken speech. This is the only way in which we can account for the existence of synonymous roots, which become more plentiful as the language which we are handling is less developed. Thus the Caribs express the same notion by very different roots, according to Adelung;[1] and Professor Key

[1] Mith. iii. 2, 686, *cf.* Rochefort, 364.

is not the only person who has been astonished at the immense number of radicals in Sanskrit which all mean "to go." We have already had occasion to notice in a preceding page the fertility of savage tribes in inventing new words, and the rapid change in the vocabulary that takes place among them. Perhaps one of the most striking instances of this in recent times is to be found in the island of Tasmania, where, with a population of no more than fifty persons, there were no less than four dialects, each with a different word for "ear," "eye," "head," and other similarly common words. Even our own semi-fossilised language has not altogether lost the power of striking out new roots, as may be proved by a reference to a slang dictionary or a scientific encyclopædia; and this may give us some idea of the boundless inventiveness of language before it had been crystallised by convention and a fixed society. In fact, just as the languages of the world with which we are acquainted have arisen out of the wrecks of numberless forgotten attempts at speech, so the roots presupposed by the lexicon are the selected relics of an infinite wealth of primitive sentence-words; for here, too, as elsewhere, natural selection has come into play, and the progress of civilisation has been to unify and minimise the inexhaustible prodigality of nature. In the same way, the indefinite variety of meanings which it was possible to evolve out of each sentence-word was gradually reduced, until every idea had its own appropriate sound, and the sentence was resolved into its individual words, like the word into its individual letters. But this individualising of the isolated word is the last result of time and thought; and so far as our data warrant us to infer, there was never a period when the root existed in its naked simplicity, any more than there was when the letter or the syllable existed apart from the root. Both are figments of the grammarian and the lexicographer, the convenient analyses of the modern student. Flection in the Aryan tongues implies a preceding flection upon which it was modelled; and a large proportion of the radicals, as we have seen, can only be used for the purposes of comparison by being treated as bases. This at once makes them dissyllables, that is, no longer monosyllabic roots — the same conclusion to which we are led by a consideration of such words as *bhûs*, *bhûm*, *sthât*, *sthâtar*, with identical significations; and when we recollect that *k* was constantly followed by *u*, we see that there is a whole class of roots like *loqu-or*, which could never have existed in a monosyllabic form in spoken speech.[1] Forms such as *ad-mi*, which present us

[1] Fick (in his "Ehemalige Spracheinheit der Indogermanen

with the bare radical immediately attached to the later inflection of the epithet-epoch, had better be explained as the consequences of phonetic decay, like our own English monosyllables, than as the evidences of an imaginary "root-period," since the tendency of language is towards attrition and contraction rather than extension and increase.

Another one-sided theory, which has for some time formed part of the doctrine of roots, is; that we must seek in them for the origin of language. Accordingly we have had attempts to derive them from the imitation of natural sounds, or from emotional interjections, or again from a kind of intuitive inspiration. Geiger believes that they have originated in the endeavour to imitate the gestures and muscular expression of emotion; Bleek would evolve them from the cries of animals, or rather the inarticulate sounds made by the anthropoid apes. The failure of these attempts, the impossibility of supporting any one of them by

Europa's"), following in the wake of Ascoli, has proved convincingly the existence of two *k*'s in the parent-Aryan, one of them passing into *kw* (*qu*) in certain of the European dialects. Havet, criticising Fick in the *Mémoires de la Société de Linguistique de Paris*, ii. 4 (1874), in an article entitled "L'Unité Européenne," shows that the two *k*'s are to be tabulated thus:—

Primitive *k* = Ital. *k* (*c*); Greek *κ*; German *h*; Aric or East Aryan *ś*; Slav. *s*; Lith. *š*.

Primitive *kw* = Aric *k*, *t́*, *p*, *kw* (*ku*); Gaelic *k*; Cymr. *p*; Latin *kw* (*qu*); Osco-umbrian *p*; Greek *π*, *κυ*; Ionic *κ*; German *hv*, *f* (*p*), *h*; Lettoslav. *k*, *p*, *kw* (*ku*).

the facts of language alone, has brought about a reaction against inquiries into the origin of language at all, and the Société de Linguistique of Paris has refused to receive any papers bearing upon the subject. But because the determination of the matter lies beyond the boundaries of Glottology taken by itself, it by no means follows that it is either useless or insoluble. On the contrary, Glottology is an historic science, and we can never, therefore, understand the problems of language properly until we have solved the riddle of its origin. But this can only be done by the aid of other sciences; Glottology cannot go beyond the limits of language, and physiology and psychology must explain the rest. As glottologists, we have to begin with roots; they are the first facts to which we can ascend. The decomposition of the roots themselves, the germs out of which they have grown, belong to other branches of study. All that we can do is to ascertain clearly the nature of these roots and to fix their limits; to determine, in short, where language first takes its start, and ceases to be the inarticulate, unconscious utterance of instinctive desire. The difficulty that meets us here is one that presents itself everywhere to the student of nature. There is no break, no sudden gap in nature; all follows in a regular unbroken order. All sharp lines of demarcation, therefore, must be artificial; our genera and species, our strata and our periods, in fine, our classifications generally, exist only for the purposes of science. Ideal types there certainly are, around which the phenomena group themselves; but the groups pass insensibly one into the other, and we can only draw our lines of division to a great extent arbitrarily. This is the case with language; we can determine on which side of the line language must be placed, and on which side mere inarticulate cries, but the line itself is a shifting one, and can only be laid down approximately. To believe, therefore, that roots are simply interjections or the imitations of sounds, is to confuse the two sides of the line of division, and to ignore the difference between language and inarticulate utterance. Roots are not emotional or imitational cries, although they may have grown out of them; but the investigation of the process has nothing to do with the science of language. The Aryan dictionary may be reduced to a certain number of radicals; but, after all, we have only found the origin of the dictionary, not of language. Consequently it is beside the mark either to quote instances of derivatives from interjections or natural sounds, like the Chinese *ngŏ* "stop," and *miau*, "cat," in defence of the "pooh-pooh" and "bow-wow" theories of the origin of speech, or to attempt to refute them by showing that supposed examples of imitation, like *thunder* or *raven* (*corvus*), turn out to have their origin in roots of very different sound. The utmost that Glottology can do is to show that words have actually been derived from both these sources within the historic period; and in that case analogy may justify us in concluding that the primitive man *may* have arrived at his roots in a similar manner. But there is no proof of this, so far as philology is concerned; and although the mind may pass from vague natural cries into the higher forms of speech when it has come to a state of consciousness, it is hard to see how the process could have been performed when the mind was yet unconscious—how, in other words, the mind could have passed from unconsciousness to consciousness and its expression. To say that this happened through intuitive inspiration is merely to state the question in a different way. We want to know where this inspiration came from, and how the mind first became conscious. But this is plainly a matter for psychology and not Glottology; and we can only see this much, that as language is the outward expression and embodiment of conscious thought, it must have had much to do with the development of consciousness, which becomes possible when thought can make itself objective, and so regard itself. Language is the counter-side and utterance of society; with society it begins and with society it ends. Before society there is no language properly so called, because there is no conscious thought, no intercourse between man and man; and consequently our linguistic researches will be bounded by the limits of social science and social archæology. As we cannot get beyond the family in the one, so we cannot get beyond the existing monuments of speech in the other.

It is clear, then, that Glottology must confine itself within the boundaries of the period of roots, and transfer its attention from the question of their origin to the investigation into their nature. In a former chapter I have endeavoured to point out that roots are by no means necessarily monosyllabic, and that the theory that they are so is one of the idola generated by the over-weight given to the Aryan family. It is bound up with the belief that the Semitic radicals were originally biliteral. The latter motion has been much encouraged by the analytic character of Aryan, and the essential difference between the two families of speech has been overlooked. But although the attempt to resolve the Semitic roots into more ultimate elements breaks down, it does not at all follow that the result is the same in the Aryan group.

Throughout this reigns the spirit of analysis, and it is very possible, therefore, that the Aryan roots are capable of still further decomposition. Composition and infliction are the distinguishing features of this family of speech, and the so-called root-period may be only the closing era of a still older root-period. This probability is strongly confirmed by a fact which it is hard to explain from any other cause, the occurrence, namely, of roots with similar meanings which differ only in the final consonants. Thus we find beside *bhâ* (φημί), *bhan* (φαίνω), *bhas*, and *bhav* (φαῦος, *favilla*); beside *sta* (*stare*), *stap* (*stipare*), *stambh* (*stamp*), *star* (στερέος), *stal* (*stellen*), and *stav* (σταυρός). In accordance with this, Professor Pott has sought to analyse the so-called roots, and to make out that all those which enclose two consonants are compounds, so that the earliest form of Aryan would have resembled the Polynesian dialects, in which each syllable must end in a vowel. A large proportion of these compounds, Pott believes, contain a preposition: thus *pinj*, "painting," comes from *api* (ἐπί) and *anj*, "anointing." Professor Curtius[1] urges several objections of great force against this view. In the first place, these compounded roots are treated in word-building just like other primitive

[1] "Grundzüge der Griechischen Etymologie," pp. 33-41.

roots, and whereas initial *api* in Sanskrit may become *pi*, this is never the case in Greek. The loss of the vowel, therefore, is a peculiarity of Sanskrit, and could not have occurred in the parent-Aryan. Then, secondly, there was no such close and intimate amalgamation of the preposition and the root in early times as is necessitated by Pott's analysis. Even in Greek and Sanskrit the nominal and independent origin of the prepositions is so clearly felt that the augment and the reduplication are inserted between the preposition and the verbal form. Latin and Greek themselves possess but few compounded roots in common.

But although Pott's theory must be resigned, it is yet certain that many of the roots are really compounds. The radical *yu* cannot be separated from *yug* and *yudh*, or the radical *tar* from *tras* and *tram*, *trak* (*torqu-eo*) and *trap* (*trepidus*), *trib* (τρίβω) and *trup* (τρύπ-ανον). Curtius[1] suggests that the longer forms are really compounded out of two other roots, *yudh*, for instance, being amalgamated with *dha* ("do"), and the *k* in *trak* being the same as the guttural which distinguishes λιθακ from λιθο. In this case the compounded roots would have originally been dissyllabic, *yu-dha* and

[1] "Zur Chronologie d. Indogermanischen Sprachforschung," pp. 28-30 (2d edit.)

*tar-ka.* The suggestion is undoubtedly a true one. We can hardly explain in any other way such roots as *vridh* and *ridh,* "growing," *dâ* and *dam,* "binding;" and the theory would be very consistent with the view that the root-period, as far as it existed at all, was a period of rudimentary inflection, which preceded the more advanced epoch of epithet-making. The theory is also borne out by the analogy of the Turanian languages. This group is still getting but scanty attention from glottologists, and, until lately, we could only study it in modern idioms. Accadian, however, has given us a background for comparison older than the language of the Rig-Veda; and the clear transparent character of the Turanian group enables us to obtain more certain results than where we have to contend with all the obscurities of phonetic decay. Now, the Accadian roots, simple as they appear, nevertheless contain compounds in which the elements are as closely amalgamated as they would be in the Aryan roots were Curtius's opinion correct. Thus it seems probable that the word *is,* "a heap of dust," has been compounded with another word *me,* "a multitude," in order to form *mes,* "many." The latter word would be of great antiquity, if, as I believe, the final *s* which marks the third person plural of the past tense is a remnant of it. We thus have composition in Turanian, in which the two factors are so welded together as to become practically one word, carried back to a very remote period; and yet the genius of the Turanian languages is thoroughly averse to composition at all.

But we must never forget that we may easily carry analysis too far. We cannot judge the primitive savage by our rules of simplicity. On the contrary, simplicity is the result of progress and culture; the further we go back, the nearer we approach the natural state, the more do we meet with the intricate multiplicity of nature. Nothing can be more intricate, more complex, than the grammar of the Red Indian or the Eskimaux; the simplicity of our own grammar is the result of a long series of comprehensive generalisations and analyses of thought. Out of the manifold comes the simple, out of the multitudinous the single. All progress in philosophy and science is the reduction of the many to the one. It is the same with the lexicon as with the grammar. The meaning of words begins with a confused vagueness, out of which definite forms with definite significations are gradually evolved. Language is the expression of thought; and the first ideas were as much undifferentiated embryos as the jelly-fish on the shore or the beehive life of primeval man.

There was no unity in them; idea had not yet been subordinated to idea; but each was the mere individual impression of the moment, with all the vagueness and complexity of a sensation. Accordingly, we must not expect to find simplicity of form, any more than simplicity of content or signification, in the root-period; and the reversal of this is the most serious argument against Pott's hypothesis. As Bleek points out, many of our involuntary sounds, such as sneezing, for instance, are by no means simple and monosyllabic; and whatever may be the origin of language, it is certain that on the phonetic side—the side, that is, of the non-mental physiological machinery—we can draw no distinction between emotional cries and articulate utterance. The clicks of the Hottentot cannot be called either simple or easy; and yet it is impossible to explain these as a later accretion to the language; they go back to the very roots of it, and may possibly be a relic of what once characterised most of the other languages of the world, but has since been lost through the influence of phonetic decay.[1] Phonetic

[1] Clicks and diphthongs have disappeared "in the grammatical elements of the Hottentot language," "though three-fourths of this language may be said to contain clicks," according to Bleek's "Comparative Grammar of South African Languages," i. p. 47. The same writer quotes from Von Klaproth the assertion that clicks occur in the Circassian tongue; "and two clicks are distinguished in the T'iche language, spoken in Guatemala, of which an old Spanish grammar is in manuscript in Sir G. Grey's library."

decay is but another name for laziness, for the effort—for effort it is—to save trouble in speaking; and it is the great principle of change in all languages. We can no longer talk of the interchange of letters, except loosely; sounds can only pass into one another in accordance with strict physiological laws, and the action of these is determined by the endeavour to facilitate pronunciation. *K*, the harder sound, may become *h*, but the reverse cannot take place unless other laws interfere. When, therefore, we find that an English *t* answers to a Greek *δ* and a German *z*, we cannot suppose that the more difficult *t* has been adopted instead of the easier *d*; and yet, to assume that the Gothic *t* has remained faithful to the original sound, while the *d* of Sanskrit, Greek, and Latin exhibits phonetic decay, would leave the High German *z* altogether unexplained. The only interpretation of the facts which is allowable is, that all these sounds have been independent differentiations of one original obscure sound which contained within itself the other clearer consonants; just as the meaning of the root-word has been gradually worked out, until the undeveloped conceptions that lay implicit in it have been severally marked off one from the other.[1]

[1] This primitive indistinctness of uttered sounds will not be sufficient, of course, to explain the phenomena of Grimm's law.

My friend Mr Sweet has come to the conclusion that primitive man could only roughly distinguish between sounds, just as he could only roughly distinguish between ideas and the relations of grammar. The belief is borne out by all the facts which we have at our disposal. The musical ear is as much the creation of a high civilisation as the eye of the painter; and the modern savage finds his music only in the rudest and coarsest high-pitched notes. It is naturally the same with phonetic speech. The appreciation of the delicate distinctions of sound which have resulted in poetry and music on the one hand, and in languages like Greek on the other, is unknown to the barbarian. The Sandwich Islander could not discover any difference between *c* and *t;* and when we rise higher in

Indeed, the mere fact that the Aryan family had arrived at a comparatively high stage of culture before the different branches of it separated from each other, shows that the speakers had left the root-period and its adjuncts far behind. Nevertheless, it has exercised a certain amount of influence upon the curious shifting of sounds which Grimm first pointed out, as in the case of *l* and *r:* the rest will be due to tribal idiosyncrasies, acted upon by climate and food, and assisted by the power of analogy. As for the original alphabet which is supposed to have been possessed by our remote ancestors, consisting of the letters *a*, *i*, *u*, *l*, or *r*, *n*, *m*, *h* (with *gh*, *dh*, and *bh*), *s*, *g*, *d*, *b*, *k* (*kw*), *t*, and *p*, it is, like the root-language, a logical, not an historical, starting-point. It is the result of the analysis and comparison of later forms of speech, and as little an historical reality as the *jus gentium* which the Romans believed they had arrived at by combining all that was alike in the laws and customs of existing nations and excluding the rest, or the "natural religion" of the divines of the last century.

the scale of civilisation, we see the Chinese transforming *Christ* into *Ki-li-sse-tu.*[1] The further back we push our phonological researches, the greater becomes the number of neutral sounds. Ancient Egyptian made no difference between *r* and *l*, and a comparison of roots would show that the same was the case in the parent-Aryan. Arguing from the alphabet, we should conclude that Sanskrit was once unable to distinguish between *b* and *v*, and Assyrian writes *m* and *v* with the same character. Finnish has but eleven consonants, and no Polynesian language more than ten; while some Australian dialects contain only eight with three variations.[2] All this would go far to show that the number of sounds possessed by early language was extremely small, and that these were mostly of a neutral, indistinct character, and what we should consider difficult to pronounce. A satisfactory explanation would thus be afforded, to a certain extent, of the phenomenon

[1] This inability of the Chinese to pronounce many of the consonants with which we are familiar is curiously illustrated by the strange transformations which Hindu names and words have undergone in the Chinese Buddhistic literature, and which formed such an obstacle to the interpretation of this until M. Stanislas Julien showed how Buddha had become Fo; Benares, Po-lo-nai; or Brahma, Fan. In contrast with the Chinese transformation of *r* into *l* is the Japanese transformation of *l* into *r*. According to Fabricius, the women in Greenland pronounce *k* at the end of words as *ng*, and *t* as *n*.

[2] Max Müller, "Science of Language," ii. 167.

before alluded to, the existence, namely, of roots in the Aryan family which differ in the final consonant or consonants, but which cannot be separated from one another, owing to their similarity of meaning, and the identity of their initial or characteristic sound. The same is yet more conspicuously the case in the Semitic group, where roots repeatedly occur which agree in signification, but have different letters, though of the same class. Thus קצץ, קסס, גזז, גזה, גזם, גזע, גזל, גזר, חדד, גדד, קדד, גדה, גוז, חצץ, חצה, קצע, קצר, כסח, כסם, חצה, all seem to contain the idea of "cutting," and little distinction can be made between נוד, נדד, and נדה.[1]

The root-period, therefore, was characterised by complexity, indistinctness, and vagueness in sound, meaning, and grammar. It was but a reflection of the hive-like community, in which the parts were as yet undistinguished, and the several factors of society lay undeveloped in a single embryonic germ. It was a life of the senses rather than of the mind, in which the past and the future were equally ignored, and language was employed in the service of the bodily wants, principally of hunger. Consequently we cannot expect to find any traces of spiritual and intellectual conceptions in this early stage of articulate

[1] Renan, "Histoire des Langues Sémitiques," pp. 96-99.

speech. The oldest roots are of the most purely sensuous description, and the words which denote the higher ideas of religion or mind are derived from these by the help of metaphor, metaphor itself having its basis in the object of sense. Thus in the Aryan family, Θεός Ζεύς, was "the bright" heaven, *anima* and *spiritus* are "the wind," and *soul* comes from "the heaving" of the sea. The Semitic *ruakh*, "the breath" of life, is simply the breeze, and *el*, "God," is "the strong" one. The numerals have been arrived at in the same way: *three* was originally "that which goes beyond" (root *tar*, *trans*, &c.), *four* was "(one) and three" (*cha-twar*), *nine* was the "new number" (*navam*).[1] Even the pronouns themselves may have a similar sensuous origin.

This brings me to the last *idolum* connected with the doctrine of roots to which I shall refer. It is generally known as the theory of Pronominal Roots, and assumes that language at its first starting possessed a large number of words which had a demonstrative meaning only, and formed a great part of the material of inflection. The theory is another result of the attempt to analyse

[1] The fact that the formation of these numerals belongs to the epithet-stage, *three* being named from its excess, or *seven* from its "following" (*saptan*, ἑπτά from ἕπω, *sequor*) the foregoing numbers, shows the comparatively late origin of the Aryan numerals.

flection by a comparison of the Aryan languages alone. We meet with certain roots, such as *ta, sa, ya,* which we cannot trace back to any other signification than that of the demonstrative pronoun. Because our data fail us, however, we are not justified in asserting that the demonstrative meaning was the original content of these roots. Our ignorance does not allow us to do more than affirm that these roots had a demonstrative signification so far back as we can go. But to suppose that such was their first and original force leads us into great difficulties. We may pass over the objection that the inventors of language would not have found such words mutually intelligible, as this might be explained by the instinctive uniformity of understanding which pervaded the beehive community; but how could the savage elaborate them without any idea of contrast? *Here* implies *there*, *this* implies *that*; but in the root-period, in the beehive life, all was *here* and all was *this*. This is the essential nature of words with the chaotic vagueness of meaning which we have seen characterised the so-called roots, as well as of a life of the senses, in which man is conscious of the passing moment only. Moreover, what need could there have been for such words, when the root contained within itself all the signification that could be expressed in speech, primarily denoting the individual object, and secondarily—since there was no idea of contrast, and so of distinction between the individual and the general—all individual objects? Any further specification that was required could not be pointed out in language; it called for the finger and the eye. If language starts with sentences, it cannot start with the demonstrative, which is not a sentence. But observed facts in other families of languages do not support the pronominal theory. In Japanese the same word may stand for all three persons; but this is not because it was primitively a demonstrative, but because it was a substantive, such as "servant," "worshipper," and so forth.[1] Chinese *ki*, "place," has become the

[1] See, too, Pott, "Die Ungleichheit menschlicher Rassen," pp. 5, 6, who remarks that even in German all possible pains are taken to avoid the use of the second person, and that where "*Er* and a feminine *Sie*" fail, recourse is had to the uncivilised method of denoting the personal pronoun by means of a substantive. The use of the simple pronoun belongs to the later era of culture, abstraction and simplification, and expressions like "Allerhöchstselbst" are a survival of barbarism. The Chinese scholar will say *ts'ie* ("the thief") instead of "I," and *tsián* ("bad") and *ling* ("noble") are used for "mine" and "thine" (Endlicher: "Chines. Grammatik," pp. 258-89). "The inhabitants of Ceylon," also, according to Adelung (Mithr. i. 233,) "have seven or eight words to denote the second personal pronoun." Cf. the ceremonial languages mentioned above, pp. 215, 216.

Wherever the pronoun has been successfully analysed, even in the inflectional languages, it has turned out to be an old substantive, which gradually came to lose what Mr Earle would term its presen-

relative, and the Semitic relative, whatever its derivation might be, was properly the demonstrative. It is the same with Malay and Siamese, which possess an extraordinary number of pronouns of the first and second persons, employed according to the rank or age of the speaker, but which are really so many substantives. A close similarity has been observed in many languages between the demonstrative and the substantive verb, and this again has in several instances been

tive meaning and to become merely symbolic, or what the Chinese call an "empty word." For English examples see Earle's "Philology of the English Tongue," 2d edit. p. 227 *sq.* The introduction of the pronominal-root theory into Semitic grammar has done much mischief, and the splendid philological labours of Ewald and Dillmann have a good deal to answer for in this respect. A more searching analysis, however, is revealing the true nature of those Semitic words whose origin and etymology have been solved by the easy hypothesis of "pronominal roots." Thus Praetorius (in the Z. D. M. G. xxvii. 4, 1873) has shown that the Ethiopic words *lălī* and *cīyā*, which when combined with suffixes express the nominative or accusative of the personal pronoun, and have been referred to "primitive demonstrative stems" by Dillmann, really signified originally "separation" and "entrails." I have myself been as guilty as any one in this matter, and have endeavoured in my "Assyrian Grammar" to explain the Assyrian *mala*, "as many as," by two pronominal roots. Dr Schrader, however, has demonstrated its derivation from *malā'*, "to fill," and thus vindicated its substantival character. Since we find that all those pronouns which can be successfully analysed are nothing more than worn-out substantives, we are justified in concluding that the assumption of a pronominal root is but another term for ignorance. "A word like the French *car*," says Mr Van Eys ("Dictionnaire Basque-Français," p. v.), "would pass for a root were we not acquainted with its etymology."

traced back to a sensuous origin. In the same direction points the formation of the demonstratives by a change of vowels, of which Mr Tylor has collected so many instances, and to which others might be added. Thus in Javanese *iki* is "this," *ika* "that," *iku* "that there;" in Japanese, *ko* is "here," *ka* "there;" in Zomba, *na* is "this," *ni* "that;" in Carib, *ne* is "thou," *ni* is "he;" in Brazilian Botocudo, *ati* is "I," *oti* is "thou;"[1] in (African) Tumali, *ngi* is "I," *ngo* "thou," and *ngu* "he." Such a distinction by phonetic means alone implies a late period of linguistic development; one of the forms must have preceded the other; and in this case there would have been no contrast, no *this* and *that*, and consequently no possibility of expressing the demonstrative. It is plain that substantives, and not pronominal words, would first have been differentiated in this way; and accordingly we find the Carib *baba*, "father," contrasted with *bibi*, "mother;" the Mantschu *chacha*, "man," and *ama*, "father," with *cheche*, "woman," and *eme*, "mother;" the Finnic *ukko*, "old man," with *akka*, "old woman;" and the African Eboe *nna*, "father," with *nne*, "mother," where a pretended pronominal root makes its appearance. Similarly the distinction between the primary numerals is denoted in

[1] Tylor, "Primitive Culture," vol. i. pp. 199-201.

the same manner in many languages; thus in Lushu, *tizi* is "one," *tazi*, "two;" "three" and "four" are *ngroka* and *ngraka* in Koriak, *niyokh* and *niyakh* in Kolyma, *gnasog* and *gnasag* in Karaga, and *tsúk* and *tsaak* in Kamtschatkan. But the expression of a grammatical relation by internal phonetic change clearly cannot belong to a period when the broadest differences of sound were confused together, and the utilisation of delicate vowel-distinctions to denote *nuances* of meaning was utterly unknown; and accordingly, we find not only the Aryan languages employing vocalic changes to represent verbal differences of signification only gradually and tardily, but even Semitic, in which internal vocalic change plays so large a part, has developed the three case terminations *-u*, *-i*, *-a* out of an original *a*, while the Bedouin even now pronounces his vowels so indistinctly that it is often impossible to say which vowel precisely is represented. In fact, the pronominal root theory is the product of the belief that the inflectional stage of Aryan was preceded by an agglutinative stage. Without the assumption of pronominal roots, which might mean anything or nothing, it was found impossible to explain many of the case-endings. But the matter seems but little mended when we lay down that the nominative and genitive singular as well as the plural number are all formed by means of the same pronominal suffix with the common signification of "that."[1]

There is one point connected with this subject of roots which must be touched upon before we finish the present chapter. The several members of the Aryan family, while agreeing in the main body of their roots, yet exhibit others which seem peculiar to each. Greek, Latin, Teutonic, each appear to possess a certain number of radicals which cannot be attached to roots found in the cognate languages without doing violence to all

[1] Professor Curtius endeavours to meet this difficulty by the assumption of different periods at which the nominative and genitive were struck out of the same colourless mould. I have already discussed his theory (p. 151), and have only to add here, that no explanation is afforded by it as to how it was to the same bare root or theme (stem) that the same suffix was attached with such astonishingly different results, or how the pronoun that had formed the chief cases of the singular could again pass through the same process of agglutination and forgetfulness, and then turn out a plural! Jacob Grimm ("Ueber Etymologie und Sprachvergleichung," *Kl. Schrift.* i. 312), while accepting the doctrine of pronominal roots as existing during the assumed period of "flection-building," yet asserted their ultimate identity with concept or verbal roots. He has been followed in this view by Schleicher ("Compendium," p. 642, 2d edit.) and Benfey, who would have the pronouns to be verbal radicals. But such a theory gets rid of only half the difficulty—the impossibility of conceiving how a "pronominal root" came into existence, and the fact that modern dialects, which admit us to some of the secrets of language-making, derive the pronouns from old substantives. How themes and flections were created by these empty shadows of forgotten substantives is still left unexplained.

the laws of the change and development of signification. There are many words the etymology of which can never be settled by Glottology, or, to speak more accurately, which refuse to be compared with allied words in other dialects. To attempt to discover a derivation for every word in the Greek Lexicon will only end in error and discomfiture. We seem forced to conclude that the different branches of our race have, beside their common stock of roots, others of native and peculiar origin and growth. The residuum of unconnected roots which scientific philology leaves in each Indo-European language is an evidence that language is still living, is still the outward expression of an active progressive society. Literature and civilisation will do much to restrain that unbounded license of striking out new words which distinguishes the idioms of savage tribes; but our own age and country will still produce such inventions as *absquatulate* and *swoggle*, which cannot be reduced to any common Aryan radical. They have come into the world fully formed, however much they may contain sounds similar to those in words of like meaning; and this single fact is a striking commentary upon the belief that our ancestors once spoke a language of roots. The root is the unconsciously conceived mental block, as it were, out of which our words are shaped; but to imagine that it was ever consciously realised in speech by a race which was afterwards to evolve inflection by some unexplained means, is not only improbable, but opposed to the data before us. As Professor Pott has said[1]—"There is no inward necessity why roots should first have entered into the reality of language, naked and formless; it suffices that, unpronounced, they fluttered before the soul like small images, continually clothed in the mouth, now with this, now with that form, and surrendered to the air to be drafted off in hundred-fold cases and combinations."

[1] As quoted by Professor Max Müller, "Lectures," second series, p. 85.

# CHAPTER VII.

## THE METAPHYSICS OF LANGUAGE.

THE term "Metaphysics of Language" has not been very happily chosen. It can only be defended upon the ground that pure being and pure thought are identical, and that the generalisations which sum up the several phenomena introduce a mental element foreign to the phenomena themselves, and may therefore be considered to partake of a metaphysical character. From this point of view all scientific laws will be more or less metaphysical; and we can hardly refuse this title to such transcendental conceptions as that of *force*. A conception like this has nothing answering to it in material nature. We see certain phenomena happening cotemporaneously or in succession, and we imagine a bond or power of which these are the result and manifestation, and to which we give the name of *force*. Yet, after all, this power is merely a mental product which we project into the world of the senses. Similarly the fundamental postulates of mathematics pass beyond the reach of direct experience. We know very well that, so far as our experience has extended, when we place two things by the side of two other things we have four objects before us; but what that conception of four is in itself is a matter of which the senses alone cannot inform us. There are some tribes who cannot count beyond three, or rather, are unable to generalise so far as four. What numbers are in themselves, what they mean and how they originate, or whether they are universally true, are metaphysical questions. However much their verification may belong to observation and experiment, the radical ideas of number generally and of the numbers specifically fall under the sphere of metaphysics. The metaphysics of language, accordingly, will be those general mental conceptions which underlie the phenomena of articulate speech, and to which an induction of the latter will conduct us. Thus we shall have to place under this head all inquiries into the origin and nature of gender or of declension, the nature of these in an historical science necessarily implying a knowledge of their origin. Such inquiries are no new thing. From the days of Plato's Kratylus downward attempts have been made to solve the obvious questions raised by a consideration of language. The Greek disputed as to whether language originated by convention (νόμῳ) or by nature (φύσει), and according to the system of philosophy he adopted, ranged himself on either side. The modern form of the discussion would be whether or not the relations of grammar, along with the words which expressed them, grew up spontaneously and instinctively, or were settled by an arbitrary compact among the first men? or, in other words, whether grammar is an invented art or the necessary development of mind? I say grammar, and not vocabulary, because although it was the single word which at first sight seems to have attracted Greek speculation, it was really the relation of the word to the mind and the grammatical fulness of meaning which was implicit in it. The word was regarded from the side of its content, and not of its outward form; and this perhaps was inevitable when the native language alone was known, and education was oral rather than literary. The attention is not so likely to be centred upon the external sound of words until they are written down and analysed into syllables and letters. Hence it is not surprising that the early speculations into the character of articulate speech did not result in a formal grammar until the Greek language had been brought into collision with the Latin, and the critical era of Alexandria had succeeded to the old political life of Greece. A regular grammar begins with Dionysius Thrax, who utilised the philological lucubrations of Aristotle and the Alexandrian critics for the sake of teaching Greek to the sons of the aristocratic cotemporaries of Pompey at Rome. Before his time, the Sophists, notably Prodikus, had made a rough classification of the principal parts of speech for the purposes of oratorical study; but without the contrast afforded by another language, these classifications could not but remain confused with rhetoric, and devoid of all method and thoroughgoing arrangement. Indeed it is hard to understand how any real analysis of a language can be made unless the idea has been suggested by the comparison of another: the grammatical labours of the Assyrian scribes in the time of Sardanapalus, and of Chayyug and his cotemporaries in the tenth century, were due to a necessary knowledge in the one case of Accadian, and in the other of Arabic; and it is very possible that the Sanskrit grammarians were excited to their work by the native dialects, which had been quickened into activity and raised to the level of respectability by the spread of Buddhism.

The elaboration of a methodical grammar brought about a more definite treatment of those speculations into the nature of language which had before been current. With a system of rules to which every one was obliged to conform, the belief in the conventional origin of grammar became more and more prevalent. Thus, in the noun, the nominative was regarded as the typical, fundamental case, from which the oblique cases were so many "fallings," *casus* (πτώσεις), so that the whole internal relation of the inflected noun became a declension. It had declined, fallen off, from its primitive correct form and meaning. In this way a systematic theory of the origin and nature of the cases was tacitly assumed, which fitted in well with the philosophic creed of the last century, when society was explained by a social contract and religion by interested artifice. It was easy enough to furnish an answer to any questions that might be asked regarding the primary meaning of the relations of grammar: the thoughts and feelings of the eighteenth century were transferred to the first men, and ready explanations were given in accordance with the arbitrary philosophy of each "illuminated" savan. This *à priori* mode of going to work, however, is more easy than satisfactory. We have no more reason for accepting the opinion of one thinker, based upon a hasty review of certain selected phenomena, than that of another; what we require is the generalisation obtained from a conscientious *à posteriori* induction in accordance with the slow critical comparative method of science. Our generalisations, transcendental as they may be, must be the final result of a careful survey of all the phenomena which are at our disposal. If we would get at a settlement of the various questions raised by grammar, such as what is gender or what is declension, we must set to work with our available materials, first reducing the different parts of grammar into their original form, so far as is possible, and then by the help of comparison determining what was the meaning implied by these original forms.

One point, however, we must not overlook. The analysis of the material is not the same as the analysis of the mental. All that we can do is to penetrate to the earliest marks of thought, the most primitive utterances of society, and infer from these outward symbols the view of the world and the condition of the mind which so expressed itself. It is not the symbol that we want to discover; it is what that symbol stands for. To mistake the symbol for the symbolised is the error of those who would develop the inward out of the mechanical, and find a ready explanation for the various relations of grammar in the accidents of phonetic decay. But between the two there is a gulf which cannot be passed. The conception of the dative case, for instance, was intellectual, not formative, in its origin. It was evolved out of the developing thought, not out of an accidental difference of sounds. All that the outward symbol can do is to *assist* developing thought by means of association. The symbol recalls to the mind a certain idea, and the likeness between two symbols will suggest a likeness between the two ideas which they severally represent. The Latin *sestertiûm* was originally the contracted genitive plural of *sestertius;* but the termination *-um* called up the idea of a neuter nominative of the second declension, and hence arose the new substantive *sestertium, sestertii.* But no previously-unknown idea was struck out by this; the conception which answered to the termination *um* already existed, and by the very nature of the case necessarily existed. A rightly conducted investigation into the metaphysics of language can only lead us back to the oldest symbols of thought; the thought which lies behind these most be reached by an application of the general principle of the uniformity of intellectual action at all times and in all places.

We may take, by way of illustration, the question of gender. What, we may ask, was the source and primary signification of the sexual relation of nouns? It cannot have been a primitive necessity of speech, since there are many languages which altogether want it: and some of these, like the Chinese or the Accadian, belonged to races that have taken high rank in the history of civilisation. The theory, therefore, that would account for gender by assuming that our first ancestors so far confused subject and object as to impose the conditions of the former on the latter, fails to satisfy all the facts. Besides, this confusion lay not so much upon the side of the subject as upon that of the object; the primitive savage was overpowered by outward nature, and immersed, as it were, in nature, not the converse. The objective case of the personal pronoun is older than the subjective; indeed, the subjective element in human consciousness and speech is only slowly and gradually evolved. Even in fetichism, the object retains all its characteristics, the subject merely imparting to it the vaguest possession of power; and the worship of dead ancestors is far from being a step in advance. Gender could only originate, according to the theory, in the transference of the characteristics of the subject to the object, and this implies at once awakened consciousness and quick imagination. In this case, however, we should expect to find the existence of genders rather among the pioneers of Asiatic civilisation than among the rude forefathers of the Slavonic tribes. The theory fares the usual fate of *à priori* attempts at explanation; and Grimm's suggestion, that gender was a kind of delicate insight into the distinction between things, has no better fortune. In actual fact, we do not find any delicate insight into nature in the modern barbarian; and the endeavour to explain the phenomena of language as the results of spontaneous growth and instinctive apprehension is nothing more than to state the problem in new words. All such unverified hypotheses are shipwrecked at once as soon as we consider that, whereas there are three genders in the Aryan group, and eight in the Nama Hottentot dialect, Semitic and old Egyptian have but two, while what Bleek calls the prefix-pronominal languages of South Africa possess a large number of genders, in one instance as many as eighteen. This curious circumstance gives us the clue to the origin of gender, and Bleek has accordingly put forward a theory which is based upon an inductive comparison of phenomena, and fully accounts for all the known facts.[1] He believes that the nouns, when combined with pronominal suffixes, which were originally nothing more than explanatory substantives, could be replaced by their corre-

[1] See his paper on "Concord, the Origin of the Pronouns, and the Formation of Classes or Genders of Nouns," in the *Journal of the Anthropological Institute*, i. 1872.

sponding pronouns, and these determined what we call the gender. Thus, masculine, feminine, and neuter were primarily only so many different pronouns, each of which appropriated a class of substantives that custom had amalgamated with the same, or allied, pronominal suffixes. The prefix-pronominal languages of Africa admitted a larger number of combined and separate pronouns than the Aryan group, and consequently the number of genders possessed by them is larger than is the case with our European dialects, Kafir having no less than thirteen classes of nouns, and one dialect as many as eighteen. In the Semitic verbs, a difference of gender is plainly expressed by a difference in the constitutive pronouns, as may be illustrated by such examples as the Ethiopic *gabar-ca*, *gabar-ci*, "thou art strong," masculine and feminine, or the Hebrew *k'dhal-tem k'dhal-ten*, "ye are killing;" and the absence of gender in the agglutinative and isolating languages, which do not make use of formative pronominal suffixes may be accounted for by the want of these derivative elements. Indeed, the exceptions to this which have been detected in a few of these languages by Castrén and Schott unmistakably confirm such a view. A feminine ending in *-a* occurs among the Kottes, and another in *-m* among the Yenisei-Ostiaks (among whom also *fun*, "daughter," stands by the side of *fup*, "son"). Now this *-a* or *-m* is simply *am*, "mother," just as in Accadian "daughter" was denoted by *sal-tur*, literally "woman-son." So in Tibetan the masculine termination *-pa*, *-po*, *-pho*, *-bo*, is the word which means "father," and the feminine suffix *-ma* or *-mo* is "mother."[1] In these cases the primitive substantives have not yet become mere pronominal suffixes. Such, however, must have been the origin of all these suffixes, for even in the Aryan family the theory of pronominal roots rests on a foundation of sand.

Upon the hypothesis, however, as Bleek puts it forward, two cases formed with different pronominal elements like the nominative and accusative would require to be assigned to two different genders. Moreover, we should expect the Aryan verbs as well as the Semitic to exhibit a distinction of gender, and the Turanian idioms ought to distinguish to some extent between the personal pronouns, however genderless their substantives may be. Man and woman, for instance, or animate and inanimate, ought not to be represented by one and the same personal pronoun, any more than the first personal pronoun in Semitic by the same

[1] In the Sonorian dialects of America, gender can only be denoted by the addition of words which signify "man" and "woman" (Buschmann, Abhandlung. d. Berlin. Akademie, 1869, i. 103).

form.[1] This is all the more requisite, in so far as these pronouns are old forgotten nouns. Bleek's theory, therefore, must be modified: satisfactory as it is in its main features, I should prefer to state it in the following way:—Out of the endless variety of words that might have been set apart to denote the personal and demonstrative pronouns, common use selected a certain number; each of these, through habit, euphony, or affinity of sense or sound, was associated with an ever-increasingly specified class of nouns, and where the pronouns continued different, the classes of substantives connected with them continued different also. Thus in Zulu the pronominal *bu* has ceased to have any meaning of its own; but it is employed to form abstracts such as *u-bu-kosi*, "a kingdom," and may be used alone like a pronoun to represent these, just as though we were to use *dom* to represent the whole class of words with which *dom*, *e.g.*, *kingdom*, is compounded, saying, for instance, "the *dom* of England." The classes of nouns so created perpetually tended to become more defined and numerous. The Aryan languages rarely show us that uncertain wavering between

[1] The Haussa has developed a distinction between the genders of this pronoun. Besides *ka* and *ki* for the second person, and *shi*, *ya*, *sa*, for "he," "him," *ta*, *ita*, *tai*, "she," "her," we have *ina* masculine, and *nia* and *ta* feminine, for "I" and "me" (Schön. Vocab. of Haussa Lang., p. 13).

two genders, that is, the substitution of two different pronouns, which we so often find in Semitic; and where the majority of words with a common termination were of a certain gender, all other words with the same ending were referred to the same gender. We see the process arrested in an early stage of growth in such idioms as the Moxa and Abiponian, in which a large number of common words have inseparable pronoun prefixes not unlike the Hebrew use of אדני, or the (Taic) Kuki numeral affix *ka* and prefix *pa*. Indeed, these numeral suffixes can be shown to have the same origin and intention as the pronominal suffixes of South Africa, although the final result of creating classes of nouns distinguished by what we call gender has not been so perfectly attained. Thus, in Burmese, the numeral termination changes according to the object numbered, "two men" being *lu nhit-yauk;* "two fowls," *kyet nhit-gaung;* "two pagodas," *tsadi nhit-chu;* in Mikir, *bang* is prefixed when individuals are enumerated, *jon* when inferior animals, *hong* and *pap* when inanimate objects; and in Malay, *êkor*, "tail," has to be added to the numeral whenever cattle are spoken of, as *sa-êkor kerra,* instead of *sa kerra,* "one monkey." Further advanced on the road to gender is the phenomenon that meets us in the Tshetsh language in the Caucasus, where adjectives and the substantive verb change their initial letter after certain substantives: *e.g.*, *hatxleen* WA means "the prophet is;" *hatxleen* BA, "the prophets are;" *waso* WA, "the brother is;" *wasar* BA, "the brothers are."[1] The change here must be ascribed to the attempt to substitute for class-grouping by the help of independent suffixed words, class-grouping by means of phonetic distinction only; sound rather than sense has been the principle at work. We find the same mode of procedure in the Wolof article, the initial of which has to be altered so as to correspond with whatever is the first consonant of its noun. Possibly, the way to this was led by the use as articles of various separate substantives which began with different letters; and when once the ear had become accustomed to a consonantal harmony between the article and the majority of nouns to which it was joined, and the original independent meaning of the words employed for it had been forgotten, nothing would have been easier than to extend the harmony to all instances, and establish the general rule that the article and its noun must commence with the same consonant. Such, at least, was the case on a small scale in old Egyptian. Here the sign of the feminine was the affixed *t*, the universal Semitic feminine ending.

[1] See Shiefner's "Versuch über die Thusch-Sprache."

When the definite article in the singular was used with this, it required the form *ta*—plainly a repetition of itself—in place of the masculine form *pa*. This change of form is what we call gender; whereas it was really an attempt to mark out the substantive more definitely by guarding it, as it were, with the same suffixed noun set at the beginning and at the end. It was thus separated from the rest of the sentence, and proved the yet living consciousness of the origin and force of the feminine termination. Gender, consequently, is by no means engrained in the nature of things. It is a secondary accident of speech, ornamental, perhaps, from an æsthetic point of view, but practically highly detrimental: and it is curious that modern English has, in this, as in so much else, gone back to the simple beginnings of the sexual relations, and distinguishes gender only by means of the corresponding pronouns. It is true that the return is but apparent; we can never get rid of our intervening history; and whereas gender started from transferring the differences between the pronouns to the substantives associated with them, we now transfer the inherited differences of meaning in the substantives to their representative pronouns.

An examination of the available data of Glottology has thus led us by the *à posteriori* road to the original conception which lies at the bottom of gender. It is meagre enough, and very unlike the magnificent poetic insight which *à priori* theories have attributed to our remote forefathers. Let us now see whether we can ascertain, by a similar method of procedure, what was the germinal notion that has resulted in the formation of a plural number. Nothing seems to us more natural, nay, more necessary, than the existence of the plural; we might suppose that its roots go deep down into the very beginnings of language; and yet there are two facts which militate most clearly and decisively against such an opinion. The first fact is the extended employment of a dual. All over the globe, in Aryan, in Semitic, in Turanian, in Hottentot, in Australian, we meet with a dual both in substantives and in the verbs, though the dual becomes more and more disused with the progress of culture and the increased use of the plural. Now, it is plain that there must have been a very good reason for this dual, which seems to us so utterly superfluous, and it is also evident that there was a time when the idea of plurality did not comprehend the idea of duality as well; and yet "two" is the first plural conception to which we can attain. The second fact to which I have alluded is the later formation of the numbers after "two" in so many languages. In our own Aryan group, *three, tres, tri*, has the same root as the Latin *trans*, our *through*, Sanskrit *tar-âmi*, and simply means "going beyond." Our earliest predecessors, accordingly, must have exhausted their power of definite numeration at "two," and have regarded all beyond that as a vague, indefinite, and therefore unintelligible series. Observation of actually existing savage races affords abundant illustration of this. The aborigines of Victoria, according to Mr Stanbridge, "have no name for numerals above two;"[1] the Puris of South America call "three" *prica* or "many" and "the New Hollanders," says Mr Oldfield (of the western tribes), "have no names for numbers beyond *two*."[2] Some of these, it is true, can now count on their fingers as high as "five," or even higher; but the acquisition of this power has been too recent to have impressed itself as yet upon the language. All this goes to show that the conception of plurality was not part of the primary stock-in-trade of mankind, and that the plural was preceded by the dual. Other facts may be added in support of this. The group of African languages which are termed Khamitic by M. d'Abbadie want a plural

[1] *Transactions of Ethnological Society*, i. 304.

[2] Quoted in Mr Tylor's instructive chapter on "The Art of Counting," in "Primitive Culture," vol. i. pp. 218-46.

in the substantives altogether; and the Amara can only say *fŭrŭsn ayŭhu*, "I have seen horse," leaving it to a future question to decide whether horse is one or many.[1] In Accadian, again, the pronoun *bi* is indifferently "he" and "they;" and as the formative affixes are appended to the whole series of words to which they refer, the plural sign is attached to the adjective only when an adjective is conjoined with a substantive, as in *dimir gal-galene*, "the great gods," *dimirri-ene* being "gods" when used alone.[2] In the case of the Khamitic idioms, it is difficult to ascribe the want of a plural to phonetic decay, as in our own "sheep," since the defect extends throughout the nouns; much less to the influence of Semitic neighbours

[1] In the Sonorian languages of America, according to Buschmann ("Abhandlungen d. Berliner Akad.," 1869, i. 122), "the simple word in the singular serves also for the plural." This is the most customary usage of the Cahita, where *mama* means "hand" and "hands;" *oou*, "man" and "men." Similarly in Tepeguana, *novi* is "hand" and "hands;" *yuyupa*, "star" and "stars." So, too, Gallatin ("Trans. of the Amer. Ethnol. Soc.," i. p. 287) says of the monosyllabic Othomi, that its nouns are altogether indeclinable. The plural is generally distinguished from the singular by the prefixed article, *na* in the singular, *ya* in the plural; both being our article "the." *Ye* means "hand;" *na ye* "the hand," *ya ye*, "the hands." The plural is also sometimes expressed by substituting the particle *e* for *ya*.

[2] M. d'Abbadie has drawn my attention to the fact that this is exactly paralleled by the Basque *yaun handi-ek* ("the great lords"), "the adjective being likewise postfixed, and taking up alone the plural article (*ak*)."

who had substituted collectives, or broken plurals as they are commonly called, for the original plural forms. A slight advance upon this utter powerlessness of passing beyond the singular in thought is the formation of the plural of the personal pronouns in the Tumali of Africa. Here the pronouns *ngi*, "I," *ngo*, "thou," and *ngu*, "he," which are distinguished from one another only by a modification of the vowel, are changed into plurals by the addition of the postposition *da*, "with." Hence we get *ngi-n-de*, "we," *ngo-n-da*, "ye," and *nge-n-da*, "they." It will be noticed that phenomena which approach inflection are met with here, in the insertion of the fulcrum nasal and the vocalic mutation in the first and third persons; but there is still no clear consciousness of anything except the singular number: the second factor, which ought to be coupled by the postposition, is left a mere blank, reminding us of those savage tribes who can only denote the relations of the verb by accompanying a word with significant gestures. But not only do we meet with languages which do not possess any plural forms, we also find many others in which the formal expression of plurality has never passed beyond that of dualism. In the language of the Bushmen, the plurals are throughout formed by reduplication; and this is but one way of saying that the doubling of a thing is the furthest point of multiplicity to which the mind of the speaker can attain. To repeat a word in order to express the idea of more than one, is to identify plurality with duality, and to imply the priority of the latter. And nearly all our evidence makes for the belief that the formation of the plural by this means is one of the oldest contrivances of language. Thus the Accadian was still able to form plurals in this way, as in *kur-kur* or *kur-kurra*, "the mountains," though he preferred to do so by the help of the postfixes *mes* ("many") and *ene*. Canarese even now makes use of reduplication to create collectives, and the Basque preposition *zaz* shows traces of the same process; so in Malay *raja-raja* is "princes," and *orang-orang*, "people."[1] The idea of the superlative, as an intensification and increase of the visible individual qualities, cannot be

[1] The Tepeguana uses several kinds of reduplication to express the plural. (1.) The simple word is doubled, as in *du*, "mother," pl. "*duddu*;" *qui*, "house," pl. "*quiqui*." (2.) The first syllable only is repeated, as in *naxa*, "car," pl. *nanaxa*; *tara*, "foot," pl. *tatara*. (3.) This repetition is accompanied by a change of the consonant, as in *buy* or *vui*, "eye," pl. *vupui*; *voca*, "stomach," pl. *voppoca*. (4.) An initial vowel is reduplicated, as in *ali*, "child," pl. *aali*; *ogga*, "father," pl. *oogga*; *ubi*, "woman," pl. *uubi*. (5.) The second syllable of the word is doubled, as in *alguli*, "boy," pl. *aliguguli*; *mavidi*, "lion," pl. *mavipidi*. (6.) A vowel in the middle of the word is repeated, as in *him*, "gourd," pl. *hiim*; *gogosi*, "dog," pl. *googosi*; *alali*, "boy," pl. *alaali*. (7.) A *v* or *b* in the middle of a word is changed into *p*—"an echo of the reduplication,"—as in *cavaio*, "horse," pl. *càpaio* (Buschmann, *loc. cit.*).

separated from that of plurality; and superlatives are made by reduplication from the Mandingo *ding-ding*, "a very little child," to the Accadian *galgal*, "very great." It does not appear, however, that the specific conception of duality was the one most prominent in this primitive expedient of speech. When we consider how often reduplication is used simply to intensify the imitation of natural sounds, and to denote their continuousness, as in the Dayak *kaká-kaka*, "to go on laughing loud," or the Tamil *muru-muru*, "to murmur," or to express the length and continuity of an action, as in the reduplicated Aryan perfect, we are inclined to believe that the contrivance of reduplication was adopted by language before it had arrived at a clear idea of duality, and while it was still struggling to pass from the single individual to a more general concept. The most obvious means of expressing this vague endeavour was the repetition of sounds; and when once thought had thus made itself objective in articulate speech, it was comparatively easy to acquire a clear and distinct conception of duality and separation. Before this, all beyond *one* would have presented itself as a misty and indefinite repetition of one. In this case reduplicated plurals would once have represented, not merely an indistinct amplification of the individual, but a definite idea of two individuals, and the further extension of this to denote the plural only shows the poverty of invention among those races who have retained the primitive dual form to express the plural.

In some of the North American languages, we may actually see the process going on, whereby the conception of duality, when once clearly defined, extended itself to that of plurality. In Cherokee, the dual of the first person is divided into two, the first of which is used when one of two persons speaks *to* the other; the second, when the one speaks *of* the other to a third. Thus *inaluiha* is "we two (*i.e.*, thou and I) are tying it;" *awstaluiha*, "we two (*i.e.*, he and I) are tying it." Here the idea of the limitation of the dual on the side of plurality has been distinctly attained. The process is to be observed still more plainly in the Papuan dialects, in which the personal pronouns possess not only a trinal form, but also exclusive and inclusive forms. In Annatom, for instance, *ainyak* is "I;" *akaijan*, "you two + I;" *ajumrau*, "you two − I;" *akataij*, "you three + I," *aijumtaij*, "you three − I;" *akaija*, "you + I;" *aijama*, "you − I." So in Mallicollo, *inau* is "I;" *khai-im* "you," and *na-ü*, "he," while *na-mühl* is "we two, exclusive of others;" *drivan*, "we two, inclusive of others;" *kha-mūhl*, "you two;" *na-tarsi*, "you three;" *dra-tin*, "we three;" and the specification of number actually rises as high as four, *na-tavatz* being "you four," and *dra-tovatz*, "we four." It is difficult to understand how a people could have reached the point of setting apart a special form to denote the number four, and should yet have not made what seems so short a step in advance, and attained the notion of plurality. The abstracting and generalising faculty was wanting, and the speaker was still unable to get beyond the individual object of sense. It is evident, however, that *tovatz* or *tavatz* must be merely the numeral "four," which is tacked on to the singular personal pronoun, just as in the Taic languages a plural numeral is attached to a singular noun; the Burmese *lu nhit-yauk*, "two men," for example, meaning literally "man two." Perhaps we may compare our own "ten foot," "ten stone," like the Hebrew use of the tens from 20 to 90 with the singular, as in *'esrim 'ir*, "twenty cities;" or the employment of collectives, which may be regarded, from one point of view, as a survival of the inability of primitive man to conceive the plural. The collective sums up under a single head the idea of plurality, and thus embodies the last result of generalisation and classification; whereas the primeval noun, like the primeval sentence, was unable to reach the simplest classification, and so was obliged to enumerate each separate individual, although, owing to this very incapacity to generalise, the universal lay implicit in the noun, waiting to be developed out of it when the time came. We cannot correctly call it a singular, because there was no plural: no singular existed until the idea of a dual was struck out.

We may even call in the aid of *à priori* arguments, whatever these may be worth, in support of the view that the dual is older than the plural. So long as men lived in the primeval beehive community, there was no need of any clear expression of multiplicity. As the individual, however, emerged from this early state, he would arrive at more definite ideas of number; one necessarily implies two, and the immediate wants of a savage life would often require the employment of language. But these wants were circumscribed, and the primitive barbarian, like modern savages, would have been extremely chary in his use of words. His simple necessities would easily be satisfied by a single neighbour; and time would elapse before the isolated nomad came to mix freely with a large circle of human beings. Primarily, therefore, his requests would be addressed to one other person only, and the dual accordingly would suffice for all his wants. Consequently we are not astonished at finding that analysis has been supposed to teach us that the Aryan plural *asma* is compounded of *ma* + *sma*, "I and he," and not "I and they," *tusma* (whence Sanskrit *yushmâ*, with the insertion of the semi-vowel and the subsequent loss of the dental) being similarly "thou and he." In this way, moreover, we can alone account for the existence and persistency of a dual, which seems so superfluous by the side of a plural; with the latter already in use it is hard to understand the elaboration of the former.

The priority of the dual, however, is contrary to the opinion which makes the dual in Aryan and Semitic merely a lengthened form of the plural. The Aryan plural is formed by a postfixed *s*, which has been compared with the preposition *sam*, *sahâ*, and the *s* of the singular nominative and genitive, as if there were any compatibility between these, or no difference between a preposition and a post-position. Now it is no doubt tempting to regard the dual as an amplification of the plural forms; but a few words will show clearly how improbable this really is. In the first place, the assumption of an uniform plural in *s* in the parent speech cannot be sustained by the side of the second declension in Greek and Latin, or of neuter bases in *i* and *u* in Sanskrit, where the nominatives do not exhibit any vestiges of an original sibilant. Then, secondly, however easy it may be to get the dual *sâs* out of the plural *sas*, it is absolutely impossible to get at once *sâs* and *aus* out of *ams*, the old accusative plural, and *sâms*, the genitive plural. Moreover, we may ask what warrant we have for postulating the change of *m* into *v* and *u* in the parent Aryan? So far as our data go, it is unheard of. And if we grant the possibility of a transformation of *sâms* into *aus*, how comes *swâs*, the conjectural pattern-form of the plural locative, also to become *aus*? This, indeed, is to presuppose the desperate expedient of a metathesis, which is contra-indicated by the usual loss of the final syllable in the Sanskrit *-su*. But the last difficulty is the greatest of all. The dative and ablative plural in *-bhyams* may readily become *bhyâms* in the dual; but unfortunately the instrumental dual has exactly the same form, while the instrumental plural, though derived from the same formative, *bhi*, is not *bhyams*, but *bhis*. The most stout-hearted philologist will find it hard to extract the same phonetic result out of a lengthening of *bhyams* and *bhis*. The fact, however, suggests another explanation. It is undeniable that *bhyâms* and *bhyams*, whence come the Sanskrit *-bhyas*, the Latin *-bus*, the Gothic *-m*, and the old Norse *-um*, are closely connected with one another; but both, as has been said in a former chapter, are derived from the post-preposition *bhi*,[1] and must have been applied to their present purpose during the period which falls within the province of Glottology; consequently they do not belong to the original flection of the Aryan noun. *Bhis* is also taken from the same independent root, and it is very probable that both *bhyams* and *bhis* existed as separate plurals, the first as an accusative, and the second as a locative (for *bhins*), before they were attached to other vocables,[2] We are here dealing with an instance that is altogether different from that of flection proper, where the inflections cannot be separated from the noun in which they inhere, and show no signs of having ever been independent roots. Now if *bhyâms* forms the dative, ablative, and instrumental in the dual, while *bhyams* performs this office only for the dative and the ablative in the plural, the instrumental being denoted by *bhis*, the simplest mode of explaining the relation of the two is to assume the prior existence of the dual, the plural not coming into general use before a further differentiation of cases had taken place. When the plural of these cases first became fixed, the instrumental had already been separated off from the dative and the ablative. Why the vowel of the dual should be

[1] *Abhi* would be the instrumental of an old noun, *a* or *â*.

[2] This is indicated in the Rig-Veda by the non-operation of the laws of Sandhi, as in the instrumental *marut bhis* instead of *marud-bhis*. See, however, Appendix II.

longer than that of the plural may perhaps be learned from a consideration of the Semitic languages. In these, while the Hebrew plural was *-īm* (from *-am*), the Aramaic *-īn* and the Arabic *-ūna*, the dual in these dialects was respectively *-áim*, *-ain*, and *-áni* or *-aini*. So, too, in Assyrian, the dual ended in *-ā*, the usual masculine plural being in *-i*. Now a comparison of the Semitic languages leads us to the conclusion that the plural primarily terminated in *-āmū*, so that the original dual was probably *-a'amu*, which expressed the reduplication of the object by the long-continued repetition of the pure primary vowel. A close analogy to this may be found in the idiom of the Aponegricans, in which "six" is *ita-wuna*, and "seven" *itawu-ú-una*: the same principle is at work in the extension of *ouatou*, "a stream," among the Botocudos of Brazil, into *ouatou-ou-ou-ou*, "ocean," or the Madagascar lengthening of *ra-a-atchi*, "very bad," from *ratchi* "bad." If the repetition of the primary vowel in Semitic, therefore, with the mimmation sounded after it (as in the singular), was intended to represent the double character of the object, the dual would have been formed upon the singular, not upon the plural, and the latter would rather be a contraction of it, the vowel being contracted in so far as the idea expressed by the plural was less definite than that expressed by the dual. The final case-ending *-u* would have been copied from the singular.

From the numbers we naturally pass on to the cases. These, as their name implies, are regarded as so many fallings-off from the *casus rectus*, or nominative, which is held to be the typical form of the noun. This view, however, which is really based on the logical analysis of a developed grammar, is not borne out by scientific investigation. The "naming" case of the noun, whose title to the name of case was itself disputed, seems after all to be a later addition to nominal declension. Everything seems to point to the accusative or objective case as the most primitive form of the noun. This is clearly patent in Semitic, where the so-called case-ending in *-a* has been retained in Ethiopic, Arabic, Assyrian, and apparently Hebrew, to mark the accusative, the later modifications of this original sound having been appropriated to create the nominative in *-u* and the genitive in *-i*. So, again, in Aryan the objective *mâ* "me," is still found as accusative in Sanskrit, while its priority is shown, not only by the verbal termination in *-mi*, but yet more by the compounded form of the nominative Sanskrit, *aham*, Greek ἐγὼν, Latin *ego*, Gothic *ik*. Whether or not this is made up of *ma*, which has first become *va* (as in the dual and plural of Sanskrit and Teutonic), and then been dropped altogether, and *ga*, an emphatic enclitic, which has given birth to the Vedic *gha* and the Greek γε, at all events ἐγὼν is a less simple and ancient form than με. It has been aptly remarked, that this is only in accordance with the ordinary facts of infantile life. The child says "Charley does this or that," before he learns to say "I do this or that." The existence of neuters, the nominatives of which end in *-m*, points in the same direction. Here the idea of life, and therefore of subjectivity, is put out of sight, and consequently the conception of objectivity has been so fixed in them, that when other classes of things came to be conceived as capable of originating actions, and were therefore assigned a particular flection when regarded in this way, the neuters were relegated to a class by themselves, and preserved the old common termination for what now became divided into nominative and accusative. The outward form kept up a recollection of that primitive state of things in which man still regarded himself, and all about him, as objects, and had not yet realised that he was a subject, and the originator of action, still less had projected this power into the objects about him. The agglutinative languages made no distinction between the nominative and accusative, thus reflecting, as in so much else, the early condition of human intelligence and speech.

Next to these cases, the most important part of the noun-declension is the genitive. But the relation which we express by this must originally have been but imperfectly, if at all, comprehended, if we are to judge from the grammatical phenomena of the agglutinative tongues. Thus in Accadian the relation of genitive and governing noun was primarily denoted merely by placing the former after the latter, as is still the case with Taic and Malay; and it was only gradually that this simple method came to be supplanted by the suffixing of words like *lal*, "filling," and *da*, "side of," to the second noun. Here, then, the relation would seem to be nothing more than what we term "apposition," that is, where two individual notions are placed side by side without any further effort being made by the mind to determine their exact relations beyond the mere fact that one precedes the other, and is therefore thought of first. Hence we may say that there was a time when the genitive, as such, did not exist, and we have to discover, as far as is possible, how it came into being. Now we are all well acquainted with the distinction between what is called the objective genitive, where the governed word is the object of the other (as in *amor Socratis*, "love felt for Socrates"), and the subjective genitive, where the reverse takes place (as in *Socratis amor*, "love felt by Socrates"). The distinction corresponds to the difference made in formal logic between predication and inhesion in a proposition, the attribute being included in the subject in the one, and including the subject in the other. The genitive relation can be looked at under either one of these two aspects, and consequently we ought not to expect to find the grammatical relics of all languages pointing to one and the same process. This race preferred to conceive the relation, when it had once arrived at it, under the one point of view, that race under another. The meaning of the relation itself, however, was not that of simple dependency, which it has since grown into. The Semite centred his attention upon the governed word, in agreement with that synthetising tendency which has displayed itself in his language, his literature, and his religion. The governing noun was placed first, and its accent and importance transferred to the following genitive, so that the whole became a kind of compound pronounced in one breath, in which the latter part alone had prominence assigned to it. The so-called genitive termination in *i*, which the second substantive takes in Assyrian, is but a modification of the accusatival *-a*, and consequently goes back to a time when the nominative did not exist. The periphrastic genitive, which placed the relative (or rather originally the demonstrative) pronoun between the two nouns, analysing the genitive relation into "love that (is) Socrates," and so equalising the two ideas, must be referred to a later period. The Aryan procedure was the exact converse of the Semitic, and would suffice of itself to demonstrate the separate origin of the two groups of languages. Here the mind fixed all its attention upon the governing noun, suitably to the genius of a race which was eminently practical, and by its close observation of objects has been the originator of inductive science. It was the governed noun the dependency of which was marked out by suffixes, and which naturally came first in pronunciation, thus directing the attention to the more important governing word, which was last heard. The mind was turned towards the object, not towards the source or end of that object. These, on the contrary, were conceived as so many attributes, which accidentally adhered to the principal object of thought. It is the same in the pronominal-prefix idioms of South Africa. The Bâ-ntu genitive agrees with the gender of the governing noun just as much as the genitival δημό-σιο-ς of the Greek must agree with its substantive;[1] thus in Zulu, *i*-SI-*tya* S-*o*-M-*fazi*, "the

[1] So in the Tibetan languages adjectives are formed from substantives by the addition of the sign of the genitive, as *ser-gyi*, "of

dish of the woman." The last instance, taken in conjunction with what has been said above upon the origin of gender, will throw much light upon the primitive signification of the genitive relation. The same pronominal word which has been attached to one substantive is attached to another when the idea expressed by the latter is sought to be brought into connection with the idea expressed by the first. If we assume that the primary meaning of *si* was "mass," the words *i*-SI-*tya* S-*o*-M-*fazi* would properly be read "mass-dish mass-woman." It is but a new application of the old law of the syllogism in logic, or of the principle which Mr H. Spencer has shown to be the ground of all science. Two things are brought into connection and equivalence one with the other by means of a third. In the present case, two ideas were first set over against one another, and expressed in language in such a way that one of them came to be always associated with the other, and with the ideas cognate with the latter, until it was reduced at last to a mere formative, constituting a class; and then by the help of this pronominal formative other ideas, not cognate with the idea originally set over against the decayed prefix, were

gold," "aureus," from *ser*, "gold;" and in Hindustani the genitive takes the marks of gender according to the words to which it refers (Max Müller, Lectures, 1st series, p. 106).

united with it in thought. In this manner the genitive would have grown out of apposition. Equipollent conceptions could be placed side by side in apposition, and one of these, after being crystallised into a grammatical form, became the medium of combining new conceptions with the conception with which it was united. This, however could only be the case where the objective genitive was the type of the relation. Languages like the Semitic, in which the subjective genitive was the type, never rose beyond an apposition wherein the first factor was subordinated to the second, and consequently never possessed a true genitive, any more than the Malay and the Taic languages generally. The insertion of the relative pronoun between the two factors, which may be made in Chinese by *tchi*, a word originally signifying "a place," is nothing else than an analysis of the apposition. The agglutinative plan of affixing a word of independent meaning to the governed noun is equally little a genitive; it is really a verbal clause; and the Accadian *enu Huru-lal* may just as well be translated "the lord fills Ur," as "lord of Ur" ("Ur-filling").

Before closing our list of illustrations of what is meant by the Metaphysics of Language, it would be well to take an example from the verbs. I have already tried to point out in a former chapter how a comparative study of languages leads us to the conclusion that the aorist is the oldest tense. Let us now see what we can learn about the person-endings, the chief characteristic of the verb so far as form is concerned. In Chinese, position alone decides whether a word is used as a verb, a substantive, an adjective, an adverb, or a preposition. Place *ngó*, "I," before a root, and it becomes the first person of a verb, just like "I ride" in English. The form of the language has scarcely advanced beyond the rudimentary stage in which the distinctions of the several parts of speech were all unknown, and lay undeveloped within the embryo of a single monosyllable. The agglutinative languages show further progress. Accadian can not only say *mu-gar*, "I made," and *mu-nin-gar*, "I made it," like the Chinese *ngò wêï* and *ngó wêï tschi*, but has proceeded to create a present by extending the last syllable of the radical, and so appropriating to it a special verbal form, just as in Tibetan we get *nga jyed-do*, "I do," from *jyed* "to do." Immense is the advance from this early stage to such broken-down forms as the Basque *duzu*, "thou hast him" (compounded of *d* "him," *au*, "have," and *zu* "thou"), or the Ostiak conjugation, where the three persons of the singular of the first two tenses of the indicative respectively are *madâdm*, *madân*, *madâ*, and, *madâu*, *madâr*, *ma-*

*dáda.* In all cases, however, we find that the forms resolve themselves into a combination of the root with the personal pronouns, these being sometimes affixed and sometimes prefixed. In Accadian, as in Basque, both processes could take place; but as a general rule the Turanian idioms of Asia have remained true to their instinct of postfixing the determinative words. It is the same in old Egyptian and with the Aryan verb, though a difficulty meets us here. It has been maintained that *ad-mi*, *at-si*, "I eat," "thou eatest," go back to the two first personal pronouns, in spite of the change of the dental of the second person into a sibilant, and the dual and plural forms *-vas*, *-thas*, and *-mas*, *-tha*, make this indubitable. But the third person is not so easy to explain, and Bleek has even ventured to derive it from a conjectural *ti* = "do," which has made the perfect of the Teutonic languages. The singular *-ti* might be discovered in the demonstrative, which has helped in the declension of the Sanskrit third personal pronoun, but the plural, *-nti*, which cannot be separated from it, still remains unaccounted for. The nasal cannot have been a mere phonetic insertion, nor is it likely that its derivation is to be sought in an assumed demonstrative pronoun *an*. Whatever may be the difficulties, however, connected with the third person, it is possible that the first person of the verb may be traced back to the original objective forms of the personal pronouns. But this implies a time when such a combination did not exist, a time when the personal pronouns were not yet fossilised out of their earlier general significations, and when a verbal force must have been given to the root in a different manner. It is noticeable that in Accadian *enu-mu* meant at once "my lord" and "I am lord," and this vagueness of meaning implies a very faint realisation of the distinction between the two principal parts of speech; while, on the other hand, the Japanese personal pronouns, true to their substantival origin, may be used to denote all three persons alike. Now here, as elsewhere, the dialects of savage tribes let us into the secrets of early language, and we find that the Grebo of West Africa can distinguish between "I" and "thou," "we" and "you," solely by the intonation of the voice, *mâ di* being equally "I eat" and "thou eatest," *a di*, "you" and "we eat." Nay, more than this; according to the Rev. J. L. Wilson, even these pronouns are but rarely employed in conversation, it being left to gesture to determine in what person a verb is to be taken; *ni ne*, for instance, being "I do it" or "you do it," according to the significant gestures of the speaker, just as in Mpongwe *tŏnda* means "to love," *tōnda* "not to love."[1] Spix and Martius describe a similar condition of speech among certain Brazilian tribes, with whom the projection of the mouth in the direction intended serves to make the words "wood-go" signify "I will go into the wood." Such a state of things is indeed hard to realise, with no pronouns and no verbs; and yet out of it grew first the conception of action in relation to the person, and then in relation to time. Men were slow in arriving at a distinction between one's self and another; the three personal pronouns could not have come into existence until after the genesis of a plural, and the idea of a subject-pronoun was evolved last of all. The verb would seem to have been at first not unlike the genitive. Primarily the rough-hewn chaotic word, with its undeveloped potentiality of meaning, was accompanied by visible action in order to impart to it the signification of agency or intention; afterwards a substantive was brought into juxtaposition to it, the sense of the compound being settled by outward action or by the circumstances of the case; and finally, these substantives, worn down to personal pronouns, became differentiated, and, joined in apposition with the roots, formed a kind of compound in which something—eating, doing, or the like—was attributed to the pronoun.[2] As

[1] Wilson, Gram., p. 32.

[2] In the Polynesian languages, the verb has never succeeded in

in the instance quoted above from the Accadian, or as in so many Turanian languages, Magyár, for example (where it is only by using different pronominal words that *kés-em*, "my knife," can be distinguished from *vár-ok*, "I wait," the aorist *vár-t-am* being actually identical), the verbal form was simply a genitive, and has to be explained like all other genitives. Were we to represent it symbolically, we might say that "expecting = me" was the source both of "my expectation" and of "I expect." The position of the pronoun in Aryan is alone to be noticed: it follows instead of preceding its governing noun; and this reversal of the usual order of words implies not only that the personal pronouns had been fixed before the verbal forms became crystallised, but also that the feeling that these pronouns were different from all other substantives, and that the power of the individual over action was omnipotent, was from the very earliest times ever present to the Aryan mind. It still required one step further, however, to ascend from these merely personal relations to that conception of time which with us lies at the very foundation of the verb. It is a conception that is still unknown to many races of men, and which is

coming into existence at all. The Dayak, for instance, says "he-with-jacket-with-white," instead of "he has a white jacket on," replacing the verbal notion by the adjectival (Steinthal, "Charakteristik," &c., p. 165).

conspicuous for its absence among the polysynthetic languages of North America. The New Caledonian, with whom "yesterday" and "to-morrow" are unknown terms, or the member of the beehive communities of the Old World, had no need, and no occasion, to mark the lapse of time in their monotonous and vegetable existence. The category of space historically precedes the category of time.

Further illustrations of the Metaphysics of Language are, I think, unnecessary. Enough has been said to show what is meant by the phrase, and the way in which this part of Glottology can be worked out. A comparative analysis of words leads us to the earliest linguistic contrivances for expressing the relations of grammar. They are but the fossilised embodiment of the thought which they clothed; and we are thus enabled to penetrate to the germ and starting-point of those conceptions which are summed up in an ordinary grammar. They are the mental forms which we finally reach, and which have developed into all the elaborate grammatical machinery of modern speech. We get back, as it were, into that very thought in its most original form which has been reflected in spoken language. We enter the world of ideas, and, like the physicist with his doctrine of force, find ourselves dealing with metaphysical facts.

## CHAPTER VIII.

### COMPARATIVE MYTHOLOGY AND THE SCIENCE OF RELIGION.

LANGUAGE, we have said, is the mirror of society, because it is the embodiment of thought. Every word has a history, and that history is really a history of the mind. The two correlatives cannot be separated from one another: thought is but the internal, language the external. Form and content, creator and created—these are other ways of expressing the same thing: the statue does not represent more truly the artistic imagination of its sculptor than does the word the mind that shaped it. And just as the statue will react on the artist, and produce, as in Egypt, a conventional conception of beauty and proportion, so in a greater degree will the plastic word react on the mind of man. The two sides of the prism, the inward and the outward, act and react one upon the other; and where the sense of objectivity is strong, or the absolute nothingness of the mere empty husk of the word is forgotten, words are likely to become our masters, and to dictate to us the meaning of things. If the Greek with his autonomous individualism could speak of the ἀξίωσις λόγου—the appreciation which he set upon the utterances of his own lips—the law-loving, abstraction-worshipping Roman, on the other hand, knew only of the *vis verbi*, a fitting echo of military martinetism. Language is a natural growth as well as an artificial production. It has developed along with the awakening consciousness, and much of it will be at best but semi-conscious. At the beginning there was no clear distinction between the parts of speech or the objects which were denoted; all lay chaotic and undeveloped in each embryonic combination of sounds, and these inevitably called up erroneous ideas, and laid the foundations of a fetichism which confounded together the agent and the patient. But more than this; language, like the rocks, is strewn with the fossilised wrecks of former conditions of society. Words which were once pregnant with meaning may either put on new significations in consequence of social changes; or long use and acquaintance may deprive them of their sense, so that the sole meaning they possess is their mere sound; or, again, their original force may be forgotten, and they may survive as proper names or in connection with obsolete ceremonies; or, lastly, they may be confused with other better-known words, and bring about a confusion of ideas. Who now connects the same conceptions with such terms as "democracy" or "church" as they conveyed to our ancestors? "Shall" and "will" have become auxiliaries, unmeaning by themselves; "Jove" and "Yule" no longer remind us of the bright vault of heaven or the burning wheel (old Norse *hjul*) that symbolised the circle of the year, while "beefeater" and "Brasenose College" show little trace of the waiter at the side-table (*buffetier*) or of the brewing-house (*Brasen-huis*) from which they sprung. The words in which one period of society struggles to express its knowledge and meaning may become the misunderstood shams of a later generation, and the explanation of them which is demanded by the mind serves only to perpetuate the delusion and stereotype an imaginary world. Indeed, the first act of the young consciousness is to ask what is the reason of that which it sees about it? The formation of a language itself implies a desire to know objects by naming them, and so distinguishing them one from the other. Every name that is given is the summing-up of all attainable knowledge concerning a thing; it contains within itself the answer which man attempts to make to that ever-recurring question "why?" and all the knowledge and experience which he can bring to bear upon it. But the knowledge and the answer of the first men must have been very different from that of a more cultivated era of humanity. The Athenian of the age of Periklês would view the world with eyes very unlike those with which the primitive Aryan gazed upon it. The old name would not express the new meaning; and if it had not expanded with the growing knowledge of the speakers, it would of necessity cramp and confine the signification within the limits originally assigned to it, and cease to reflect the living knowledge of the day, and to be anything more than an antiquated symbol. Words have a life, because the society which produces them has a life; and just as the old forms of society become dead and misleading, so also do the words which shadow them forth. They no longer answer truly to objects, and therefore objects must be made to answer to them; and thus a dark cloudland is built up upon these worn-out husks, hiding nature and reality from the mind and the belief.

Now this is mythology exactly. Its creations move, like the ghosts of Homer, in an unreal fairy-land, and their sole basis is the names which are given to them; for these names are the heirlooms of a traditional past—the heritage which has come down from the giants of old time; this is their only title to existence and respect. The traditional past, therefore, which has given them their existence, must furnish the key which shall unlock them. We must track the names back historically, until we reach the age when they were living and full of significance. Mythology is founded upon words, and the history of words, therefore, must explain it.[1] But we must not forget that, after

[1] Mr Fiske, who sees clearly that a myth is not the result of the forgetfulness of a word or phrase, but of the thought which underlay them, very truly says ("Myths and Myth-makers," p. 214), "The myths, and customs, and beliefs which, in an advanced stage of culture, seem meaningless save when characterised by some quaintly-wrought device of symbolic explanation, did not seem meaningless in the lower culture which gave birth to them. Myths, like words, survive their primitive meaning. In the early stage, the myth is part and parcel of the current mode of philosophising; the explanation which it offers is, for the time, the natural one—the one which would most readily occur to any one (?) thinking on the theme with which the myth is concerned. But, by and by, the mode of philosophising has changed; explanations which formerly seemed quite obvious no longer occur to any one; but the myth has acquired an independent substantive existence, and continues to be handed down from parents to children as something true, though no one can tell why it is true. Lastly, the myth itself gradually fades from remembrance, often leaving behind it some utterly unintelligible custom or seemingly absurd superstitious notion." Elsewhere he adds (p. 195), "The physical theory of myths will be properly presented and comprehended only when it is understood that we accept the physical derivation of such stories as the Iliad myth in much the same way as we are bound to accept the physical etymologies of such words as *soul, consider, truth, convince, deliberate*, and the like. The late Dr Gibbs, of Yale College, in his 'Philological Studies,' . . . . describes such etymologies as

all, words will only explain the external side of mythology. It is true that this is its chief and most important side; but, without an inward and sustaining spirit, mythology could not have lasted so long and so persistently as it has done, and have blinded the eyes to its manifold absurdities. There must have been an element in it which appealed to the heart of man, and preserved it from being relegated to the nursery, like the fairy tales which yet claim the same origin as the gorgeous mythology of the Greek poets. This element was the religious instinct. Behind the outward veil of the myth was enshrined the belief in God and the soul, more and more concealed and over encrusted, it may be, in the course of generations; but still there it abided almost unconsciously, and kept the old mythology from premature death. It is clear that we are here dealing with a similar case to that which we described in the last chapter. As we get at the original conceptions which underlie the several relations of grammar by a comparison of the forms which denote them, so in mythology we must dis-

'faded metaphors.' In similar-wise, while refraining from characterising the Iliad or the tragedy of 'Hamlet'—any more than I would characterise 'Le Juif Errant,' by Sue, or 'La Maison Forestière,' by Erckmann-Chatrian—as nature-myths, I would at the same time consider these poems well described as embodying 'faded nature-myths.'"

cover the spirit that has given it birth by an inductive comparison of the various forms with which it has clothed itself. These are words and phrases, and consequently Comparative Mythology is but a branch of the Science of Language.

But the religious idea can make use of other means of expression besides mythology. What we call a religion differs from mythology in the same way that a civilised state differs from a savage tribe. The one is organised and artificial, the other is spontaneous and natural. There is no longer a sort of dim half-consciousness of spiritual being; the individual has awakened to a consciousness of himself and his relations to others. In a beehive community morality is impossible, much less a worship of one God; it is only when the conception of the individual had been reached that the idea of responsibility begins, and with it both morality and the endeavour to obtain a personal salvation. The savage knows nothing of all this; sin and moral impurity are words which he would not understand; his only idea of happiness consists in abundance of food; the only evils from which he prays to be delivered are material discomforts. A religion must be organised and individual; and this implies tradition and literature on the one hand, and on the other hand a hierarchic aristocracy, in so far as individualism presupposes distinction and superiority. To call fetichism a religion, therefore, is a misuse of terms. Where every man is his own priest, there is no system in which one man knows the will of the gods better than another. Rome had no religion until the days of the Empire, for its organised cultus was political; and religion in Greece was confined to Delphi or the Orphic hierophants. The individual character of a religion is universally recognised; where history can present us with no founder like Buddha or Confucius or Christ, later legends delight to trace back its ceremonies and organisation to some single Numa Pompilius.

But the founder must have materials to work upon. There must be the religious instinct, without which all religion is impossible; there must be a hallowed stock of traditional beliefs and rites; and, above all, there must be a willingness on the part of the people to accept the system that is formed out of them. The founder of a creed generally comes forward as the reformer of a past unorganised cultus, and if he would succeed, he must strike a chord in harmony with the wants and wishes of his age. Buddha preached a gospel of freedom from the intolerable yoke of castes and Brahmanical despotism; Mohammed broke up the aristocracy of Arab traders, and proclaimed equality before one God and one Prophet to the sons of the desert; and Joseph Smith flattered the sensuousness of American enthusiasts and the millenarian dreams of uneducated Protestantism. Mythology necessarily precedes a religion. It may be extirpated by its successor, or it may be taken up and absorbed into it; or it may linger on side by side with the new creed, sometimes in alliance, sometimes in antagonism. It never follows it, however; for the myths which so often gather round the person of the real or imaginary legislator are borrowed from older legends, and do but find a new hero to whom to attach the venerated stories of the timeworn folklore. The saints of Christendom have taken the place of the gods and demigods of Pagan antiquity, and the deities of the Veda became the evil spirits of Zoroastrianism. *Tritâ*, the Hindu power of night, and *Ahi*, the serpent of darkness, change, in the Avesta, into the human Thraêtaona, the son of the first man, and Azhi dahâka, "the biting snake," which he destroys; and the transformation is completed when the religion can no longer assimilate the old mythology even thus far, and Thraêtaona and the serpent become the Feridun and Zohak of Firdusi—the Kyrus and Astyages of the Greeks. Assimilation of pre-existing beliefs must necessarily be the work of a new religion; the beliefs will be modified and arranged; but if the religion is to make its way, it cannot afford to ignore the current superstitions and practices of the country. Indeed, these will colour it the further it spreads and the more it appeals to the uneducated portion of society; and it is no strange thing for a religion which begins with a protest against the popular idolatry to end by becoming inextricably mixed up with it. Even if this does not happen, however, it is plain that, in order to understand a religion rightly, we must know the meaning of the mythological elements which it incorporates and rests upon, and of the terms which are its own watchwords. These change with the change of knowledge and circumstances and generations; and a Church will often be found fighting over the signification of a word which originally bore an import quite other than any dreamed of by the combatants. The interminable wranglings and divisions that have been carried on in modern Europe over the questions of the Eucharist and the ministerial orders would have been unintelligible to the first Christians. The battle is one of words; but the insertion of an *iota* was once sufficient to deluge Alexandria with blood. Here, then, Glottology, with its calm scientific dispassionateness and its rules of sound comparison, is needed in order that we may comprehend the origin and growth of religious ideas, and of the dogmas which endeavour to express them. In so far as the science of religions consists in comparing words with words, dogmas with dogmas, and in tracing the development of the one out of the other, in so far it is, like mythology, a branch of the science of language, and this, too, apart from its embodiment of mythological elements, which, as we have seen, demand the key of Glottology.

But there is another reason why the comparative study of religions calls for the glottologist. The oldest and the most interesting are locked up in the recesses of dead languages, and it is only the scientific method which can accurately explain much that is most important in the language of the Rig-Veda, and still more of the Zend-Avesta. The traditional renderings of Sanskrit pundits are often grotesque, often the result of modern misconception; and some of the most valuable disclosures of the old Hindu hymns, which have helped to explain the problem of mythology, would never have been made without the application of glottological laws. Even the Old Testament cannot afford to dispense with this assistance: whether or not Samson is the Melkarth of Tyre and the Herakles of Greece can only be decided by Comparative Philology. The same holds good of the Science of Religions if we regard it from another point of view. Every system of religion consists of a certain number of doctrines which circle round some central one, and the meaning of this is all important if we would understand the system. But doctrines alter, although the words in which they are formulated do not; and to discover their original import is to discover the original sense attached to the words. A good example of this is the *Nirvana*, the point about which the whole system of Buddhism revolves; and until we have accurately settled the primary signification of this word, and the historical modifications which it has undergone in various ages and among various races, we shall never properly know what Buddhism is. Religion is the most spiritual, and therefore the deepest and most enduring, expression of society; and if the history of society is to be sought in language, yet more emphatically must the history of religion be.

Before, however, we can venture to compare religions together, we must establish the scientific study of mythology upon a firm and satisfactory foundation. As a branch of Glottology, it must be investigated upon the same principles and in the same way. We must never forget that it is a dependent science, and is, therefore, not to be treated as though the higher science did not exist. To draw conclusions from a comparison of myths which are not supported by etymological evidence is altogether unwarrantable. If Comparative Philology can show that Paris is the Paṇis of the Veda, the robbers of the bright cow-clouds of the dawn; that Helen is Saramâ, the dawn goddess; and that Akhilles, who dies at the western gate of Troy, is *Aharyus*, the sun, from the Sanskrit *ahar*, "day," then the burden of the Iliad may well be the old fight between the night and the morning, the old story of the victory and death of the solar hero around the walls and battlements of the sky.[1]

[1] The evidence of Comparative Philology here, as elsewhere, finds its counterpart and confirmation in the evidence derived from a comparison of the myths themselves. The Homeric siege of Troy is but a repetition of an earlier siege, when Laomedon and the walls of his city, which "like a mist rose into towers" at the song of Apollo, were conquered and overthrown by Herakles; and of the siege of Thebes, which was hardly less famous in Greek story than that of Troy. To seek for fragments of history in either of these is like looking for gold in the rays of the sun. The legend, it is true, had localised itself, in the one case in Thebes, in the other case in the old Mysian town of Ilium; but such a geographical setting is necessary for all myths. It is possible that struggles between the Semitic companions of the "Eastern" (Kadmus) and the inhabitants of Bœotia may have occasioned the selection of Thebes, just as Ilium may have been the centre of unrecorded conflicts between Ionic settlers and Asiatic natives. Dr E. Curtius is doubtless right in ascribing the origin of the popular lays out of which the Iliad has grown to the period of the Greek emigration to Asia Minor, when fugitives from the Peloponnesus and from Athens came flying from the Doric invaders, carrying with them their traditions of ancient Akhæan glory and power among the hills of Argos. It is thus that we can explain the curious mixture of regal autocracy and Ionic democracy, such as would prevail among struggling colonists, which meets us in the Homeric poems,

But to resolve Orestes into the sun and Semiramis into the morning is to step beyond the limits allowed to us, and to assert what cannot be proved. In comparing our myths we must never lose sight of the etymological part of the subject, since it is this which gives security to our conclusions. Unless the features of a myth unmistakably resemble those of another, more especially in the smaller details, we should be very cautious in setting it by the side of another, where the proper names are not transparent. There is no doubt as to the meaning of the names of Phœbus and Hyperion, and we may therefore class them with other solar myths without hesitation, even supposing that the outlines of the stories told about them were vague and general; but to discover the sun on the horizon of the sea in the frog-prince of the fairy-tale is to transgress the boundaries of scientific evidence, and incur the charge of riding a hobby too hard. Besides the care which must thus be taken to make language the ultimate ground of our comparisons, we must be on our guard against that hankering after unity which has been so fatal to glottological progress. The *general* laws of Comparative Mythology, like the

as well as the strange confusion between the opponents of the Greeks in Mysian Troy, and on the banks of the Mysian Xanthus, and those Lykian Troes who contended with them further south in the neighbourhood of the Lykian Xanthus.

general laws of Comparative Philology, must be obtained by the widest possible induction of instances; we must collect our myths from every race and climate under the sun, and we shall often find that some low and despised tribe of savages can furnish us with a clue to the laws we are seeking. Mythology, like language, is a reflection of the human mind; it belongs more especially to what we may call the natural era of mankind;[1] and since the framework of the mind and the circumstances which surround the life of the savage are much the same everywhere, we shall expect to meet with a common similarity and obedience to general laws in the myths of all nations. But we must not go further than this, and, in disregard of all linguistic testimony, derive the stories of Aryans, and Finns, and Kafirs, which resemble one another, from one and the same

[1] Myth is the necessary form in which thought finds its expression among uncivilised peoples. It is to the savage and the child what history is to us; and just as contemporaneous literature accompanies history, so does oral tradition accompany myth. There is a mythical geography and a mythical philosophy, as well as a mythical history, if the expression may be allowed; geography must begin with its Odyssey, philosophy with its Eris and Erôs, and history with its heroic age. The child and the savage merge the subject and object into one, and can draw no distinction between them; the objective *me* preceded the subjective *ego*, *aham*, while, on the other hand, the creations of the imagination were regarded as being as much realities as the events and objects of everyday life.

source. Where language demonstrates identity of origin, there will there be identity of origin among the myths, but not otherwise. To imagine that the coincidence of legends among two races unallied in language means anything more than the common uniformity of intellectual action in the mythopœic age is to repeat the mistake of bygone writers, who believed that the story of a flood among different peoples bore witness to the Biblical deluge. With them the belief was excusable, for they had been taught the existence of a single primeval language and the transformation of the heroes of Genesis into the personages of heathen mythology. But where there is no disposition to see Noah in Kronos, and his three sons in Zeus, Poseidon, and Aides, the indiscriminate lumping of myths together, without any heed to the requirements of Glottology, is altogether indefensible.[1]

[1] Mr Fiske well says ("Myths and Myth-makers," p. 160)—"The mere fact that solar heroes, all over the world, travel in a certain path and slay imps of darkness, is of great value as throwing light upon primeval habits of thought, but it is of no value as evidence for or against an alleged community of civilisation between different races. The same is true of the sacredness universally attached to certain numbers. Dr Brinton's opinion that the sanctity of the number *four* in nearly all systems of mythology is due to a primitive worship of the cardinal points becomes very probable when we recollect that the similar pre-eminence of *seven* is almost demonstrably connected with the adoration of the sun, moon, and five visible planets, which has left its record in the structure and nomenclature of the Aryan and Semitic week."

There is yet another fault of which we must beware. Mythology has a setting in geography and history. Myths move in an unreal world of their own, a dead reflection of this world, distorted by the childlike ignorance of primitive man. Hence there is a mythical geography, a mythical history, and a mythical philosophy. When the original physical reference of the myth had faded away from the memory, it was necessary for the story-teller to hang his tale upon some fact, or person, or place. When this was once found, and the needful local colouring imparted, the myth continued to circle around it, and to attract fresh elements, until a change of conditions transferred the circle of myths so formed to a new local centre. To look for any traces of history here is obviously out of the question. Even granting that the mythical element has been grafted upon a real person and a real fact, the latter were but the framework, which was wholly swallowed up in the animating mass of mythic matter. Not history, but folklore was what was wanted; and nothing perishes so quickly as names which have no meaning, which are merely the proper names of actual men, and not the crystallised reflections of a popular tale. The memory of the past dwells but little in the mind of the uneducated; the battle of Minden in 1759, little more than a hundred years ago, is utterly forgotten in the neighbourhood; and, according to Hahn, all that Skanderbeg's countrymen remember of him is a marvellous escape which never took place;[1] while the oldest Albanian genealogy cannot mount beyond eleven ancestors. The "Niebelungen Lied" is a most instructive example of the relation between myth and history. The Sigurd of the Edda, who gains possession of the bright treasure of the Niflungs or clouds by slaying Fafnir, the serpent of winter, and after delivering Brynhild from her magic sleep, is made by Gunnar to forget his betrothed and marry her daughter Gudrun or Grimhild—a crime to be avenged by his murder at the hands of Gudrun's brothers; again to be avenged, after Brynhild has burnt herself on Sigurd's pyre, like Herakles on Mount Œta, by Atli, Brynhild's brother—this Sigurd of the Edda reappears in the old Saxon tale of "Dietrich of Bern." Dietrich or Theodoric rules at Bonn, the earlier name of which was Bern; and Etzel, the Atli of the Scandinavian version, is the younger son of Osid, the Frisian king, who conquers Saxony from King Melias, and lives in Susat, the present Soest, in Westphalia, while the Nibelungs or cloud-children dwell at Worms. But the story, as we have it in the great German epic of the twelfth century, has

[1] Von Hahn, "Sagwissenschaftliche Studien," i. 62, 63.

undergone yet another change. Bern has become Verona, Dietrich Theodoric, the famous Gothic conqueror of Italy, and Etzel, Attila the Hun. The Jörmunrek of the Icelandic myth, who slays Swanhild, Sigurd's posthumous son, is now Hermanric, the Gothic king at Rome; and Sigurd or Siegfrid himself, with Brynhild and Gunnar (Gunther), are identified with Gundicar, the Burgundian victim of Attila and the Austrasian Siegbert, who reigned from 561 to 575, married Brunehault, defeated the Huns, and was murdered by his brother's mistress, Fredegond. But in spite of these coincidences, and the historical colouring that the latter versions of a literary age have given to the old Teutonic myth of the waxing and waning of summer, we know that neither history nor even historical names are to be sought for in the legend. The Attila of history died two years (453) before the birth of the historical Theodoric; and Jornandes, who wrote at least twenty years before the death of the Austrasian Siegbert, was already acquainted with Swanhild, the child born after Sigurd's death. If more were needed, the Icelandic and Saxon versions of the story would prove the mythic antiquity of the names of the heroes. Similarity of name or local celebrity may cause a myth to entwine itself about some personage or event of actual history; but the latter thus far cease to belong to history, and, unless supported by cotemporaneous evidence, must be relegated to the ideal land of poetry. The life of Mohammed is full of mythic elements; fragments of old Arab folklore have fastened themselves upon it; and were there no other record of the Prophet's existence, we should have to assign him to the same category as the Rishis of Brahmanism. The Charlemagne who has taken the place of Wodin, as in the group of stars which we still call Charles's Wain, belongs to myth, and not to history. Myth has accidentally attached itself to an actual personage, but it is not the myth which tells us this. To seek for facts of ethnology and tribal migration in the mythology of Greece is but to modernise Euhemerus, who found a Kretan king in Zeus, and a Pankhæan conqueror in Uranus. To prop up conclusions so derived by an appeal to local names is to argue in a circle. We know that nothing is more liable to corruption than the names of places and tribes; and the attempt to explain their new forms will either itself originate the myth, like the arrow that Little John "shot over" *Shotover* Hill (Château Vert), or occasion the old folklore to localise itself among them.[1] The architectural remains of the Pelopon-

[1] When I was at Carcassonne, I was told that the town derived its name from one of the cathedral bells, which was christened

nesus bear witness to a powerful dynasty such as that which the Homeric poems represent in the Akhæan princes; but unless coeval monuments be discovered to corroborate the legendary picture, we must not look for further historical facts in the Iliad and Odyssey.[1] And even in this case we

*Carcas* according to the forms of the Roman Catholic Church. When the bell was first rung the people shouted out, "Carcas sonne!" A parallel to this etymological myth will be found in the name of the Swiss mountain Pilatus. The word is really *Pileatus* ("the capped mountain"), due to the cap of cloud which so frequently rests upon its summit. But of course the popular legend brings Pilate hither from Galilee, and makes him drown himself, in the bitterness of remorse, in a small snow-lake near the top of the mountain. When once the myth had fixed itself here, natives and visitors, in spite of the evidence of their senses, insisted on believing that the characteristics of the lake were worthy of the catastrophe of which it was supposed to be the scene. Merian (in 1642) describes it as "situated in a secluded spot, deep and fearful, surrounded by dark woods, and enclosed to prevent the approach of man; its colour is black, it is always calm, and its surface is undisturbed by the wind." It is remarkable that a French range of hills in the neighbourhood of Vienne bears the same name as the Swiss mountain, and from the same cause. Vienne, however, was actually the spot to which Pilate was banished; and the accidental coincidence is a striking instance of the impossibility of discovering historic fact in a myth, although we may know from other sources that it has accidentally fastened itself to a real event. Close to Vienne is a ruin called the "Tour de Mauconseil," from which Pilate threw himself into the river, according to the legend of the country, just as he did on the summit of Pilatus. The value of a popular legend may be judged from the fact that the tower is really a *tête-du-pont* built by Philippe de Valois.

[1] Dr Schliemann's recent discoveries in the Troad show that Ilium was as real a place as Thebes, and that the warrior bands who chanted the deeds of Akhilles and Agamemnon transferred the

should learn the facts, not from the epic, but from far different sources. All that the poems can do is to reflect the manners and beliefs of the age in which they grew up, and, however much modernised they may be in their present form, to set before our eyes the society of a period out of which was to spring the glorious culture of Athens. The scientific student of mythology must always remember that he is dealing with the mythic element only; historical facts *may* be imbedded in it—upon this point he cannot decide; but unless these facts are discovered by historical means, no amount of ingenuity and conjecture can extract them from the myth.

As in language, we must be careful to distinguish in mythology between what is native and what is borrowed. It would be worse than a mistake to treat as a pure and original myth the hybrid conception which resulted from the amalgamation of Herculus, the old Italian god of enclosures (from *arceo*), with the Greek sun-god Herakles; or of Saturnus, the patron of sowing and agriculture, with Kronos, who owed his existence to his son Kronion, "the ancient of days"

old tales of the siege of the sky by the powers of light to their own struggles with the coast population of Asia Minor. The myth takes its colouring from each generation that repeats it, and clothes itself with the passions and the interests and the knowledge of the men in whose mouths it lives and grows.

(χρόνος). Nothing but confusion would come out of such a comparison. In this matter we have to refer to history wherever this is possible, and, as in the case of the latter Roman mythology, discover what elements have been imported from abroad; where it is impossible to do this, language is our only guide. Glottology alone can warrant us in tracing myths to the same origin, and Glottology also must inform us which of them come from a foreign source. In no other way, for instance, could the story of Melikertes, the Tyrian Melkarth, be traced to a Semitic derivation; or, on the other hand, could Minôs be referred to the Aryan *man* and *manu*, instead of being coupled with the Egyptian Menes, "the founder" of the state. It may sometimes be difficult to detect the presence of an alien myth: like borrowed words that assume native inflections, the borrowed legend may clothe itself in a familiar form. But until the two elements are separated, the comparative mythologist is not certain of his primary facts.[1]

[1] The story of the Kyklops in the Odyssey is, as it seems to me, an instance of a myth which has been borrowed by the Aryans from their Turanian neighbours and predecessors. W. Grimm (*Abhandlungen d. Akademie d. Wiss. zu Berlin*, 1857), in an article on "The Legend of Polyphemus," points out that the episode of the Kyklops, while forming a complete whole by itself, fits awkwardly into the story of Odysseus, and varies both in style and matter from the rest of the Odyssey. Thus Odysseus is no longer the

Again, we must distinguish from the myth a good deal that is often confounded with it. The myth is the spontaneous and necessary outcome of the young mind, which takes its own subjective fancies as the true objective answers to the questions inspired by the world around it. Very

far-sighted hero of epic song, but a foolhardy and cunning trickster. Grimm goes on to point out that similar tales exist in many other parts of the world. The one-eyed giant, who lives on human flesh, and is finally blinded by a hero whom he entraps into his cave, but who escapes under the belly of a sheep or ram, and then taunts the monster, reappears among the Turkish-Tatar Oghuzians, where he is called Depé Ghoz ("eye-in-the-crown"), the hero being Bissat (Diez: "Der neuentdeckte Oghuzische cyclop, verglichen mit d. homerischen," 1815). In the Servian tale (collected by Wnk Stephanowitsch Karadchitsch, No. 38), the pupil of a priest plays the part of Odysseus, and in the Finnish (as given by Bertram), Gylpho, a poor groom. In the latter version the Kammo or Cyclops has a horn in addition to the one eye in the forehead, and is not only blinded but put to death (as in the Oghuzian version), without, however, any mention being made of the hero's escape by the help of the sheep. In the Karelian legend reported by Castrén ("Reseminnen från åren 1838-44," p. 87), the Cyclops is "humanised" by having two eyes assigned to him, one of which is blind; and the Transylvanian version still further rationalises the myth by giving the giant two sound eyes, which are both destroyed by the hero, who throws into them the boiling fat of his two elder brothers. In this version, as in the Servian, the giant is finally drowned. "The Romance of Dolopathos," translated from a Latin work of John the Monk into French verse (about 1225), which Grimm believes to have been derived from the East, also allows the giant two eyes; and an Esthonian tale found in Rosenpläntner tells how a thresher blinded the eyes of the "devil," under the pretext of curing them, and, as in the Odyssey, lost him the sympathy of his friends by giving his own name as Issi or "Self." In the Oghuzian, Servian, and Transylvanian versions, as well as in the legend of Dolopathos, the Homeric account is amplified by a magic ring or staff, which the

different are the conscious and deliberate allegory and fable, which generally have a moral intention, and therefore belong to the period of religion. In the one the material is lifted up to the spiritual—it is an effort to express the higher yearnings of

Cyclops presents to the hero, and which clings to the latter's finger, or compels him to shout out, "I am here." This part of the myth has apparently been rationalised in the Odyssey. Grimm further quotes a similar tale from the Harz (which has probably been influenced by the Homeric one, however), and the third adventure of Sindbad; and alludes to the Norwegian stories in which a maiden escapes from a witch under a sheep's fleece, and two boys meet three monstrous trolls, who have but one huge and transferable eye between them, like the Graiai of Æskhylus. M. Antoine d' Abbadie tells me of a similar story to that of the Kyklops, which he met with among the Amharic-speaking tribes of Abyssinia, and remarks, that though a man with one eye in the centre of his forehead is a conceivable monster, the escape of a man under the belly of so much smaller an animal as a sheep is an inconceivable impossibility. He has also kindly sent me an account of the Basque Tartarua or "one-eyed" Cyclops. This monster is a man-eater who lives in a cave, and is challenged by one of three brothers. The latter lops off one of the arms of the Kyklops, and renewing the challenge next day, lops off his head; then kills one or two other Tartaruas, fights a body without a soul, kills it, and delivers the three daughters of a king. He kills also an intelligent eagle and a hare; and the three brothers finally marry the three sisters. The body without a soul reminds us of the Norse story of "The Giant without a Heart in his Body" (in Dr Dasent's "Norse Tales," pp. 64 *sq.*), which reappears in Southern India (according to Miss Frere's "Old Dekkan Days"), as well as in the Finnic legend written down by Castrén of the giant who kept his soul in a snake which he carried in a box with him on horseback, or in the Samoyede myth of the seven robbers who hung up their hearts on a peg and were destroyed by a hero (whose mother was a prisoner among them), with the help of a Swan-maiden whose feather-dress he had stolen.

the soul by the known and visible things of sense; in the other, the spiritual is brought down to be veiled in the material. The allegory is the product of individual invention, designed either to conceal the higher knowledge of the initiated from the profane gaze of the unlearned, or to explain and bring it home to them by the aid of metaphor. It differs from the fable in not making the brute animals the mouthpiece of its meaning. The beast-fable seems to be one of the earliest creations of the awakening consciousness. It was known to the Egyptians at least as early as the reign of Rameses III.; and "Reynard the Fox" has its analogue among the Kaffirs. Prof. Mahaffy conjectures that Africa, the land of animal-worship, was its original home; and he mentions, in corroboration of this view, that the first essays in composition made by the Vai-Negroes, after Doalu's invention of a syllabary, were fables about beasts.[1] At any rate, beast-fables were peculiarly appropriate to Egypt, where

[1] "Prolegomena to Ancient History," p. 391. The suggestion, however, does not seem altogether tenable. Mr G. Smith has recently found fragments of a collection of beast-fables which belonged to a certain Assyrian city. One of them is a dialogue between the ox and the horse; another between the eagle and the sun. It is difficult to suppose that this collection was borrowed from Egypt, and it is more probable that the beast-fable was the independent creation of more than one people. It would be the natural form of political satire under a despotic government. The modern gypsies have beast-fables of their own, which cannot be ascribed to any foreign source. (See Leland.)

"Oppida tota canem venerantur, nemo Dianam." Animals live and move like ourselves, and yet between us and them lies a great gulf, which we cannot cross to discover what their thoughts and feelings are. The primitive races of men, accordingly, regarded them with awe and wonder; sometimes they were the sole companions of the hunter and the herdsman, sometimes they were the organs of departed spirits or divine beings—the true root of totemism, which has made the Malayans look upon the *orang-otang*, or "man of the woods," as the possessor of superhuman wisdom.[1]

[1] I cannot believe that totemism was the origin of beast or ancestor worship, much less of fetichism and mythology, except so far as the principle of reaction came into play, since a tribe must have had some semi-religious reason for adopting a certain object or animal as its badge and representative. It was not a mere symbol, like the figures of modern heraldry, but a mysterious representative of the clan, which bound it together like the common ritual of a Roman *gens*. The animal was sufficiently on a level with man to be substituted for him; but it was also sufficiently divine to stand for the whole community, and not for the individual alone. Totemism, though springing from the same root as mythology, was powerless to effect the development of the latter. A striking example of this is to be found in Dr Brinton's "Myths of the New World" (pp. 161 *sq.*), where an account is given of Michabo, "The Great Hare," whom the various branches of the Algonquin race, from Virginia and Delaware to the Ottawas of the north, regarded as their ancestor. "The *totem*, or clan, which bore his name was looked up to with peculiar respect." But Michabo, like the other legislators and founders of America, was really a solar hero, the brother of the snow, who had his home on the verge of the east, whence he sent forth the luminaries on their daily journey. His identification with the hare is but an etymological

Besides allegory and fable, another kind of fiction has to be distinguished from myth. It is not necessary to mention the imaginary chronicles of medieval monks, whose seclusion from the work-a-day world and morbid dwelling upon self brought about an inability to separate truth from falsehood, or the interested inventions of patriots or ciceroni. But writers, more especially among the Greeks, have in all good faith ascribed eponymous ancestors to tribes and races, in the belief that gentle names *must* have thus originated, and that consequently the existence of populations called Hellenes and Assyrians was a sufficient proof of a Hellen and an Asshur. The notion has the same foundation ultimately as the myth which arises from the attempt to explain the signification of a forgotten word; and when once it has become

accident. His name is derived from *michi*, "great," and *wabos*, which, though it means "hare," properly signifies "white," whence come numerous words for "morning," "east," "day," and "light." It was "The Great White One," therefore, and not "The Great Hare," from whom the Algonquin drew his descent. The selection of the hare as its unifying symbol by a particular tribe was due to the feeling which saw the "mystery of divinity" in the brute creation, like the beast-worship of Africa or the metempsychosis of Indian philosophy; but such a feeling could not produce a mythology—a richer and wider belief was needed for this. (See, however, Mr H. Spencer, "Essays," iii. 4, though his speculations are based on the wild and unscientific theorising of Mr M'Lennan in his articles on "The Worship of Plants and Animals," i. ii. iii., *Fortnightly Review* 1869, 1870.)

popular, and has been encrusted with the floating mythology of the people, it passes into a genuine myth.

Such, then, is the method, and such are the dangers, of our new science. Already have conclusions been arrived at which clear up this obscure province of human history, and enable us to trace the development and perversion of the religious spirit. In these researches Comparative Mythology, as a branch of Glottology, cannot dispense with the help of other sciences, more particularly of Ethnology. The latter has allowed us to penetrate back into the very roots of the old Theogonies. We learn that the religious instinct first exhibits itself in the worship of dead ancestors. Society begins with a hive-like community, the members of which are not individually marked out, but together form one whole. In other words, the community, and not the individual, lives and acts. But the community does not comprise the living only; the dead equally form part of it; and their presence, it is believed, can alone account for the dreams of the savage or the pains and illnesses to which he is subject. In this way the conception of a spiritual world takes its rise. The spiritual, however, is recognised only in the sensuous. It is a sensible image or a sensible feeling which convinces the barbarian of the existence of the supernatural. The spirits are but part and parcel of the community to which he himself belongs. There is no difficulty in embodying them in the objects around him. In his dreams they appear to him in corporeal shape, and when his tooth aches he thinks that he feels the gnawing of the malignant ghost. Hence they are supposed to take up their habitation in animals and material things. The Hurons believe that the souls of the departed turn into turtle-doves; and the Zulus consider certain green and brown harmless snakes to be their ancestors, and accordingly offer them sacrifices. In fact, all serpent-worship has had this origin, the serpent that crawled along the ground, and was thought to eat dust, seeming peculiarly fitted to be the representative of the buried corpse. "Serpens Libavitque dapes, rursusque innoxius imo Successit tumulo, et depasta altaria liquit." The Pythagorean saying that the human marrow after death was changed into a serpent is but a later form of the old idea; and the Accadian god of the house, as well as of cities and wisdom, who was symbolised by the snake, was primarily the earth, reminding us of the answer of the Telmessians to Krœsus, ὄφιν εἶναι γῆς παῖδα. The ascription of spiritual existence to material objects was from the first inevitable among those who had not yet retained individual and subjective consciousness. Objects equally with persons appeared in dreams, and it was the ghost of the food that was offered, and the ghost of the flint-weapon that was buried, which delighted the dead and supported him in the spirit-land. As yet there was no distinction between the form and its content. Now the cause of the worship paid to the spirit, and, in short, of any recollection of him at all, was fear or the desire of food. Terrified by dreams or tormented by disease, the savage would try to appease the angry ghost, while the sole source of a continuous cult was the appetite. It was to obtain the needful supply of food that the daily sacrifice was made and the daily prayer addressed. It was the animal wants of early man that kept the light of the religious instinct unextinguished. When, therefore, the conception of the spiritual had passed from mere ancestor-worship, mere adoration of one's own bodily feelings, to the second stage of object-worship, those objects which directly influenced the acquisition of food would receive the principal homage. Fetichism, by localising the spiritual, instead of leaving the remembrance of it to the chance of a dream or an illness, first made it possible to select the objects which were to be accounted divine, and to remind the worshipper of his religious duties by having his gods perpetually before his eyes. But the religious ground and kernel of fetichism is the cult of the deceased forefathers of the community.

With fetichism the germs of a mythology make their appearance. The objects worshipped are, as I have said, those upon which the satisfaction of hunger mainly depends. The arrow, the spear, the harpoon, the fruit-tree, such are the gods of the lower races. Their investiture with independent life shows that man is still in the infantile stage in which the object and the subject are confounded together. Human action is attributed to the inanimate, and the work of the hands is described in language as effecting all those results which we now predicate of nature.

When once, however, human action has been transferred to an inanimate object, a number of phrases have been stereotyped in language which will survive into an advanced condition of knowledge. Ceasing to represent the knowledge of the day, they will create an ideal world, illuminated by traditional reverence and the halo of divinity; and thus the foundations of a mythology are laid. So the marvellous *Sampo* of the Finnic Kalewala is the last relic of a time when the quern was invested with the attributes of religious sanctity. Unquestionably, however, myths which go back to the period of fetichism are rare. It rather survives in the symbols which are attached to different divinities, in the wand of Hermes and the arrows of Apollo, or in the refined conceptions of Agnis, "the fire," and Hestia, "the hearth." The period of fetichism was not one in which the capabilities of language were much tried; the savage was still chary of his words, and unconcerned at the loss of old ones, while the verbal idea of action was still struggling to express itself. But out of fetichism came a higher order of things. Through the medium of conceptions like that of "fire," primitive man transferred his religious associations from the objects which his own fingers had wrought, or which lay immediately about him, to those whose nature he could not explain, whose working he could not influence, and whose power he himself had felt. The bright vault of heaven, the toiling sun, the raging thunderstorm, these were now his gods. The old motive that drove him to select his deities was still strong; the divine beings that he honoured were those that seemed to give him his daily food or to withhold it when they were angry. The feelings of terror once inspired by the appearance of the departed in sleep were now confined to the gods of night, whose subterranean abodes well agreed with the sepulchres of the dead. It was only in dreams that these could afflict him; they could not bring the prey or nourish the plants on which he lived; and consequently the worship that he paid them was forced and scanty. It was the brightness of the day and the sun, and more especially of the dawn, when man goeth forth to his labour and his search for food, that absorbed almost all his religious care. As Von Hahn has acutely remarked,[1] the small part played by the moon in mythology is in great measure due to the little share it has in providing for human necessities. To the sun, on the contrary, the mainstay of life, the altar smoked and the hymn ascended. Man was content not to look for his gods beyond the atmosphere, beyond the space between the earth and the sky, since here alone were to be found the powers which enabled him to live and be conscious of a higher existence.

But the instincts that underlay fetichism were only transferred to less coarse and unintelligent objects. There was a worship of nature instead of stocks and stones. The old confusion between object and subject was still present, the old childish ignorance that had fixed its religious intuition in lifeless things. The new gods, therefore, were endowed with human action; and when men came to be more self-conscious and informed, they found their language teeming with expressions which could only be explained by remembering that the phenomena of the atmosphere had once been divine

[1] "Sagwissenschaftliche Studien," p. 92.

beings, whose actions were the actions of men. But this had been forgotten; and so there grew up an ever-increasing mythology. As the old names and phrases became more and more obscure, popular etymologies were invented to account for them, and Prometheus, the *pramanthas* or fire-chark of the ancient Aryan, crystallised into the wise representative of forethought, who stole the fire of heaven for suffering but finally victorious humanity. Mythology, however, had no past, just as it had no future. It came down from a period when the verb had not yet realised the idea of time, and when the substantives which denoted the individual objects still served to express also both action and will. The labours of the sun were the same day after day; there was no tense to describe them except the aorist.

It is obvious that what we have called the Epithetic Stage of language would have been the most fruitful soil for the birth of mythology. An epithet is necessarily a metaphor, implying action; and when we call the moon "the measurer," we at once personify it, that is, ascribe to it the action of a man. But not only was there thus from the first a mythic element introduced; the epithet, being equally applicable to a variety of objects, would tend to confuse their qualities together, and when one special application of it was preserved through religious sanctity as a mere name, all the original meaning and reference being lost, a number of incongruous attributes, derived from other applications, would be associated with it. In fact, in proportion as a community has advanced towards the epithetic stage, the mythological wealth of its language is large. Myths are the traditional relics of the way in which primitive man confounded his own subjective sense of power with the objects which animal needs had led him to consecrate as gods, as well as of the attempts made to explain them when the state of society and knowledge which had produced them was changed. They rested upon the religious instinct, and it was this that saved them from perishing.

The results of Comparative Mythology have not escaped misconception and objection. It is no doubt hard for those who have been brought up to regard the myth as a corruption of revelation or a perversion of an historical fact or a sacerdotal allegory to disabuse themselves of their belief. It is harder for those who have been accustomed to hunt for fragments of history in the mythology of a nation, under the guidance of a special divination, to acquiesce in the decisions of a study which declares that all such labour is in vain, that myth is to uncultivated man what history is to us, and that any historical references that may be imbedded in it can only be discovered from ordinary historical sources. The method, however—that of comparison—by which these conclusions are obtained is the method of science, and, if properly carried out, can alone lead us to scientific truth; but it must not be held responsible for the rash statements of over-hasty disciples, who are not contented with the restrictions imposed by our evidence. Just as we shall never be able to give the derivation of every word in the dictionary, so we shall never be able to explain every individual myth; and the endeavour to do so necessarily brings discredit upon the conclusions arrived at on sufficient data. We must be content with general rules and the explanation of the larger number of myths. The two chief objections, however, raised against the results are, on the one side, that they presuppose in primitive man too high an imagination, and, on the other side, that they ascribe to him too feeble an imagination. We might leave these mutually destructive statements to neutralise one another, but it is better to clear up the misunderstandings upon which they are based. We are told, then, on the one hand, that to believe that our barbarian ancestors were always busied in describing the wonders of the dawn and the daily progress of the sun through the sky in richly poetical metaphors is simply absurd. The country boor is blind to the beauties of nature, and the savage cares only for his selfish animal lusts. But it is precisely the latter fact which solves the difficulty. It was just because the dawn and the sun and the fire seemed to provide him with the food which he needed that primitive man regarded them as his gods and invested them with human power. The poetical dress which has been thrown over them is a necessity of language. Poetry consists in metaphor, personification, and terseness; and all these were the inevitable characteristics of early speech, when the spiritual could only be understood through the sensuous, and when object and subject were inextricably blended together. It is scientific language that is furthest removed from poetry; the savage still talks in poetic metaphor, and the earliest compositions are in verse. The rhythm that underlies the myth is the lyric rhythm of speech—the most exquisite of all music; and the deep insight that pervades it is the naive simplicity of childlike humanity, and the religious conviction which it would express. As for the contrary objection, that our forefathers could not have had such a poverty of ideas as to confine all their attention to the phenomena of the atmosphere, it is answered by the same consideration, that the choice of the objects of mythology was dictated by the circumstances in which the first men were placed. We do not find that the range of ideas possessed by the modern savage is very great, and the very growth of mythology implies that the imagination increased with changing conditions. That the elements were only modified, enlarged, and combined, but not added to, is due to the religious core to which mythology owed its preservation. Indeed, without the religious instinct, mythology would have had no existence at all; it originated not in the imagination of the poet, but in the requirements of worship. As a matter of fact, however, the assertions of the comparative mythologist, whether likely or unlikely, are no subjective theory, but the plain reading of the evidence before us. In many cases, at least, the Rig-Veda, our earliest Aryan monument, *does* show that a Greek legend had a solar origin; and so long as we keep to our data, we can find nothing to support us in tracing back our European mythology to anything else than atmospheric phenomena. If there were any primitive myths of a different derivation, we have no means left of detecting them. Nor is it in the Aryan family alone that the same conclusion is necessitated, although the inflective character of the language and the extensive development of the epithetic stage would lead us to expect to meet with more mythology here than anywhere else.

The myths of other races, wherever their meaning is transparent enough, wherever the proper names are capable of analysis, are all atmospheric and celestial. Thus the Eskimaux have a legend about the moon—how he met a girl in a dark hut at a festive gathering, and declared his love by shaking her shoulders. She smeared her hand with soot and marked him: but when a light was brought she found it was her brother, and fled, ever pursued by him through the sky, where the moon is always chasing the sun with a dark spot upon his blackened cheek. The Assyrians, again, borrowing apparently from their Accadian predecessors, told how Allat or Astarte, "queen of heaven, with crescent horns," descended from the sky through the seven gates of Hades, leaving at each some one of her adornments—her earrings, her necklace, her girdle, her anklets—so that at last she reached the land of the dead, where the sun of winter was sleeping, stripped and empty; to return again, however, and receive back at each gate the ornaments she had left behind. No one can fail to see here the waning and waxing moon, any more than to understand how the sun-god can be addressed in an old Babylonian hymn as the opener of the bright locks of heaven.[1]

[1] The more I examine the mythology of the ancient non-Semitic population of Babylonia, the more clearly does the solar origin of

The last two arguments urged against the scientific interpretation of mythology are, firstly, the elastic limits and vague and general characteristics assigned to the myth; and, secondly, the narrow local restrictions to which it is often subject. It is said that any story of life and death and marriage, any tale in which the hero migrates from east to west, ought, upon the theory, to be admitted

the larger part of it appear. Thanks to the agglutinative character of the language, the proper names are always transparent, and so, in spite of the strange transformations which the various divinities have undergone, carry their primitive meaning and nature upon the face of them. But it is not only the long-buried records of old civilisations that are rising up, as it were, to confirm the conclusions of Comparative Mythology; the self-evident myths of modern barbarians all tell the same tale. A typical instance is the charming legend of the Esthonians which Professor Max Müller has given in his "Introduction to the Science of Religion," pp. 386-89. "Wanna Issi," it relates, "had two servants, Koit and Ammarik; and he gave them a torch which Koit should light every morning, and Ammarik should extinguish in the evening. In order to reward their faithful services, Wanna Issi told them they might be man and wife; but they asked Wanna Issi that he would allow them to remain for ever bride and bridegroom. Wanna Issi assented, and henceforth Koit handed the torch every evening to Ammarik, and Ammarik took it and extinguished it. Only during four weeks in summer they remain together at midnight; Koit hands the dying torch to Ammarik, but Ammarik does not let it die, but lights it again with her breath. Then their hands are stretched out and their lips meet, and the blush of the face of Ammarik 'colours the midnight sky.'" The significance of the myth would be plain, even if we did not know that *Wanna Issi* in Esthonian means "the old father," *Koit* "the dawn," and *Ammarik* "the gloaming." The New Zealand stories of Maui, the sun-god, which will be found in Tylor's "Primitive Culture," pp. 302, 309, are quite equal to any of the mythological products of the Aryan mind.

into the circle of solar myths. In fact, so general are the features which are attributed to the myth, that it is possible to transmute any individual whatsoever into an image of the sun, just as Archbishop Whateley banished the great Napoleon to the realm of fable. But all this proceeds upon the mistaken assumption that it is only necessary to compare two legends together to determine their character. On the contrary, a scientific comparison must conform to all the rules of the special science; and since Comparative Mythology is but a branch of Glottology, we must not advance one step without the safeguard of language. Hêraklês is the sun, not only because his life and labours are those of other solar heroes, but also because his own name discloses his origin from *swara*, "the splendour of heaven," like the names of those with whom he comes in contact—Augeias, Deianeira, Iole—in his struggles and in his death. The second objection is even less plausible. When it is asked why the story, for instance, of Kephalos and Prokris, the rising sun and the dewdrop, should have been so local in character that no allusion to it appears before the time of Apollodorus and Ovid, we can only reply, why is it that so many old words are utterly obliterated in the language of the country, and yet crop up in these latter days of linguistic research in obscure provincial dialects? Our good old English *laik*, "to play," only lurks now in the corners of the northern counties, just as many a myth of pre-Homeric Greece survived in the mouths of illiterate peasants, to be discovered and recorded in the days of court dilettanti and antiquarian book-makers.

When once the question of mythology has been settled, we can proceed to the comparative science of religions, or, if we might coin a word, of Dogmatology. What we have to do here is to compare and classify the various religious systems that have prevailed in the world, and to trace their connection, origin, and development. It is, of course, only the external form and shell with which we are concerned; the religious spirit which inspires them must be left, as in mythology, to other students. We have nothing to do with the truth or falsehood of particular religions; that is a point which must be handed over to the theologian. Nor is it our business to ascertain the history of a special creed, and the unfolding of its dogmas; the quarrels of Catholics and Arians, the disputes of Nestorius and St Cyril, are of little consequence to us; what we want are the general results, just as Glottology makes use of materials provided by the specialists in each language. Still less have we to deal with the biographies of religious founders or reformers; for all that Dogmatology requires, they may be mythic personages. It is the ideas, or rather the forms of the ideas, which they utilised and arranged, and the way in which these were afterward modified and added to, that have an interest for us. As in most cases we can arrive at these only by the aid of language, the science of religions will need the control of Glottology as much as does Comparative Mythology. As yet the science of religions has made but little progress. We are still engaged in collecting materials, in learning to read the sacred books of the East, and to ascertain what it is they have to tell us. Nevertheless certain general outlines, within which the conclusions of the new science will have to be comprehended, have already been sketched. We have come to see that religious systems and their development are obedient to general laws, like everything else, and that each race of men has shaped its system in a manner of its own. The isolating Chinese differs in his form of creed from the inflection-using Aryan and Semite, and these, again, carry out their religious ideas in a different way; but a general likeness is to be observed between the latter. As Buddhism and Zoroastrianism have come forth from the bosom of Brahmanism, so have Christianity and Mohammedanism from Judaism; and just as Buddha preached the equality of men, in contradistinction to the aristocratic creed of Manu, so the exclusiveness of the Jew has given place to the universality of Christianity; while the prophet of the Avesta was not less clear in his sharply-cut dualism, out of which Monotheism was to spring by the absorption of good into evil, than was the prophet of the Korân in his doctrine of one God. Indeed, Buddhism and Christianity present closer analogies than that of mere derivation. Just as Sakya Muni appeared about 600 years before the birth of Christ, so did Mohammed about 600 years after that event: 300 years after its institution Buddhism was made the state religion by the powerful monarch Asoka, by whose orders a general council was convened to settle matters of faith and discipline, just as Constantine was converted, and the Council of Nikæa assembled by him, A.D. 325. The monasteries of Christendom find their parallel in the monasteries of Buddhism, the Pope of Rome in the Lama of Tibet; and the image-worship, the proxy-prayers, and the elaborate ceremonial of the medieval Church are not more unlike the divine morality of the Sermon on the Mount than are the adoration of relics, the praying machines, and the rites of the Buddhist hierarchy unlike the simple code of morals and life which their founder bequeathed to them.[1]

Much that is now dark in dogma may be cleared up with the advance of our comparative researches. Here, as elsewhere, it will be found that we inherit the forgotten beliefs of our forefathers. The words, the phrases, the practices, have descended to us from the past, but we have put into them a new spirit and a new meaning. The founder of a religion, however great he may be, however much, as his disciples believe, a prophet of God, or even God himself, has yet to deal with men. He must work upon the ideas current in his age; and though he may give them a fresh direction, still their comprehension and carrying out will be limited by the intellectual knowledge of the recipients. And as this will vary from generation to generation, so will the ideas themselves vary, and catch the colour of each succeeding century.

[1] Professor Max Müller, in his charming "Lectures on the Science of Religion" (p. 105), adds another parallelism between the two religions:—"Buddhism, being at its birth an Aryan religion, ended by becoming the principal religion of the Turanian world;" just as "Christianity, the offspring of Mosaism, was rejected by the Jews, as Buddhism was by the Brahmans, . . . and became the principal religion of the Aryan world."

## CHAPTER IX.

### THE INFLUENCE OF ANALOGY IN LANGUAGE.

The phenomena of phonetic decay are among the first to attract the notice of the student of language. They show themselves, as it were, upon the surface of speech; they force themselves upon the attention; and the slow and gradual change that goes on in language seems, at first sight, to be due to them alone. The wear and tear of words and their meanings which is continually taking place, however little perceived by the passing generation, is like the wasting of the rocks by air, and water, and ice, that, through the long series of geological ages, has piled up the crust of the earth, scooping out the valleys and moulding the everlasting hills. And just as this constant process of destruction has blotted out myriads of intermediate links between successive forms of life, bringing about the so-called imperfection of the geologic record, so, in language, the action of phonetic decay has left us but waifs and strays of former states of speech, and obliterated words and forms which alone can explain the origin of what is left, or affiliate languages one to the other. It is not wonderful, therefore, that phonetic decay has assumed an exaggerated importance in the eyes of philologists, or even been brought forward to the exclusion of all other principles which affect linguistic growth. Its very name, however, shows that it cannot be a principle of universal application. Phonology is but a subordinate part of Comparative Philology, dealing at most with its material, not with its content. And though in philology material and content can only be arbitrarily separated one from the other for the purposes of scientific analysis, inasmuch as language is but the outward expression of thought, yet a principle which primarily deals with the external alone must be of limited and not general range. In fact, when we come to look closely into the matter, we shall find that phonetic decay is largely influenced by another and wider principle, that of Analogy. This is a main element of change in the signification as well as in the outward form of words; and just as phonetic decay wastes and destroys, so analogy repairs and reconstructs. The one is the agent of destruction, the other of construction, though they both spring from the same root of human laziness.

One of the most important of the functions of

analogy is the production of a new grammar. Grammar is not only the skeleton of a language, but the very life-blood of it as well, and the changes that take place in it are in large measure occasioned by the agency of analogy. But analogy may be either false or true; indeed, in the history of speech we shall see that false analogy has as often been at work as true. A large number of feminine nouns in French, like *étude* and *voile* have arisen from the mistaken comparison of the plural neuter ending in *-a* with the similar termination of the singular of the first Latin declension. And so, as the majority of the substantives belonging to this declension were feminine, mind and ear came to associate the idea of the feminine so closely with the termination *-a* as to assign that gender to all words whatsoever which ended with this particular vowel. The instinct here led to a false conclusion; that is to say, it ignored the true history and significance of certain linguistic forms; and this confusion and violation of the regular historical development of speech is all that is meant by the philologist when he speaks of the false in language.

But analogy does not act upon forms alone. Both matter and form are alike subject to its influence. While, on the one hand, the relations of grammar, the rules of syntax, and the content and meaning of words grow changed and altered by its subtle operation, the external shape and character of the vocabulary, on the other hand, also becomes insensibly transformed. No doubt the two processes of change go on, for the most part, side by side, since we cannot, except on paper, separate the inner essence of a word from the material in which it is expressed; but there is no more fatal error than to assume that a new conception or a new grammatical relation can arise out of mere phonetic change. They are due to analogy, not to phonetic decay. It was not the neo-Latin pronunciation and external form of *voile* that caused it to be feminine, but the fact that a particular external form had already been appropriated to the feminine gender in a preponderant number of instances. The inward in language, as in other things, cannot be originated by the outward, however much the outward may be originated by the inward. It was to be a vehicle for internal thought that language first came into existence; and the popular etymologies, which modify the outward form of a word in order to harmonise it with an intelligible idea, still bear testimony to this.

Now the principle of analogy may be ultimately traced partly to the desire of saving trouble, partly to the natural instinct of imitation. It is easier for the vocal organs to repeat the same sound than to attempt a new one, while the repetition of the same idea, or the expression of an analogous one, involves less exertion on the part of the mind. Habit is a ruling power in life, and sounds or ideas to which we are accustomed rise uncalled for to the intelligence and the lips. Every one must have experienced the difficulty of pronouncing some sound in a foreign language to which there is nothing similar in his own; and in proportion to the strangeness of the sound will be the vocal effort to produce it. The more regular the inflectional system of a language, the more readily do we learn it; and the ease with which a knowledge of Italian, as compared with German, may be acquired results to a great extent from the superior regularity of its inflections. The tendency of all linguistic progress is to reduce the number of anomalous forms, and bring them all, whatever may have been their origin, under one and the same type. Thus in modern Greek certain declensions have become the prevailing models in accordance with which substantives are declined, and words like *φύλαξ* have long ago become *φύλακος*.[1] This process of assimilation of sounds and gram-

[1] So in the Ionic of Herodotus. The modern Greek declines innumerable words which formerly belonged to different declensions after the type of *ταμίας*; as *βασιλέας*, *γ'ροντας*, *ἄνδρας* &c.

matical terminations is accelerated by contact with another language. Exceptions and irregularities, which seem quite natural to a native habituated to their use, are always hateful to the foreigner, inasmuch as they require a greater effort of memory and attention. To say nothing of the general loss of inflections, many of which had grown otiose, the preponderance of the plural in *-s* in English is due to the Norman invasion, as well as the softening or dropping of the guttural aspirate in words like *enough* and *though*.[1] Assimilation, so frequent a cause of phonetic change, is wholly occasioned by the attempt to avoid pronouncing a fresh sound, and by allowing analogy to operate upon an adjacent letter; and other phonetic changes are extended and stereotyped in speech by means of the same principle. But it is not phonetic change alone that is influenced in this way by the wish to save trouble. Nothing is harder than to think out a new thought or to grasp a totally new idea; hence the conceptions applicable to one set of phenomena are transferred to an entirely different, and perhaps even contradictory, set; and simi-

[1] The effects of the movement set on foot in this direction by the Norman invasion were very slow in being brought about. It was not until the seventeenth century that the guttural sound had disappeared uniformly in the South of England, and it still flourishes in the North. When Butler wrote in 1633 it is clear that it had become altogether extinct in the South. See A. J. Ellis, "Early English Pronunciation," vol. i. pp. 209.214.

larities are ingeniously detected between the most dissimilar things. It was long before the several relations of space, time, and manner came to be distinguished from one another, and we may even now hear expressions used of time which can strictly be employed of space alone. So, again, the wealth of meanings contained in our dictionary is the result of the endeavour to get at new ideas without having to take the trouble of inventing them. The words *post* and *arm* may be selected as illustrations of the roundabout way in which the human mind goes to work to increase its store of conceptions. From the simple idea of a thing *placed* or *set* we have a myriad derivatives, from the stake fixed in the ground to the medium of modern correspondence. Similarly, analogy has extended the signification of *arm* to the weapon a man carries, a channel of the sea, or the power of law. If Curtius is right, no better instance can be found of the extraordinary transformations of meaning undergone by words than the Homeric adjective φοξὸς, which, derived from the root *bhaj*, "to bake," originally signified a vessel of baked clay, and finally came to be applied to the head of Thersites, the peaked shape of which resembled the household *amphora*, with its pointed bottom for sticking in the ground.[1] When we consider the

[1] Curtius, "Grundzüge der Griech. Etymologie," p. 172 (2d edit.)

manner in which the lexicon is enlarged and altered by the action of analogy, and the unlikely cases to which we find it applied, we may well be cautious in assuming the primitive independence of two roots which agree in sound but differ in meaning.[1] It is not more difficult to understand how the name of the *guinea-pig* could have been given, and, what is more, accepted, among people acquainted with the swine, than to comprehend how the South Sea Islander could call the dog a pig, or the Kuriaks the ox "the Russian elk" (*Ruski olehn*).[2]

We have now to examine the influence of analogy in language as affecting its matter and its form. And first, as regards its matter. Here we find it bringing about changes in accent, in quantity, and in pronunciation generally. False rather than true analogy is the guiding principle; that is to say, the historical reasons for a certain pro-

[1] Donner has a short but instructive article in the *Zeitschrift der D. M. G.*, xxvii. 4 (1873), on root-formation in the Finnic-Ugrian languages, in which he points out that the great transparency of the Ugrian family of speech allows us to see the passage of one signification in a root into another of a wholly different kind, accompanied by a modification of the vowel. Thus *kayan* is "to ring" and "to lighten;" *kar-yun* and *kir-yun*, "to cry," but *kir-on*, "to curse;" *kah-isen*, *koh-isen*, *kuh-isen*, "to hit," "stamp;" *käh-isen*, *köh-isen*, "to roar;" *keh-isen*, *kih-isen*, "to boil." The Turanian idioms conceal their radicals so slightly that this development of meaning is still living and still traceable in them.

[2] See Pott, "Etymologische Forschungen," II. i. pp. 125-139 (2d edit.) "The New Zealanders are stated to have called horses large dogs" (Farrar, "Origin of Language," p. 119).

nunciation are forgotten, and a word is made to conform to what, from some cause or other, has become the favourite and most common type. Thus the general tendency of our own language is to throw back the accent as far as possible; and accordingly words like *balcony* and *illustrated*, which fifty years ago were pronounced with the accent on the penultima, are now usually sounded *bálcony* and *illústrated*. *Contemplate* and *blasphemous*, in which Tennyson and Milton preserve the penultimate accent, are now almost always accented on the first syllable;[1] and *revenue* has long followed their example. Sooner or later analogy is pretty sure to force all exceptional cases into harmony with what has become the prevailing rule of pronunciation.[2] In no other way, again, can we explain how it is that whereas

[1] "When I contémplate all alone" (Tennyson, "In Memoriam," lxxxiii. 1). "O argument blasphémous, false, and proud!" (Milton, "Paradise Lost," book v.) The change that has taken place in the pronunciation of *tea* since the reign of Queen Anne is of a similar nature. Pope has—

> "Soft yielding minds to water glide away,
> And sip, with nymphs, their elemental tea."
> —"*Rape of the Lock*," canto i. (so, too, canto iii.)

[2] In a paper read before the Philological Society (March 1875), Mr J. Payne pointed out that many words in the Midland dialect are of old French origin, though disguised by the accent, which has been transferred from the final to the first or second syallable in accordance with the English rule of accentuation. Thus *enchantoúr* has become *enchánter*; *batáile*, *báttle*; *lábber* is for *laboúr*, *fúzzen* for *foisón*, *Marry* for *Marié*, *tice* for *enticér*, &c.

Irish and Bohemian accent all their words on the first syllable, Welsh and Polish accent all theirs on the penultima.[1] Welsh and Irish on the one side, Bohemian and Polish on the other, are dialects too closely related not to oblige us to believe that there was a time when the common idiom out of which they have severally developed was pronounced in the same way; but circumstances caused a particular mode of accentuation to become fashionable in each of the separated dialects, and the whole stock of words in each was thereupon gradually brought under the dominant type. It must have been much the same with Latin and the Æolic dialect in Greece. We now know that the regular throwing back of the accent as far as possible was the late product of the action of analogy, and not the survival of a primitive practice. The normal Greek accentuation agrees with that of Vedaic Sanskrit, even in such seemingly arbitrary cases as the different position of the accent in the numerals *pánchan* πέντε, and *saptán*, ἑπτά; and Doric Greek has more truly preserved the paroxyton of the third person plural in the second aorist, which primarily ended with a long syllable

[1] Whitney, "Language and the Study of Language," p. 96. The accent, however, is not all over Ireland on the first syllable. O'Donovan states that the poets of the north and south of Ireland are no longer in metrical harmony with one another because they place the accent so differently.

(ἐτύπουτ), than has the classical dialect, where the ancient form of the word has been forgotten, and the tendency that became a dominant law in Æolic and Latin has been followed.[1] Intimately connected with accent is quantity; and in this also the modifying influence of analogy has been active. A good example is afforded by the Latin rule, which allows a vowel before a mute followed by a liquid to be either long or short. Thus we have *latēbræ* or *latĕbræ* from *latēre*, *scatēbra* or *scatĕbra* from *scatēre*; and Horace addresses the fountain of Bandusia as "splendidior *vĭtro*." Now, by all the laws of prosody, the first syllable of *vitrum* ought to be as long as the middle syllable of *latebræ* and *scatebra*, since the word stands for *vis-trum*, that is, *vid-trum*, from the root *vid*. But in numerous instances the vowel before the double consonant was short by nature, and since this could be lengthened when necessary, the belief grew up that any vowel before a mute and a liquid might be either long or short, and so a naturally long vowel came to be used as a short one wherever the exigencies of the metre demanded it. Much the same has happened with words terminating in *d* or *t*. The majority of vocables which ended in a dental had the vowel of the last syllable properly short; and accordingly all such syllables

[1] Ahrens, "De Dialect. Doric," p. 28 *sq*.

came to be regarded as short, whatever may have been the original length of the vowel. Hence it is that we find words like *sed*, the old ablative of the third personal pronoun, or *sit*, the contracted form of the optative *siet* with long *e*,[1] employed with a short vowel. So again, in Greek, Hartel has shown that the -ι of the dative plural and the -α of plural neuters were primitively long—a fact traces of which may still be observed in Homer.[2] The short final syllable, however, of the third person plural of the verb (λέγουσι, for λέγοντι), and the short accusative termination of nouns of the third declension (ποδὰ for ποδὰμ), prepared the way for shortening every terminal -ι and -α; and when once the ear and tongue had become accustomed to the shortened form of these terminations, every fresh case that occurred had to conform to the general analogy.

But not accent and quantity only, the pronunciation of syllables and letters also falls under the same principle of change. How much, indeed, a change in the latter depends upon a change of accent may be seen from the so-called *guna*, in which the modification of the vowel is entirely occasioned by the stress laid upon it. But what-

[1] *Siet* answers to the Sanskrit optative *'syât*, the Greek εἴη for ἐσίη (=ἐσyητ).

[2] Hartel, "Homerische Studien," 1873. See Curtius in "Studien zur Griech. und Latein. Grammatik., iv. 2, p. 477.

ever may be the cause of change, when once the new pronunciation has taken a firm hold upon the speech, it gradually extends itself to the whole vocabulary; so that it may happen that a sound formerly familiar to a language dies out so utterly that the speakers find themselves unable to pronounce it when met with in another dialect. A striking example of this is to be found in the history of the guttural aspirate in English. A similar occurrence seems to have taken place in Assyrian in the case of the letter *'ayin.* This had been thinned into a modified *i* vowel, so that when they wanted to express the name of the Palestinian city Gaza (עזה), they could find no better representative of the old guttural sound of *'ayin*, as preserved in Western Semitic, than the ordinary guttural aspirate *kheth*, and so עזה (*'azzah*) was written *khazitu.*[1] The action of analogy upon pronunciation, however, is nowhere exemplified more clearly than in the adoption of foreign words. A Frenchman drops the final consonants of the names and terms which he borrows or uses, and the Englishman speaks of *Marsails* and *Paris*, of *lieutenant* and *passport.* Indeed, our own language is a most interesting monument of the profound and universal change in pronunciation that may

[1] The final syllable is the feminine termination in -ת (-*t*), which has become -ה (-h) in Hebrew.

be brought about by the influence of analogy when special circumstances give a particular mode of pronunciation a superiority in the linguistic struggle for existence. Our vowels are no longer what they were three centuries ago. The *a* and the *i* have become diphthongs, and the *e* has taken the place of the *i*. Sir Christopher Wren's cathedral is St Paul's not St Powle's, and the final *e* has long ceased to be sounded. But a change is still going on. Just as it has been remarked that French is becoming more and more nasalised, so also has it been noted that the vowels in English are continually growing more and more thinned. The broad *a* in words like *mast* or *bad* is a mark of Cockneyism, and the diphthongal sound of *u* is extending itself on all sides. The same preference for diphthongal sounds is making itself apparent in words like *either* and *neither*, the first syllable of which is beginning to be pronounced as though it were German, although the only other word in English by which such a pronunciation could be supported is the misspelt *height* from *high*. It has been pointed out [1] that the reason why we pronounce the three first vowels of the alphabet in a way essentially different from that in which they are sounded in the majority of our words is because they are so pronounced in

[1] Earle, "Philology of the English Tongue," pp. 111-114 (2d edit.)

the three vocables in most common use, *a*, *me*, and *I*; and it is a curious instance of the power of analogy that, although the numerical majority of words is against it, yet the frequency with which this peculiar pronunciation is heard in the three words just mentioned, aided by the values assigned to the three vowels as letters of the alphabet, induces us to give this pronunciation to them wherever they occur in foreign terms with the true pronunciation of which we are unacquainted.[1] But the influence of analogy will, of course, be proportionally greater where we have to do, not with the spelling, but with sound exclusively; and the power exerted by the principle over written words will enable us to understand how largely it will affect spoken words, more especially in an illiterate society. This, I think, will afford an explanation of the phenomena of Grimm's law. Accident, so to speak, may have made a particular pronunciation of some letter predominant in one of the branches of the Aryan

[1] Prof. Rhŷs says of the peculiar Welsh sound represented by *ll*, that it was produced by "the coming together of the two *l*'s, which were undoubtedly so pronounced up to a date which has not as yet been exactly fixed. Eventually this sound has much extended its domain in the language" ("The Early Inscribed Stones of Wales," reprinted from the *Carnarvon and Denbigh Herald*, 1873, p. 11). It may be noted that the same souud is to be found among the Cherokees of North America (Prof. Haldeman, *Proc. of Amer. Orient. Soc.*, 1874, p. xlv.)

family; but when this pronunciation had once fixed itself in the most commonly used words, or in the majority of them, or had approved itself to the popular taste by its greater easiness of utterance, or by some other reason, it was extended to every case found in the vocabulary. We may thus account for the remarkable uniformity and regularity in the shifting of sounds which is observed in the several members of the Indo-European group. In this instance the action of analogy would have been natural; but it may also be produced artificially. A good illustration of this is to be found in the Homeric dialect. The Iliad, and, to a far less extent, the Odyssey,[1] are the growth of generations, old epic formulæ and verses being handed down tradition-

[1] The critical labours of Kirchhoff ("Die Composition der Odyssee," 1869, and "Die Homerische Odyssee und ihre Entstehung," 1859; see also Heimreich in the *Progr. des Gym. zu Flensburg*, 1871) have made it pretty clear that the Odyssey is the amalgamation of two artificial poems, each of which was based upon ancient popular lays. The redactor would have flourished in the seventh century B.C., since not only is an acquaintance with the Argonautika displayed, but also with countries in the West, whither the Greek colonists transferred the myths originally localised in the Black Sea; while the Kimmerians (Od. xi. 14-19), who were driven out of Tartary by the Skyths, in the time of Gyges, and a little before the siege of Nineveh by Kyaxares (B.C. 660), are mentioned by name. So, too, the fountain of Artakiê (Od. x. 108) was an historical locality near Kyzikus, the birthplace of Aristeas, whose poem, the Arimaspea, first informed the Greeks about Kimmerians and Skyths; and as Kyzikus was founded between the 7th and 24th Olympiads, and a certain lapse of time must be allowed for the

ally from rhapsode to rhapsode, and imitated and incorporated in a slowly increasing body of poetry. But the imitations very frequently were based upon a false analogy. The old pronunciation had been lost; and what had really a sound philological origin was supposed to be due to metric license, and so came to be applied to totally different cases. Thus, as Mangold has pointed out, the analogy of the dicktasis or so-called resolution of the vowels in verbs in -αω, where it had a philological reason, lead to a similar resolution of the syllable in verbs in -οω, in the conjunctives of verbs in -μι, and elsewhere, where it was wholly unjustifiable.[1]

Before leaving this part of the subject, I must

attachment of a myth to the place, the story of the Læstrygonians could hardly have been introduced into the Odyssey before 660 B.C. It may be true that in the Iliad, as well as in the Odyssey, the armour, the chariots, and the dress, both of men and women, is the same as upon vases and sculptures of the fifth century, B.C., but however hard it may be to explain how this could be the case in an age of rapid change and revolution, it is certain that the subjects of the vase paintings and the Lykian sculptures, which are older than the sixth century, are taken from the Iliad alone, while it is only in the Odyssey that a reference is made to the *nine* muses (Od. xxiv. 60), and therefore to a knowledge of tragedy, comedy, prose-writing, and astronomy, and that the Attic and post-Solonian division of the month into decades (Od. xiv. 161-164), and the day into hours (Od. iii. 334), is alluded to.

[1] Mangold, "De Diectasi Homerica," in Curtius' *Studien*, vi. 1. See also Hartel, "Homerische Studien;" Curtius in the *Studien*, iv. 2; and Paley "On the Odyssey," in the *British Quarterly*, Oct. 1873.

not forget to notice how, even in the *material* of language, analogy shows itself as a creative and reconstructing principle. English has somewhat doubtfully enriched itself with several anomalous plurals by means of it. The distinction of vowel between *man* and *men*, *foot* and *feet*, was, in Anglo-Saxon, purely euphonic. The dative singular was *men*, just as much as the genitive and dative plural were *manna* and *mannum*. But the thinner form with *e* occurred more frequently in the plural than in the singular, and so, when the cases of the old language disappeared, the unmeaning difference became significant. *A* absorbed the singular and *e* the plural, instead of being merely predominant. The distinction between the present and perfect of verbs like *lead*, *led*, is of the same nature. The Anglo-Saxon imperfect was marked, not by the change of vowel, but by the flection; when this was dropped, however, the greater frequency of the obscure vowel in the past tense, owing to the inflection (*ledde*), caused it to be assigned to all the persons, and to become a characteristic of the tense. So in Greek, the distinction between verbs in -άω, -έω, and -όω was at first purely phonetic, each of the vowels being only a modification of one and the same termination which we have in Sanskrit; but in course of time, in consequence of the accidental fact that a considerable number of verbs in -οω were active and of verbs in -εω neuter, the form in -οω came to be more and more set apart to denote a transitive, and that in -εω an intransitive notion, while the form in -αω floated between the two senses. It is true that the distinction in meaning was never exhaustively carried out, but we can hardly doubt that it would have been had Greek lasted long enough and never become a literary language. It is highly probable that the significant vowel of Arabic verbs has the same history. In Arabic, *u* (and *i*, for the most part) marks a passive sense, *a* generally an active one. Now traces of this distinction are to be found in Hebrew and Aramaic, as well as in Assyrian; but what has become the rule in Arabic is at most nothing more than a tendency in the other Semitic idioms.[1]

The change of the euphonic into the significant vowel would be much easier in a Semitic than in an Aryan tongue, since analogy would be all in its favour—Semitic grammar preferring to effect

[1] Wright, "Arabic Gram.," pp. 28, 29; Gesenius, "Hebrew Gram.," § 43; Cowper, "Syriac Gram.," § 78; Dillmann, "Grammatik der äthiopischen Sprache," p. 116; and my "Assyrian Gram.," p. 72.

According to Bleek ("Comp. Gramm. of South African Languages," ii. p. 138), the vowel which terminates nouns in Bâ-ntu, and has nothing to do with the derivative prefixes, may be either *u* (or *e*) or *o*. The latter has "a passive meaning, *i* an active or causative, *a* a neutral force."

by internal vowel-change what is left to external flection in the Indo-European group; but the instances given above show that the process is not unknown to our own family of languages wherever association of ideas and sounds may favour it. In contrasting Aryan vocalism with Semitic consonantalism, it is impossible to draw any sharply-defined lines of distinction. Here, as everywhere else, however true our classification may be, yet the several classes pass insensibly one into the other, and we cannot precisely determine their boundaries. It is to this fact that the idolum of the three stages in the growth of a language mainly owes its origin.

We must next consider the manner in which analogy has acted upon the form and content of speech. This is the side upon which it has been most influential, and where its consequences have been most important. Some form suddenly gets into vogue and replaces older ones, or leaves but a few of them, which henceforth are regarded as abnormal exceptions; or, again, a new grammatical relation is elaborated in some particular case, and then extended to others more or less similar. Thus the English perfect in *-ed* has become predominant in the language. Originally *dide*, the reduplicated past tense of *do*, it was affixed to verb after verb, until only a few were left which still follow the primitive method of conjugation, and every new verb taken into use has to form its perfect by means of it.[1] The Latin perfect in *-vi* or *-ui*, and future in *-bo*, perhaps grew up in the same way, by postfixing *fuo*, *fui*, in a few instances, which continually tended to become more and more numerous. In French, every fresh verb has to belong to the first conjugation. There is no reason in the nature of things why the language should not employ words like *électrisoir*, *photographir*, but the mysterious influence of analogy has ruled that only *électrifier*, *photographier*, should be admitted into the domain of speech.[2] This is the form which, in the struggle for existence, has established itself to the exclusion of every other. Ear and mind had grown accustomed to the association of a special sound

[1] The reduplicated perfect itself, the oldest contrivance of speech for making past and extended time in contradistinction to aoristic indefiniteness, may be regarded as an instance of analogy. Here the repetition of the same sound finally came to be used to express important grammatical relations. For the widespread results of reduplication, see Pott, "Doppelung als eines der wichtigsten Bildungs-Mittel der Sprache." *Cf.* also Lubbock "On the Origin of Civilisation," pp. 403-405, who makes a curious calculation of the proportion of reduplicated words found in English, French, German, and Greek on the one side, and some of the jargons of Africa, America, and the Pacific on the other, the result being, that whereas "in the four European languages we get about two reduplications in 1000 words, in the savage ones the numbe varies from 38 to 170, being from twenty to eighty times as many in proportion."

[2] Ancessi, "L'*S* Causatif et le Thème *N* dans les Langues de Sem et de Cham," p. 72.

with a special sense, and could allow of no other. One of the most striking examples of the way in which this sometimes results in the creation of wholly new flections is the distinction of gender in the nominative singular of Latin comparatives. This arose in the historic period, and we can accordingly trace its genesis. The termination of the nominative was indifferently *-ior* or *-ios* (*-ius*), like the Greek *-ίων* and Sanskrit *-yan*, from an original *-yans*, *r* in Latin commonly standing for *s*,—*e.g.*, in *arbos* and *arbor*, *generis* (which would represent a Sansk. *janasyas*), from *genus*, &c. In Valerius Antias (apud Priscian., vii. 345), we still find *prior* used for the neuter ("senatus consultum prior"), and the title of the Fourth Annal of Cassius Hemina was "Bellum Punicum posterior;" but the connection of the idea of the neuter with the ending *-us* in such words as *opus*, *genus*, and the like, and of the masculine with the ending *-or* in such words as *honor* or *arbor*, brought about the specialisation of form which we meet with in the classical age.[1] The remarkable regularity which we find in the Assyrian conjugations has been produced in much the same way. Its artificiality is shown by a comparison of the other Semitic idioms. *Kal*, *niphal*, and *shaphel*,

[1] Curtius, "Studien zur Griech. u. Latein Grammatik," vi. 1, p. 262.

the active, passive, and causative, were taken as the three primary voices; and not only was *kal* provided with the intensive *pael*, but a *niphael* and *shaphael* were formed as well; while the secondary conjugations in *t* and *tan* were attached to each of the principal voices, including *pael*.[1]

[1] Curtius draws attention to a similar instance of abnormal regularity in the Latin conjugation ("Studien zur Griech. u. Lat. Grammatik," v. 1). After the model of *vehimini*, the plural of the middle participle used for the second person plural of the present, have been formed *vehamini* and *vehemini*, which would answer to ἐχώμενοι and ἐχοίμενοι in Greek, and even *vehebamini*, *veheremini!* Greek analogues to the latter would be μαχεσοίμενοι and μαχεσαίμενοι. The remarks of the eminent German philologist deserve being quoted:—"Analogie setzt überall im Gegensatz zu den normalen Lautverhältnissen und ursprünglichen Formen eine Art von Verirrung der Sprachgefühle durch ein dem redenden Dunkel vorschwebendes Vorbild voraus, dem die Neubildung nur äusserlich und ohne Rücksicht auf die Entstehung der Vorbilder folgt. Unstreitig ist Analogie in diesem Sinne nicht unähnlich jener Anomalie, welche die alten Grammatiker mit συνεκδρομή bezeichneten, namenlich in verhältnissmässig jüngeren Perioden der Sprachgeschichte vielfach eingetreten. Wenn wir z. B. bei Apollonius Rhodius, i. 45, die Form ἔλειπτο, bei Nonnus Dion. xxiv. 241, ἄμειπτο lesen, so sind solche Gebilde sicherlich nur nach der Analogie homerischer wie λέκτο, δέκτο, μῖκτο, κατάπηκτο entstanden und jeder Versuch, sie in das natürliche System des Griechischen Verbums einzuordnen, wäre verfehlt." Elsewhere, again ("Zur Chronologie der indogermanischen Sprachforschung," p. 6), he writes as follows:—"In no discussion upon language, not even in the analysis of forms, much less in the settlement of phonetic laws, can we dispense with the conception of analogy, which is something purely spiritual, and, as far as I can see, foreign to mere natural development. The accusative plural πόλεις can hardly be explained from the original forms πολι-νς or πολι-ας except by the lazy habit of making the accusative plural like the

Analogy, however, will sometimes bring about far more wide-reaching effects than the alteration or production of certain grammatical forms and relations. It may change the whole character of a grammar, the whole structure of a language; provided, that is, that the fundamental principles upon which it is based, the mental view of the people to which it belongs, be not violated. Thus Coptic, which was formerly an affix-language like old Egyptian and the Semitic tongues, has become a prefix-language, resembling in this respect the Berber, the Haussa, and other sub-Semitic dialects of North Africa. When we remember the formal relationship between these and the Semitic idioms, the conclusion seems forced upon us that they also have undergone the same change as Coptic, and assumed their present appearance within a comparatively recent epoch.

Analogy is equally active in the province of syntax. The analytical character of the modern European languages, of which English is the most extreme example, is largely due to its influence. The substitution of prepositions and syntactical contrivances for inflection has gradually become

nominative plural. Equally spiritual is the tendency to *differentiate*, which can be as plainly pointed out as the other. To it we owe the fact that three roots, ἀρ ἐρ and ὀρ, have arisen in Greek different in sound and meaning, out of the common radical *ar*."

the rule instead of the exception. The contact of the Teutonic and Romanic nations brought about the consciousness and analysis of the relations of grammar, which is out of the question so long as the native dialect alone is known; and the tendency to replace flection by analysis and accidence by syntax extended itself with an ever-increasing rapidity. The few remains of flection, the last relics of an uncultured age, which still exist in English, may be expected to disappear in time, even supposing that pigeon-English does not become the universal language, as a recent writer prophesies.[1] Already the inflected genitive in *-s* is more and more disused, and confined to poetry or a high-flown style, the general receptacle of antiquated forms; and it may not be long before this fossil-like survivor of nominal inflection becomes as totally extinct as it is in modern Persian, where the genitive is denoted by the short vowel placed between it and the preceding nominative. The manner in which we express the relation of the genitive must follow the common analogy, and be no exception to the analytic character of our speech. Another example of the effect of analogy upon syntax may be found in the history of the relative sentence, which has been so ably investi-

[1] See W. Simpson on "China's Future Place in Philology," *Macmillan's Magazine*, November 1873.

gated by Jolly and Windisch.[1] Comparative syntax teaches us that the relative sentence was primarily expressed by being immediately subordinated to the principal clause without the addition of any explanatory word, just as it may be in Hebrew or Assyrian poetry, and in such English phrases as "This is the man I saw." For the sake of clearness and emphasis, however, the object of the antecedent clause was repeated in the consequent by some demonstrative term signifying locality, and the attention was thus drawn to the idea intended to be signalised. Thus in Chinese, the relative *so* properly means "place;"[2] and Philippi has shown that the relative pronoun in Semitic was originally a demonstrative.[3] So it was also in our Aryan family. But after a time, this pronoun, this representative of the object denoted, came to be used in all cases, and not merely where peculiar stress was wished to be laid upon it; and when analogy had thus uniformly extended this particular employment of the word, it ceased to convey any longer a purely demonstrative sense, and resumed a relative signification, which was

[1] Jolly, "Ueber die einfachste Form der Hypotaxis im Indogermanischen;" and Windisch, "Untersuchungen über den Ursprung des Relativpronomens," in Curtius' *Studien*, vi. 1, and ii. 2.

[2] Schott, "Chines. Sprachlehre," p. 88.

[3] Philippi, "Wesen und Ursprung des Status Constructus im Hebräischen," p. 71 *sq.*

then applied by the further operation of analogy to instances in which the demonstrative could hardly have been employed.

The last illustration that need be taken is the position of the verb and objective noun in the sentence. It is remarkable that whereas the normal place of the verb in Latin is at the end of the clause, while the same rule may be said to hold good in German and Dutch, the Romance languages, which have grown up through the contact of Teutonic and Latin populations, place the verb before the objective case. English follows the same order, although poetry or a poetical style are still allowed to adopt a contrary arrangement without fear of unintelligibility. Now it would seem to us, who are accustomed to such an usage, that the verbal action ought naturally to come between its subject and the object upon which it is directed; and the fact that this is the order of ideas observed in those dialects which have arisen through the attempt of two races to render themselves mutually intelligible, would appear to support this view. On the other hand, this order is found only in the analytic stage of Aryan speech, that is, in its latest and most modern form, while the arrangement which sets the verb at the end becomes more and more universal the older the language with which we are dealing. Which arrangement, then, is the most *natural?* Not the most *simple*, for the two terms are by no means synonymous; and philology is continually reminding us that what is *logically* prior is seldom *historically* so, but that simplicity and clearness are only reached by a slow and laborious process. The answer to our present question is furnished by observation of the deaf and dumb. Deaf mutes enable us to a certain extent to make the experiment which Psammitikhus is said to have attempted, and to see what kind of language the uneducated mind would form for itself when deprived of the power of learning one of those spoken idioms which have been elaborated by preceding generations. Now it is found that the deaf mute invariably places the verb at the end of the sentence, the subject and object, to which his thought is chiefly directed, being the first to occur to his mind.[1] The alteration, therefore, which has been brought about in English and the Neo-Latin dialects in this natural order of ideas must be due to the action of some influential principle like analogy. A speaker who is imperfectly acquainted with the language of another has to ransack his memory for the names of objects and conceptions in the foreign tongue;

[1] Tylor, "Researches into the Early History of Mankind," pp. 92, 93.

in order to gain time for this, he defers mentioning the object of action as long as possible, and interpolates any other words he can between the subject and the objective noun, the verb being, of course, one of the first. So convenient an arrangement of the sentence would be more and more extended by means of analogy, until it finally became the characteristic of the language.

If analogy, however, has done so much for the accidence and syntax of a grammar, it has done everything for the meaning of words. Professor Whitney reduces the changes of signification which are perpetually going on in the lexicon to two processes—one the specialisation of the general, the other the generalisation of the special.[1] But the agent of change is analogy. A general term is applied to some particular object, or a special term to a less special instance through some likeness supposed to exist between them; new likenesses are then detected; the terms are used of fresh cases; and so the process of the analogical expansion or contraction of signification goes on indefinitely. To make our meaning plain to another, it is necessary that we should employ words which he understands, and we can only convey a new idea to him by comparing and likening it to one with which he is already

[1] "Language and the Study of Language," p. 106.

familiar. Indeed, it is not only in the instruction of others, but just as much in the development of our own knowledge, that the same contrivance is required. One idea is best remembered by being connected with another idea, no matter how fanciful the connection may be; and it would be quite impossible to recollect a large mass of isolated ideas. Knowledge is one vast chain of associations, and analogy is the principal forger of its several links. A new fact falls within our experience, a new object is discovered, or a new notion is struck out, and we at once seek to bring it within the circle of our previous knowledge, and to connect it with something with which we are previously acquainted. The name assigned to it accordingly expresses the resemblance believed to exist between the new subject of thought and the existing furniture of the mind. It has long been recognised that all the terms which denote the spiritual and abstract are derived from the physical and concrete. *Spirit* is primarily "the breath," *soul* "the heaving sea," *Deus* "the bright heaven." Language is the treasure-house of worn-out metaphors. As Carlyle has said, "They are its muscles, and tissues, and living integuments."[1]

But the metaphors belong to thought, not to

[1] "Sartor Resartus," X.

the mere outward form. Language is the expression of thought, and consequently, though thought and its expression can scarcely be separated in practice, yet, like the seal and its impression, they are really distinct; or rather, while thought can exist without expression, expression cannot exist without thought. The outward presupposes the inward, the impression presupposes the seal. The influence of analogy, therefore, under which words change their significations, is exerted upon the ideas they denote; the mind first discovers similarities between its conceptions, and these are then reflected in speech. The dried grape is called a plum when put into a cake or pudding, because it looks like the fruit of that name, and not for any linguistic reason. But although it is the content that properly modifies the form, the form may react upon the content. In this case, analogy becomes a truly creative philological principle. The simple sound of the word itself, its mere outer husk, as it were, calls up associations which create new sounds, new ideas, and therefore new words. There arises an imaginary world, answering to nothing real and substantial, which stands solely upon the basis of uttered speech. It is the creation of the external side of language, and the demiurge is analogy. There will be an unreal world either of content or of form. In the first instance, the mind will be deluded by those false notions, those Baconian *idola*, which have done so much to impede progress, and which are called *popular etymologies*. In the second instance, it is only the expression of thought that is made unreal, only the outward form of language that is forced and artificial, and we term it *poetry*. The two creations spring from one and the same source, but they represent two different stages in the growth of the mind. The mythopœic age is the period of primitive unconscious childhood and barbarism, and wherever it still exists it bears witness to a naive unthinking attitude of mind. Poetry, on the other hand, is the cultured and conscious expression of thought; its artificiality is recognised, and it can accordingly affect only the outward form. It is the spiritualising of the material, which it therefore moulds according to its will; while the etymological myth is the materialising of the spiritual, which thus becomes distorted and untrue. I am not now going to discuss the origin of mythology in general, and the cause of its continuance; I shall merely confine myself to those portions of it which are due to the action of false analogy. A large part of our Aryan mythology, as has been eloquently pointed out by Professor Max Müller, is derived from homonymes and synonymes, from phonetic decay, and the attempt to explain forgotten words.

*Daphne*, "the laurel," and *daphne*, "the dawn," came both from the root *dah*, "to burn;" what more natural than that the dawn should be changed into a laurel in her flight from Apollo, the sun-god? *Pramanthas*, "the fire-chark" of the Hindu, became the Προμηθεύς of the Greek; and the simple contrivance of the savage for the production of fire passed into the wise benefactor of man, with his brother *Epimetheus* or "afterthought." The various tribes with names, sometimes explicable, sometimes obscure, had to be provided with eponymous heroes; and the manifold appellations assigned to the same object of worship were transformed into as many separate deities. Led by a false analogy, men argued that what was different or alike in name must also be different or alike in reality; and so a whole fairyland was built up upon the mere *sound* of words. But the influence of a false analogy went even further back than this. Before the primitive man had learned to distinguish between the subject and the object, the actions and passions of the thinker were transferred to the inanimate. So the sun was compared to a charioteer or a one-eyed monster, and the thunder was the voice of God. The similes in all these cases, however, were still between ideas, not words—still belonged to thought, not to its expression; but when they had once been enshrined in language, they tended to grow and multiply, and the starting-point was no longer the inability of the child to distinguish between himself and the object, but the mere verbal metaphors themselves. As the primitive state of mind passed away, the original meaning intended to be conveyed in the traditional phrases was forgotten; the myth became purely etymological, and the solar charioteer was transformed into Phaethon, and the one-eyed monster into the Kyklops. The simple words, divested of their real signification, were associated with others which represented intelligible notions to the users of them; and out of these false analogies grew up the fantastic shapes of many a legend and myth. The human mind cannot be satisfied unless it can assign some reason for the existence of a thing, unless it can believe that it understands it. So long as an explanation is not forthcoming, it feels itself in the presence of something mysterious and supernatural, and this causes all the discomforts of fear and uncertainty. The explanation may be very far indeed from the truth; but so long as any can be given, the man is content. Now in order to explain we must compare; it is only by bringing a phenomenon within the limits of the known that we take it out of the region of the inexplicable. Hence come all those popular etymologies which interpret unknown terms by words of the same or similar sound. The eponymous heroes, already alluded to, who have been manufactured out of the names of tribes and places, are a case in point; here the attempt to assign definite conceptions to the words themselves has been despaired of, and they have accordingly been explained by what seemed the analogous instances of words without any signification of their own, but which served to denote individuals. Proper names have naturally been the special subject of popular etymologising; there is nothing else in language which so quickly and thoroughly changes its form; and yet, since everything must have a reason, the assumption is irresistible that they once had a meaning. Thus, as my friend Professor J. Earle tells me, there are two neighbouring places in Somersetshire called Saltford and Freshford. The first was originally *Sal-ford* (Sallow-ford), the "Willow-ford;" but when the Saxon *Salh* (*Salig*) died out of use, a slight change of pronunciation altered the unintelligible Salford into the intelligible Saltford, a change facilitated by the neighbourhood of the corresponding Freshford. In modern Greece, again, we see the same process taking place. Thus Athens is *Ἀνθῆναι*, "the flowery," in the mouths of the common people; Krisa is *Χρυσό*, "the golden;" and a legend of a quarrel between two brothers has fastened itself upon Delphi.[1] Not very unlike is the superstitious feeling which has transmuted the forms of words of ill-omened sound. Because an unfortunate event was called *malum*, and a fortunate one *bonum*, it was thought that the words themselves brought good and evil; and so *Maleventum* was changed into *Beneventum*, just as the Erinyes were addressed as the Eumenides, and the left hand as "the better;" or as, in modern times, the Cape of Storms has become the Cape of Good Hope, and the custom of Ta-pu is perpetually transforming the languages of the Pacific islanders.[2] But other words besides proper names lose their true form and meaning through the influence of imaginary analogies. Thus the German *sündfluth*, "great flood," has had the first syllable assimilated to *sünde*, "sin," through its application to the Biblical Deluge; and even philosophy has been deceived by the outward resemblance of the logical copula to the substantive verb, while Bacon believed in the existence of sensible qualities answering to the abstract nouns derived from attributive adjectives.

[1] Deffner, "Neograeca," p. 307, in Curtius' *Studien*, iv. 2.

[2] Among the Eskimaux of Greenland, any one who bears the same name as a deceased person changes it in order to deceive and escape from death, in the same way as among the native tribes of America and the Sunda Islands. (F. Liebrecht in the *Academy*, Sept. 1st, 1872.)

Thus far this popular etymologising is unconscious and instinctive. But it becomes more or less artificial in cases like those which meet us in the Homeric poems. Thus the old epic adjective ἐπηέτανος, "long-lasting," from ἐπὶ, ἄει, and τείνω, came to be thought to be derived from ἔτος (√Fετος, Sansk. *vatsas*), "a year," and accordingly is used in the sense of "lasting for a year" more than once in the Odyssey; while πλέες, "full," was fancied to be a contracted form of πλείονες, "more," through the false analogy of the Ionic πλεῦν, πλεῖν, for πλέον (that is, πλεῖον), and hence we will find the monstrous solecism οἰωνοὶ . . . πλέες ἠέ γυναίκες, "more birds than women," in Il. xi. 395. So, again, τέλσος, "tilth," was imagined to be identical with τέλος, "end" (as in Il. xiii. 707, xviii. 544), and the aorist infinitives χραισμεῖν, √Fιδεῖν, handed down in various formulæ and stereotyped verses, were believed to be presents, and accordingly provided with the futures χραισμήσω and ἰδήσω. The Odyssey even goes a step further than mere unconscious misunderstanding of the traditional language of the past; and the affectation of archaism observable in it, which ignores, for instance, the existence of writing, even to the extent of making a Phæakian supercargo commit his freight to memory, renders Spenser's "Fairy Queen" its best analogue, and results in a list of similar etymological mistakes.[1] A good parallel to this appearance of popular etymologising in literature may be found in some of the eccentricities of modern English spelling. *Further*, the comparative of *forth*, has thus been spelt and pronounced *farther*, under the impression that it was derived from *far*, the *th* being euphonic or something of that kind; and this erroneous etymology has reacted upon the meaning of the word. *Whole*, again, the by-form of *hale* (the Greek *καλός*), has been garnished with a *w*, through the supposed analogy of *wheel* and *whale*,[2] and *could*, from *can*, has received an *l* because *should*, from *shall*, has one; and all this in defiance of pronunciation. The authority of Webster's Dictionary has induced our American cousins to get rid of the unnecessary *u* in words like *honour*, *favour*; but instead of confining themselves to vocables of Latin origin, they have extended the practice to totally different cases, like *harbour* and *neighbour*. It is only the philologist who knows the deceitfulness of the analogy.

[1] Od. viii. 164. The Phæakians, the children of the "bright" clouds, are the representatives of *Phœnician* commerce and naval activity so far as trade details are concerned. The plain reference to the Erekhtheum of Perikles in Od. vii. 81 makes the affectation of archaism all the more startling. (See Paley, *Brit. Quarterly*, October 1873.)

[2] Earle ("Philology of the English Tongue," p. 143, 1st edit.) quotes *whote* for *hot* from John Philpot, and *wrought* for *reached* from Myles Coverdale.

But the influence of analogy upon the written form of words leads us naturally to the consideration of the way in which it has acted upon what is pre-eminently the cultured expression of thought. Poetry is artificial language; it is the endeavour to express the best ideas in the best manner possible, and, after the form has thus been elaborated, to secure it by artificial means from being forgotten. Hence come all the various contrivances of metrical feet, of parallelism, of alliteration, and of rhyme. Metrical feet, whether quantitative or qualitative (that is, accentual), is the satisfaction of the striving after analogical harmony, of the desire of mind and ear and lips for the like, which lies at the bottom of speech itself. In the parallelism of Semitic poetry material analogy passes into conceptual analogy; clause answers to clause, stanza to stanza. But the oldest device invented to imprint upon speech the poetical form, and to enable the memory to retain it, is alliteration. Here the natural tendency to repeat the same sound or combination of sounds comes into full play; and so alliteration is the essential characteristic of barbarian poetry all over the world, from the Kalewala of the Finns to the songs of the North American Indians. It has been an especial favourite with the Teutonic race; all our old English poetry is alliterative, and to this day the musicalness which we recognise in the verses of certain poets is due to this cause. Alliteration may be said to belong to the beginnings of words, and so to correspond with rhyme, which affects the ends of words. Rhyme is the fulfilment of the expectation of discovering an analogy between final sounds. It may be detected here and there in the poetry of most nations; examples of it, for instance, are to be met with in the Old Testament, and the charm of the Latin pentameter is enhanced by the rhyming of the last syllables of the two penthemimers. But it has attained its fullest development in modern European poetry. According to Nigra, its origin is Keltic; but however that may be, the Romance languages, such as Provençal and Italian, with their words terminating in the same sounds—the worn remnants of Latin flection—seemed created for the application of rhyme. No doubt the Latin poems of the Middle Ages, in which a jingle had to take the place of forgotten quantity, helped considerably towards the same end. The child of the South, rhyme, was soon transplanted to the North, and became a successful rival of alliteration in Teutonic poetry. But it could never win the same influence in languages which abounded in monosyllabic words as it had in the Neo-Latin dialects, for the simple reason that such an ornamental help to the memory ought rather to affect unmeaning and merely euphonic final syllables than words every letter of which is instinct with life and signification. Hence the strong hold that alliteration still has upon our taste; hence the fact that our greatest poems have been written in blank verse; hence, too, our preference for double rhymes, our dislike to a perpetual rhyming of monosyllables.

With poetry, the highest effort of the human mind consciously to shape and fashion language, we must close our review of the influence of analogy. I have tried to show how immense is its power throughout the whole domain of speech, and how it is present everywhere as a creative and reconstructing principle. Whether the analogy be true or false, whether it act upon the matter or the form, is of little consequence. Phonology, accidence, syntax, and signification are all equally affected by it; while the poetry of the people, which is based upon unreal ideas—ideas, that is, which have nothing actual and objective answering to them—is not less the product of its ceaseless activity than the poetry of literature, where the form alone is unreal and artificial, a language never spoken in the work-a-day world.

# APPENDIX.

# APPENDIX.

## I.

*The Route followed by the Western Aryans in their Migration into Europe.*

ONE of the historical questions raised by the study of language, and to which the study of language must furnish the answer, is the road by which our Aryan forefathers entered Europe. I assume it to have been proved that their original home was in Asia, and more particularly in the high plateau of the Hindu Kush. When Comparative Philology first sets them before our view, they had left anything like primitive barbarism far behind, and had reached a considerable degree of civilisation. They were herdsmen and cultivators, living in houses and communities, with settled customs and government, and even acquainted with the use of metals. Such a state of culture points to a comparatively late stage of development, indefinitely removed from that imaginary root-period discovered by the analyst which represents the earliest epoch of Aryan speech to which we can attain. Now, I conceive Fick to have demonstrated against Schmidt[1] that the West or European Aryans lived together in a body after their separation from their Eastern brethren in Asia, and that the different branches of the European family did not break off from the parent stock until after the arrival of that stock in Europe. Just as there was a primitive Aryan language, therefore, so was there a primitive European language; and the branching off of East and West Aryan was paralleled by the branching off of Lithuanic, Slavonic, Keltic, Teutonic, Italic, and Hellenic. The question, then, arises, Did the speakers of this primitive European language move westward north or south of the Caspian, through the Sagartian desert, Media, Armenia, and Asia Minor, or through the steppes of Tatary and across the Ural range?

The old belief was that the course taken by our ancestors was southward of the Caspian, and that bodies of the emigrants were left behind on the march in Media, Armenia, and Asia Minor. The science of language soon showed, however, that both the Medic and Armenian languages belong to the Iranic stock, and might therefore be regarded as offshoots from Persia; while Fick has lately made it clear that the Aryan dialects of Asia Minor, of which Phrygian may be considered the representative, belong incontestably to the European group. This is in full harmony with the Greek tradition that the Briges or Phrygians had originally migrated from Thrakia,[2] and with the resemblances that Plato detected between Greek and Phrygian words.[3] As I have elsewhere pointed out,[4]

[1] Die ehemalige Spracheinheit d. Indo-Germanen Europas. 1873.

[2] Hdt. vii. 73; viii. 138. Strabo, xiv. 618; x. 471; vii. 295. Arrian ap. Eustath. on Dionys. Perierg. 322.

[3] Kratylus, 410 A.

[4] *Academy*, May 30, 1874.

the want of iron in the pre-Hellenic remains found by Dr. Schliemann at Hissarlik shows there could have been no intercourse between the west coast of Asia Minor and the great metal-workers beyond the Halys. The Assyrian inscriptions, too, would lead us to infer that no Aryan nations were settled eastward of that river, at all events, in the twelfth century B.C.; and the cuneiform inscriptions found at Van and its neighbourhood are written in a language which, though flectional, is not Aryan, and probably belongs to the Alarodian group of speech, of which Georgian may be taken as a type. We find no traces of the Aryan in Armenia or even Media before the eighth century B.C. The Assyrians first became acquainted with the Medes, or *Amadai*, as they then called them, in the reign of Shalmaneser III. (840 B.C.), when they lived far to the east, the Parsuas or Parthians intervening between them and Assyria. It is not till the age of Rimmon-nirari, about 790 B.C., that they had advanced into the country known as Media Rhagiana to the classical geographers. The legends of the Vendidad represent the westward advance of the Iranians as slow and gradual, while the Aryan language of the Iron or Ossetes, in the Caucasus, is, like the Armenian and the Kurd, a member of the Iranic stock. Our evidence is complete that if the European branch of the Aryan family moved into its present home along the southern shores of the Caspian, it left no stragglers on the way, no tokens to mark its road. The Aryan dialects of this part of Asia are late emigrants from Persia, and the Aryan settlers in Asia Minor crossed from Europe to invade the old inhabitants of the country.

Now one of the most curious discoveries that have

resulted from the decipherment of the records of Assyria and Babylonia is that the whole of the district included in Assyria, Chaldea, Susiana, and Media was originally inhabited by a Turanian race with agglutinative languages, who invented the cuneiform system of writing, built the great cities, and founded the monarchies of the kingdoms of the Tigris and Euphrates, and were, in fact, the pioneers of civilisation in Western Asia. Their traditions pointed to a cradle in the mountainous region south-west of the Caspian; and the mountain of Nizir, in the land of Gutium, between the 34th and 36th parallels of latitude (the present peak of Elwand, as it would seem), was the sacred spot on which the ark had rested and mankind had found its second birthplace.

The Accadian, Susianian, and Protomedic languages, which have been brought to light by the progress of cuneiform research, are more or less closely related to one another and to the modern dialects of the Ugric group. It has long ago been shown that the ancestors of the Finns must have come from a southern Asiatic home; and the very names Suomi and Akkarak, given in their traditions to the primeval divisions of the race—Akkarak, by the way, having no longer an etymology in Finnish—are strangely like Sumir and Accad, the two cantons of Turanian Babylonia.[1] The legends of the creation, the flood, the giants, and the monsters contained in the Epic of the half-savage Voguls, resemble those of ancient Chaldea,[2] and *reuta*, the Finnic name for "iron," seems to claim relationship with the Accadian *urud*, "bronze."[3] It would

[1] Lenormant, "La Magie chez les Chaldéens," pp. 272, 273.

[2] See Adam, "Un Genèse Vogoule," in the "Revue de Philologie," i. (1874).

[3] See Lenormant, "Les Premières Civilisations," i. p. 119.

appear that the Finnic branch of the Turanian family moved northward across the Caucasus and westward of the Caspian to the Ural range; but the present position of the Tatar, Mongolian, and Tungusic members of the family, with which Accadian shares remarkable similarities both in vocabulary and grammar, would imply that the Median cradle was a second and not a first starting-point of the race. However that may be, the whole strip of country from the Caspian to the Persian Gulf was in the possession of a Turanian population at the earliest time to which we can go back; and there is little probability that the flow of Aryan migration towards Europe had begun before the occupation of this part of the world by the Turanians.

Now I have been unable to detect any traces of Aryan influence in Accadian and its allied languages. Had the Aryan emigrants forced their way through the Turanian population of the country, it is hardly probable that a few Indo-European words at least would not have found their way into the Accadian vocabulary. Of course no account can be taken of resemblances in sound and meaning that may exist between Aryan and Accadian *roots;* whatever may be the explanation of these, the Aryans had left their root-period far behind them when our European ancestors started on their westward wanderings; and if the Accadians borrowed at all, it would be fully formed words and not roots. But the Accadian lexicon is wholly free from any signs of such a borrowing; and when we consider that it is the same with the Assyrian lexicon also, we seem driven to the conclusion that the Turanian population of Media and the regions of the Tigris and Euphrates, as well as their Semitic conquerors and successors, never came into immediate contact with an Aryan tribe until the late period when Aryan Medes and Akhæmenian Persians appear upon the scene. It is not until the time of Assur-bani-pal or Sardanapalus, in the seventh century B.C., that Aryan glosses are found upon the Assyrian tablets, and these belong to the Persian branch of the family. Thus *urdhu*, the Zend *eredhwa*, is given as a synonyme of "high," and *Mitra* as a synonyme of "the sun." Everything bears out the inference already arrived at upon other grounds, that the Western Aryans must have entered Europe by a road that had led them to the north and not to the south of the Caspian.

But a further conclusion besides this may be drawn from the absence of any Aryan influence upon so ancient a monument of speech as the Accadian. If that language shows no signs of contact with Aryan, from a date indefinitely earlier than the third millennium B.C., when the Accadians had already long left their mountain-cradle in the north and had settled themselves in Babylonia, the speakers of Aryan on the one side, and of that group of languages of which Accadian is a representative on the other, can scarcely have been known one to another. The Sagartian desert must have been an effectual barrier between them, and the Caspian Gates had not yet been forced by invaders from the East.

But now there arises a very curious question. Gerland, in his book on the Odyssey,[1] has tried to show, by the help of Comparative Mythology, that the primitive Aryans lived on the shores of a great inland sea, under whose waves the sun sank evening after evening. Humboldt believed that the Sea of Aral is the remains of such an

[1] "Altgriechische Märchen in der Odyssee," Magdeburg, 1869.

expanse of water, which, at no very remote period, included the Caspian and Euxine; and this opinion has been confirmed by recent researches.[1] We should then have the primitive Aryans on one side of this vast lake, and the primitive Ugrian tribes on the other side, the desert nature of the country which lay between the two settlements preventing any communication except by water. Did such a communication by water ever take place? The evidence derived from the want of any traces of Aryan influence in Accadian enables us to answer in the negative, and the little acquaintance with maritime pursuits which Comparative Philology shows the primitive Aryans to have had confirms the conclusion. We may safely believe that our remote forefathers set out on their journey towards the West by land and not by sea, that the Sagartian desert barred their progress on the south, and that consequently the route they adopted was that which led them along the northern shores of the Caspian. Europe would therefore have been entered through Russia; and we may discover a reflection of the bleak and wintry character of the region the emigrants had to traverse in the fact that the fir (πίτυς, *pinus*, Sansk. *pîtu-dâru*s) and the birch (see p. 203) were the only trees whose names were remembered by the European Aryans after their long wanderings. The path they had chosen was again followed, as it would seem, after the lapse of many centuries, by the Scyths or Sarmatians, whose language has been proved by Mullenhoff[2] to be Iranian,

[1] See Spörer in Petermann's Mittheilungen (1868–72), and *Nature*, May 20, 1875.

[2] Monatsbericht d. Königl. Akademie d. Wiss. zu Berlin, 2 Aug. 1866, pp. 549 *sq.*

and so connected with those of the Persians, the Medes, and the Bactrians. Like the Scyths, they may have relapsed into a nomad life while passing through the inhospitable steppes of Tatary and Russia; at all events, it was not until they had settled on the western shores of the Black Sea (or possibly on those of the Baltic) that they broke up into the several races of Aryan Europe, as is shown by the agreement of the European languages in the words that relate to the sea, and in the name of the *beech*, which only grows westward of a line drawn from Königsberg to the Crimea.

---

## II.

### *Origin of the Case-endings in Aryan.*

AFTER the larger part of the preceding pages had been printed, I came across an extremely able and suggestive article by Bergaigne, which has been published in the "Mémoires de la Société de Linguistique de Paris" (tom. ii., fasc. 5), under the title, "Du Rôle de la Dérivation dans la déclinaison Indo-Européenne." I have long believed that an unprejudiced and thoroughgoing examination of the Aryan declension would show that its origin was similar to that of the Semitic noun, the cases being differentiated, as the need for them arose, out of various more or less unmeaning terminations, or "suffixes of derivation," if the latter phrase be preferred. M. Bergaigne has made it clear that this is the fact, and has thus provided a way of escape for believers in pronominal roots out of the difficulties in which they are involved. In almost every line we may trace the assumption that Glottology begins with the sentence and not the word, though it is never definitely expressed; and the only logical conclusion that can be drawn from the results of the author's researches is, that so far as the declension of the noun is concerned, it has grown out of a process of adaptation and not of agglutination. As he remarks very justly, we cannot assign the formation of the cases to the same process as that whereby they have been *replaced* in the later stage of analysis; and to suppose that a preposition (like *bhi*) could have been employed as a postposition to form a case, is not only to forget that prepositions are a very late growth, but also to ignore the distinction between prepositions and postpositions. I have myself been led away by what I believed to be the evidence of the Pada-text of the Rig-Veda to allow the agglutinative character of the suffix *bhi* (p. 284), though I have noticed that the preposition with which it has been connected is not *bhi* but *abhi* or *âbhi*, formed by means of the very suffix in question. That *bhi* originally imported no specific meaning into the noun is clear from its being common to many cases on the one hand (the dative and locative in Old Slavonic, for instance, being *te-bè*, the genitive *te-be*, and the instrumental *to-bojă*), and on the other from its being absent in certain languages in some cases in which it appears in the cognate dialects. Thus in Sanskrit we have *'sivais* by the side of *'sive-bhis*, and in Latin *dominis* or *rosis* by the side of *arcubus* or *deabus.* In the dative plural in Gothic, and the instrumental and dative plural and dual in Old

Slavonic and Lithuanian, it is replaced by *sma* or *smi*, a suffix which we meet again in the Sanskrit pronouns *ta-sma-i, ta-sma-t; a-smā-n, yu-shmā-n.* M. Bergaigne is doubtless right in making it the same "suffix of derivation" as that which we find in the Sanskrit *garda-bha-s*, "an ass," and *vrisha-bha-s*, "a bull;" or the Greek ἔλα-φο-ς, ἔρι-φο-ς, κρότα-φο-ς or κορυ-φή.[1]

The most important point brought out by his investigations is, that an essential difference exists between the strong cases (nominative, accusative, and vocative) and the weak cases, the former being primarily so many abstracts, and the latter mere adjectives used adverbially. The formatives of the strong cases (*-as* [*-ās*], *-i* [*-ī*], *-ā* [*-yā*], *-an*) continued to the last to mark abstracts like Sanskrit *áhan*, "day," *lipi*, "writing," *vrajyā*, "act of travelling," *muda*, "joy," Greek, φυγ-ή; and the same Sanskrit form *vákas* is differentiated in Greek into the plural ὄπες and the singular ἔπος. Originally, however, *vákas* expressed no distinction either of number or of gender; and how little the termination had to do with case is shown by its appearing in the oblique cases as in the Greek πόδεσ-σι or ποδῶν (= ποδέσ-ων), where the accentuation of the strong cases is followed. In short, the strong cases, with all their varieties of number and gender, were gradually evolved out of abstract nouns, which were fitted with a multitude of meaningless suffixes. Hence we can understand why the final *s* is wanting in so many plural nominatives and accusatives, or why the same suffix may belong indifferently to all three genders.

As for the weak cases, like the genitive in *-sya*, which

[1] Curtius has already anticipated him in this. See his "Zur Chronologie," &c., p. 79, and "Jahn's Jahrbücher," 60, p. 95.

has long ago been compared with the suffix of such Greek adjectives as *δημο-σιο-ς*,[1] or the Sanskrit pronouns *ta-sya-i*, *ta-syā-s*, they have all grown out of adjectives taken adverbially. In many of the forms one suffix has been added to another; thus the *-hwa* (*-swa*) and *σι* (*-swi*) of the Zend and Greek locatives unite the suffixes *-a* and *-i* to the suffix *-su*. M. Bergaigne reserves a discussion of the terminations *-s*, *-t*, and *-m*, as well as of the verbal endings to a future period; but it is plain to what origin he would refer them.

Almost cotemporaneously with M. Bergaigne's article, a pamphlet has appeared in Germany by Gustav Meyer, called "Zur Geschichte der indogermanischen Stammbildung und Declination," which embodies somewhat similar views, though the author does not go so far as the French philologist. Thus he says (p. 3)—"Here at the outset I must express my conviction that the parent Aryan contained an uncommonly great variety of formations without any real distinction [of meaning], or at all events without any apparent to us, and that this variety came gradually to be restricted through the developing classificatory power of the understanding." These numerous "synonymous formations," he thinks (p. 3), might have been distinguished from one another by tone and gesture, though all traces of such a mode of distinction are of course now lost. Meyer also makes an attempt to analyse the personal pronouns. He rejects the suggestion

[1] As *σ* in Greek is generally lost between two vowels, this suffix is perhaps rather to be referred to *-tya* than *-sya*. Both suffixes, however, performed the same function; and they bore the same relation to one another as *sa* and *ta*.

that in *agh-am* (*ego*) we have the root *agh*, "to speak,"[1] on the ground that the name of "the speaker" was too abstract for the primitive Aryan, and prefers to analyse *agham* into *a-gha-m*, tracing the first element in a number of forms which denote the third person. "This promiscuous use [of the same word]," he adds, "for the first and third persons, is plain evidence how little a distinct difference of meaning resided in these pronominal roots;" though the truer conclusion would be, that the substantives from which they have really come might be used for either one of the three persons. He goes on to observe that "the confusion between the first and second person which meets us in the stem *va-*, is even more striking." One other point that he brings out is the difficulties involved by the assumption of one uniform parent-speech. "I, on the contrary," he says, "am convinced that no small number of what we may term dialectic differences prevailed in it, which have partly been preserved in the several [Aryan] languages." Thus we seem compelled to admit the co-existence of the forms *sa* and *tas* for the demonstrative. Professor Whitney, in his new work on "The Life and Growth of Language" (p. 177), has expressed himself strongly against the views upon this subject which—after the example of Professor Max Müller—I have endeavoured to set forth in the present volume. But he seems to me to confuse the question of the origin of languages—a question which lies beyond the province of Glottology—with that of their remotest beginnings to which our data allow us to go back. As

[1] As in Latin *ad-ag-ium*, Greek *ἠ-μί*, Goth. *af-aik-a*: Curtius, "Grundzüge" (2d edit.), p. 357.

glottologists merely, we have nothing to do with the process by which languages were made; for us they can exist only in a society, and must therefore have been as multitudinous as the early communities that spoke them. Of course mutual intelligibility required that one dialect only should be spoken within the same community, allowance being made for individual differences of speech. How far similar conditions of life and thought, of food and climate, may have independently produced a similar form of language in neighbouring but isolated societies, is a question which we have no means of answering.

---

## III.

### *Language and Race.*[1]

THE fallacy that language is a sure and certain test of race is one to which few comparative philologists would now-a-days commit themselves. There is no assertion which can be more readily confronted with history, or, when so confronted, more clearly be demonstrated to be false. Language is no physiological necessity; it is not one of those physical marks which characterise race, and, like the colour of the skin or the shape of the skull, are inseparable from a man. We cannot help having hair of a particular character, or even, perhaps, a disposition of a particular kind; but we *can* help having lan-

[1] Communicated to the Journal of the Anthropological Institute

guage. A man may never speak all his life through, may never have the opportunity of speaking, but he will none the less be a man. We can easily conceive of a race of deaf-mutes who never make use of language in the ordinary sense of the word; indeed, the opinion is gaining ground among the students of philology that all articulate language has originated out of a previous gesture-language, which, of course, is the same all the world over, and could constitute no *differentia* of race. But, though language is no mark of race, it *is* a mark of society. Even the most rudimentary society could not exist without it; certainly no civilised society could do so. It is social in its origin and nature, the creation and mirror of society, as well as the bond that keeps society together. Had men always led isolated lives, any means of communication with one another would have been unnecessary, and language need never have been elaborated. Just as writing was invented for the wants of a civilised society, so we may say that language was invented for the wants of an uncivilised society. The power of articulate speech was possessed by man, like the power of making laws or of mathematical reasoning; but had it not been for social requirements it would have lain dormant, without a motive for calling it forth and using it as an instrument of intercommunication. In short, society implies language, race does not; and hence, while we may lay down that language is the test of social contact, we may lay down with equal precision that it is not a test of race.

This conclusion is borne out by a survey of the facts. The language we speak is not implanted in us at our birth. The child has painfully and slowly to learn his native tongue, though, doubtless, he inherits a certain aptitude for doing so. If he is born in England, it is English that he learns; if in France, French. If two or more languages are spoken by those about him, he is likely to acquire these languages more or less perfectly, according to the degree in which he comes into social contact with those who speak them. Languages, once well known, can be entirely forgotten, and foreign ones can become as familiar as though they were native. Children whose language was Hindustani have forgotten it utterly after a short residence in England, and it is often difficult to reproduce a sound which was constantly on the lips in childhood.

What holds good of the individual holds equally good of the community, which is composed of individuals. Here, also, the language spoken depends upon the influences surrounding the community. Whatever breaks up, amalgamates, or mixes the community has the same effect upon the language it speaks. The community must be carefully distinguished from the race. The same race may be divided into a multitude of communities, each separate and independent, and with characteristics of its own. Indeed, except under the unifying pressure of a centralised civilisation, such independent communities *must* exist in every race, and the variety and unlikeness of the communities will be reproduced in the variety and unlikeness of their languages or dialects. The diversity of manners and customs will not be so great as the diversity of speech, since the speech is a reflection of the whole body of manners and customs, past and present, in each society. The infinitely numerous societies that have existed during the long period that man has been upon the earth imply an equal number of forms of speech; and as these societies have been continually influencing one another, destroying, absorbing, modifying, and invigorating, the languages or dialects which they represent will have been in a corresponding state of flux. Indeed, the languages will have been affected even more than the societies themselves. A society may continue to exist, thanks to its customs or the influences of race, while the language it spoke has disappeared, through the daily need of communication with other and more powerful societies. Thus Jewish societies exist all the world over as separate societies with peculiar rites and customs, and apart from any question of race; and yet their language is, for the most part, that of the people among whom they are settled. The Jews of Southern Austria are emigrants from Spain, and believe that old Spanish is their sacred tongue; and the Jews of Abyssinia, of China, and elsewhere speak the dialect of the country in which they live. This is a strong case, as the disappearance of a language generally implies the disappearance of a community as a separate society. But it sets in a very clear light the fact that language is a test of social contact. Looking merely at the rites and customs of the Jewish communities, we should have no idea of the vicissitudes they have experienced and the unallied societies which surrounded them. It is not until we come to the language that this is made plain; and so good a register of social influences is the language, that even without the aid of history we could have discovered the Spanish origin of the South Austrian Jews.

Now there are not many examples of so pure-blooded a race as the Jews, in the civilised world at any rate. Even among savages and barbarians purity of descent is likely to be the exception rather than the rule. Considering the antiquity of mankind and the history of modern savage tribes, which are constantly at war with one another, or intermarrying into other clans, making wives of the slaves they capture, races as well as societies are probably somewhat mixed. In most cases, however, the type remains fixed and unmistakable; but the mere possibility of mixture—that is, of close intercourse with another society—makes it impossible for language to be a criterion of race. We cannot tell whether the same event that has befallen the Jews has not befallen other races also, and that they have not been brought into such intimate connection with a foreign language (though, as with the Jews, not necessarily through the medium of marriage) as to have adopted it for their own. Keltic is extinct among the Kelts of Cornwall and the Isle of Man, and the same fate seems to threaten the other Keltic dialects of Great Britain and France. Slavonic has similarly disappeared from Prussia, and Basque alone is left of the pre-Keltic languages of Western Europe. Keltic itself had to make way for Latin in Gaul and Spain, like Punic in Africa; and the Normans first lost their mother-tongue in Normandy, and then their new tongue in England. The Scandinavian colonies which existed in Greenland for 500 years left no traces behind them, and Arabic in Sicily and Visigothic in Spain have been totally extirpated. The Melanesians and Papuans belong to different races, and yet speak the same languages; and the same may be the case with the Finns and Lapps. A few inscriptions of doubtful meaning are all that is left of the Etruscan language. The race that spoke it was numerous and powerful; it was a language of literature and culture, and struggled successfully against Roman encroachment down to a late period; but the fragments of it that remain have been vainly compared with languages dead and living, possible and impossible, and I believe it to be the last waif and stray of an extinct family of speech. According to Humboldt and Bonpland, "A million of the aborigines of America have exchanged their native for an European language." The inhabitants of San Salvador, Nicaragua, Costa Rica, Santa Margaretha, Baradéro, Quilmos, Calchaguy, and Chiloe, have exchanged their own idioms for Spanish, the inhabitants of Rio Janeiro for Portuguese. The negroes of Hayti have adopted French; while the soldiers sent by the Sultan Selim into Lower Nubia in 1420 soon lost their mother-tongue. "Before the Christian era," as I have remarked in my "Principles of Comparative Philology," when dealing with this subject, "Hebrew, Assyrian, and Babylonian had been supplanted by Aramaic, which was fast tending to become the common dialect of the Semitic world, like Arabic in later times." The ancient agglutinative Accadian of Chaldea, in which a large and influential literature was written and the first elements of Asiatic civilisation comprised, was so completely rooted out by the conquering Semites, that the very existence of the language was unknown till the last few years. And yet so important was it as to become the Latin of the educated Assyrian, whose science and art were locked up in this dead tongue, while members of

# INDEX.

THE END.